Chinese Thought in a Multi-cultural World

Reflecting on the "clash of civilizations" as its point of departure, this book is based on a series of sixteen of the author's interconnected, thematically focused lectures and calls for new perspectives to resist imperialistic homogeneity.

Situated within a neo-humanist context, the book applies interactive cognition from an Asian perspective within which China can be perceived as an essential "other," making it highly relevant in the quest for global solutions to the many grave issues facing humankind today. The author critiques American, European, and Chinese points of view, highlighting the significance of difference and the necessity of dialogue, before, ultimately, rethinking the nature of world literature and putting forward interactive cognition as a means of "reconciliation" between cultures. Chinese culture, as a frame of reference endowed with traditions of "harmony without homogeneity", may help to alleviate global cultural confrontation and even reconstruct the understanding of human civilization.

The book will be essential reading for scholars and students of Comparative Literature, Chinese Studies, and all those who are interested in cross-cultural communication and Chinese culture in general.

YUE Daiyun is a distinguished, award-winning professor at Peking University, China. She specializes in comparative literature and has dozens of highly influential publications in the field of comparative culture and beyond.

China Perspectives

The *China Perspectives* series focuses on translating and publishing works by leading Chinese scholars, writing about both global topics and China-related themes. It covers Humanities & Social Sciences, Education, Media and Psychology, as well as many interdisciplinary themes.

This is the first time any of these books have been published in English for international readers. The series aims to put forward a Chinese perspective, give insights into cutting-edge academic thinking in China, and inspire researchers globally.

To submit proposals, please contact the Taylor & Francis Publisher for China Publishing Programme, Lian Sun (Lian.Sun@informa.com)
Titles in literature currently include:

A Thematic Exploration of Twentieth-Century Western Literature
Jiang Chengyong

Oral Epic Traditions in China and Beyond
Chao Gejin

A Study of the Urban Poetics of Frank O'Hara
Wang Xiaoling, Wang Yuzhi and Zheng Mingyuan

After Postmodernism
Wang Ning

Dual Narrative Dynamics
Dan Shen

Chinese Thought in a Multi-cultural World
Cross-Cultural Communication, Comparative Literature and Beyond
YUE Daiyun

For more information, please visit https://www.routledge.com/China-Perspectives/book-series/CPH

Chinese Thought in a Multi-cultural World

Cross-Cultural Communication, Comparative Literature and Beyond

Written by YUE Daiyun

Translated by MENG Xiangchun, Ian Hunter, and Harry Kuoshu

LONDON AND NEW YORK

Sponsored by Chinese Fund for the Humanities and Social Sciences.

First published 2023
by Routledge
4 Park Square, Milton Park, Abingdon, Oxon OX14 4RN

and by Routledge
605 Third Avenue, New York, NY 10158

Routledge is an imprint of the Taylor & Francis Group, an informa business

© 2023 YUE Daiyun

Translated by MENG Xiangchun, Ian Hunter, and Harry Kuoshu

The right of YUE Daiyun to be identified as author of this work has been asserted in accordance with sections 77 and 78 of the Copyright, Designs and Patents Act 1988.

All rights reserved. No part of this book may be reprinted or reproduced or utilised in any form or by any electronic, mechanical, or other means, now known or hereafter invented, including photocopying and recording, or in any information storage or retrieval system, without permission in writing from the publishers.

Trademark notice: Product or corporate names may be trademarks or registered trademarks, and are used only for identification and explanation without intent to infringe.

British Library Cataloguing-in-Publication Data
A catalogue record for this book is available from the British Library

English Version by permission of Zhonghua Book Company

Library of Congress Cataloging-in-Publication Data
Names: Yue, Daiyun, author. | Meng, Xiangchun, 1977- translator. |
Kuoshu, Harry H., 1955- translator. | Hunter, Ian, 1957- translator.
Title: Chinese thought in a multi-cultural world : cross-cultural communication, comparative literature and beyond / written by Yue Daiyun; translated by Meng Xiangchun, Ian Hunter, and Harry Kuoshu.
Other titles: Duo yuan wen hua zhong de Zhongguo si xiang
Description: Abingdon, Oxon ; New York, NY : Routledge, 2023. |
Series: China perspectives | Includes bibliographical references and index.
Identifiers: LCCN 2022032282 (print) | LCCN 2022032283 (ebook) |
ISBN 9781032410968 (hardcover) | ISBN 9781032410975 (paperback) |
ISBN 9781003356240 (ebook)
Subjects: LCSH: Comparative literature. | Comparative civilization. |
China–Civilization.
Classification: LCC PN879.C5 Y8513 2023 (print) | LCC PN879.C5 (ebook) | DDC 809–dc23/eng/20220928
LC record available at https://lccn.loc.gov/2022032282
LC ebook record available at https://lccn.loc.gov/2022032283

ISBN: 978-1-032-41096-8 (hbk)
ISBN: 978-1-032-41097-5 (pbk)
ISBN: 978-1-003-35624-0 (ebk)

DOI: 10.4324/9781003356240

Typeset in Times New Roman
by SPi Technologies India Pvt Ltd (Straive)

Contents

List of table	vii
Foreword	viii
Acknowledgments	ix

1	The Context of the Times: The Clash of Civilizations and the Future	1
2	The Neo-Humanism for the Twenty-first Century	22
3	The Transformation of the Post-Modernist Ethos and a New Platform for Literary Studies	30
4	The American, European, and Chinese Dreams: An Example of Cultural Transformation	37
5	Thoughts on Comparative Literature and World Literature	51
6	Interactive Cognition: The Case of Literature–Science Interaction	59
7	Interactive Cognition and Mutual Interpretation	68
8	Difference and Dialogue	74
9	Chinese Culture and the Reconstruction of World Culture	85

vi *Contents*

10 The Interpenetration of Sinology and *Guoxue* 98

11 The Three Phases of the Development of Comparative
Literature 103

12 "The Death of Comparative Literature"
and Its Regeneration 121

13 The Beginning and Early Development of Comparative
Literature in China from 1900 to 1910 126

14 Where to, Where from, and When: The Quest
of Wang Guowei 153

15 The Enquiries of Lu Xun in His Early Years 165

16 Zhu Guangqian and His Contribution to Comparative
Literature in China 182

Index 198

Table

1.1 Comparison between Sinic Civilization and Western Civilization 5

Foreword

At the dawn of the twenty-first century, humanity had hoped to usher in a peaceful, golden era, but this era of ours has turned out to be one bristling with clashes, horrors, and atrocities. Those enlightened vanguards who aim to save our endangered Earth, and aspire to peace, must gain fresh ideas, thoughts, and approaches from all possible resources to carve out new paths and prospects. In this context, multi-cultural coexistence and cross-cultural communication have risen to become today's strongest advocate for core common global values, which I have been exploring over the past decade or so.

The bulk of the 16 chapters in this book convey my fresh thoughts in this new century (many of which have already been delivered as lectures in the classroom or elsewhere) with others' opinions often solicited or juxtaposed. These chapters are arranged roughly along the line of the dramatic changes at the turn of the century, the reconstruction of thought patterns, and their significance for society and life. The negative sides of these changes find expression in, among other things, the clash of civilizations, ecological crisis, and interest-induced moral degradation. It is my conviction that the "modern" outlook on development buttressed by the accruing of material wealth, ecological destruction, and unbridled consumption will be rectified, if not replaced, by the philosophy of "sustainable civilization" based on the quality of life rather than on the hoarding of personal fortune and material pleasures. The neo-humanism for the twenty-first century promotes eco-awareness, transcendence over human-centrism, and respect for the "other", for difference, and for complementary multi-culturalism. The new sustainable civilization in question will witness human beings' effort to reconstruct a brand new view of life and the world by following a new thought pattern whose core is interactivity, complementarity, and mutual benefits. This brand new view will conjure up a brand new world. In this hugely exciting context, the field of comparative literature and culture, which is still evolving, is a key discipline that may help us all realize our best aspirations and pursuits.

Acknowledgments

The author gratefully acknowledges the substantial and significant contribution of Professor MENG Xiangchun, the chief translator, and the highly professional team he has been leading in the English translation of this book, without whose work the book would have never become what it is now. To show my due respect, I would like to list their brief profiles here, though, I assume, their names deserve better places.

MENG Xiangchun is Professor of English at Soochow University, China. He specializes in translation theory and practice, cultural translation, literary theory and criticism. He is the founder of Translation Interactology, or the Studies of Translation Dynamics.

Ian Hunter is a British associate professor who has been collaborating with Chinese researchers for over twelve years. His research interests include applied linguistics and translation studies. In 2014 he was granted the Sole Researcher-Practitioner Award for China by ETS of Princeton, USA.

Harry Kuoshu is Herring Professor of Asian Studies at Furman University. His research focuses on Chinese film and cultural studies.

They are researchers, translators, and cultural "ferrymen", enriching in their own way the global cultural ecology.

My thanks also go to the publishers, editors, proofreaders, reviewers, and all who have contributed to the improvement and publication of this book.

YUE Daiyun
Peking University

1 The Context of the Times
The Clash of Civilizations and the Future

1.1 A Review of "the Clash of Civilizations"

1.1.1 Huntington's Theory of "The Clash of Civilizations"

Chairman of the Harvard Academy for International and Area Studies, president of the American Political Science Association, and co-editor of *Foreign Policy*, Samuel P. Huntington advanced this concept in his 1993 article titled "The Clash of Civilizations" and it was later expanded into his highly influential 1996 monograph *The Clash of Civilizations and the Remaking of World Order*. His main arguments are summarized as follows:

1   Civilization is the highest cultural grouping of people and the broadest level of cultural identity essential to people that fundamentally distinguishes humankind from other species. The post-Cold War world is made up of seven or eight major civilizations and the major players in world affairs are no longer nation-states, but core states of major civilizations.

   The difference between culture and civilization is that the latter has a broader extension. Culture exists as a collection of beliefs, mainly composed of religious faith, psychological, emotional aspects and values, customs, institutions, and the resulting behavioral patterns that emerge. Religion is the primary factor that defines a civilization. Unlike the other four world religions, namely, Confucianism,[1] Islam, Hinduism, and Christianity, each serving as the religious foundation for a corresponding civilization, Buddhism is the only world religion that has been assimilated into multiple civilizations.

   Simply put, culture is created by humans, and humans in turn are cultural products, while civilization, as the highest level of cultural identity, is more inclusive than culture by its extension.

   The concept of civilization can be traced back to the first Axial Age. Karl Jaspers (1953) coined the term "axis" (of world history) in his book *Vom Ursprung und Ziel der Geschichte* (*The Origin and Goal of History*), referring to "the common frame of historical self-comprehension for all peoples" formed in the process of intellectual and spiritual development

DOI: 10.4324/9781003356240-1

2 *The Context of the Times*

between the eighth and the second centuries BCE (p. 1). The Axial Age is embodied by Confucius, Laozi, Mo-ti and Lieh-tsu among other schools of Chinese philosophers, Upanishads and Buddha of India, Zarathustra (circa 628–551BCE) of Persia, Hebrew prophets, and Greek philosophers. This Axial Age developed into diversified civilizations. World history has witnessed the rise of twelve major civilizations and the perishing of seven of them (including the Egyptian, Mesopotamian and Byzantine). The existing major civilizations are as follows:

Sinic: Chinese civilization dates back at least to 1500BCE or perhaps a millennium earlier;

Japanese: Japanese civilization, though a derivation of Chinese civilization, is distinct from the latter and emerged between 100 and 400CE;

Hindu: Arguably, the Hindu civilization emerged in 2000BCE;

Islamic: Islam came into being in the Arabian Peninsula during the middle seventh century CE and now encompasses Arab, Turkish, Persian, and Malay sub-civilizations;

Western: Western civilization began to prevail in Europe, North America, and Latin America between 700 and 800CE;

Latin American civilization and African civilization.

Huntington negates the idea of nation-states to lay a foundation for his concept of hegemony.

2 A shift in the balance of power among civilizations is under way. Asian civilizations are expanding their economic, military, and political strengths, and Islam is growing rapidly in demography. By and large, non-Western civilizations are reaffirming their own cultural values or legitimacy. Humans will witness the resurgence of non-Western civilizations and power, clash within non-Western societies and that between the Western and non-Western worlds.

In the first stage of the Axial Age, inter-cultural communication was rather slow, as evidenced by the delayed spread of some Chinese inventions. For example, printing was invented in the eighth century CE and movable type in the eleventh century, but they were not introduced into Europe until the fifteenth century. Paper making, developed in the second century CE, reached Japan as late as the seventh century and Europe in the thirteenth century. Similarly, gunpowder, a ninth-century Chinese invention, was made accessible to Europeans as late as the fourteenth century.

The second stage of the Axial Age witnessed an opposite trend. Within a few centuries, the non-Western world re-emerged, mastering most Western technologies and reviving its own cultures. A prominent manifestation is the population expansion in Islamic countries. The Muslim population constituted 18 percent of the world's total in 1980 and was projected to reach 20 percent in 2000 and 30 percent in 2025, with young people as the main contributor to the bulge. Those Islamic countries welcomed modernization but avoided Westernization. The territory of independent Islamic societies amounted to 11 million square miles in 1993, making up 21.1 percent of the world's total territorial area, compared to 1.8 million square miles in 1920, when it accounted for only 3.5 percent of the world's total.

In his 1918 book *The Decline of the West*, Oswald Spengler denounces the view of the progression of human history as linear, going through the ancient, medieval and modern stages, which he regards as an "empty figment"[2] conceived by the West. Arnold J. Toynbee also reprimands the "parochialism and impertinence"[3] underlying the Western illusion of a unified history. The assumption under this misconception is that there is only one river of civilization, and that all others either feed into it or vanish in the desert. Contemporary scholars, on the other hand, urge "the need to strive for a broader perspective"[4] and to understand "the great cultural conflicts in the world, and the multiplicity of its civilizations".[5] However, in Western societies, Western civilization is regarded by many to have the highest universality, and therefore to be superior to any others. Many Westerners dread the economic resurgence of non-Western societies, their massive immigration to the West and their possession of most sophisticated technologies. Westerners seem to be rendered helpless when facing this wholesale blending of regions and nations. Huntington contends that, under these circumstances, the "clash of civilizations" is inevitable and the hope of Western civilization to circumvent and survive such plight rests on the clash between the Islamic and the Confucian civilizations.

3   Alliances defined by ideology and superpower relations are giving way to those defined by civilization. Nations with civilizational similarities are coalescing and the fault lines between civilizations are becoming the primary lines of conflict in global politics. By such means a civilization-based world order is emerging.

At the micro level, the fiercest fault lines are those between Islam and its Eastern Orthodox, Hindu, African, and Western Christian neighbors. At the macro level, the primary division lies are between "the West and the rest", with the most intense conflicts occurring between Muslim and Asian societies and the West. The interaction between "Western arrogance, Islamic intolerance, and Sinic assertiveness" (p. 183), as Huntington concludes (1996), is believed to be the cause of future clashes, with perilous implications.

Huntington's fundamental point of departure is whether Western values and interests or those of Islam and China will be the decisive factor in global institutions, the distribution of power, national politics and economies in the twenty-first century. Islamic and Sinic societies alike, as Huntington argues, view the West as their rival and will antagonize the Western superiority with weapons of mass destruction and missiles for their delivery. In the scenario envisioned by Huntington, two camps will

4 *The Context of the Times*

be in place to counter the West, one made up of China and North Korea and the other comprising Pakistan, Iran, Iraq, Syria, Libya, and Algeria. He refers to the nuclear agreement between the United States and North Korea as a "negotiated surrender" and the treaties between the United States and Asian powers as "unconditional surrender", including renouncing the linkage of the most-favored-nation status of China granted by the United States with human rights and consenting to the caning of an American citizen in Singapore. Huntington's primary intention is to establish a civilization-based world order, or, to be precise, a world order based on Western civilization.

4   Fault line wars are characterized by prolonged duration and intermittence, intense violence, ideological ambivalence, and a low likelihood of resolution through negotiations. Reasons responsible for those wars include the following: a historical legacy of conflict; memories of fear and mutual hatred; huge changes in the demographic proportions; political, economic, and social pressures; and the urgent needs of emerging political entities. According to Huntington (1996), the solution to fault line wars mainly depends on the "interests and actions of the core states of the world's major civilizations" (p. 298).

During the seventh and eighth centuries, Muslim rule was established by the Arab–Islam alliance in North Africa, Iberia, the Middle East, Persia, and northern India; this remained stable for about two centuries. In 1095, Pope Urban II delivered a speech at the Council of Clermont, calling for a crusade to wrest the Holy Land, and Jerusalem in particular, from Muslim control, and appealed to Western European princes, Italian merchants and Catholic churches to launch an expedition to the eastern Mediterranean. Over the course of the following two centuries or so (1096–1291), eight crusades were made. As monotheistic religions, Islam and Christianity tend to deny the assimilation of additional deities and see the world in a dualistic way, or, in other words, in "us vs. them" terms. They both claim to be the one and only true faith and have a mission to convert nonbelievers to their faith. By the late twentieth century, the conflict between Islam and the West has been intensified by multiple factors, including: (1) the Muslim population growth and increasing unemployment, which spurred migration to the West; (2) the confidence of Muslims elevated by the breakdown of the colonial system and the Islamic Resurgence; (3) resentment among Muslims aroused by the West's efforts to disseminate its values and institutions and to intervene in conflicts in the Muslim world; (4) the collapse of the Soviet Union, which was the common enemy of the two parties; and (5) the unprecedented expansion of the intermingling of Muslims and Westerners, which has prompted contact among nations and their sense of self-identity. The previous power shift from Great Britain to the United States did not result in a hegemonic war thanks to the cultural kinship of the two societies. Huntington (1996) attributes many relatively small fault line wars

The Context of the Times   5

Table 1.1 Comparison between Sinic Civilization and Western Civilization

Facets	Sinic Civilization	Western Civilization
Individual	Stressing authority, hierarchy and the subordination of individual rights and interests.	Stressing liberty, equality, democracy, and individualism.
Collectivity	Attaching importance to consensus, avoiding confrontation, and "saving face".	Opposing authority, encouraging competition, distrusting government.
History	Giving priority to maximizing long-term gains and valuing history.	Forgetting the past and ignore the future.
Practice	"There are not two suns in the sky, there cannot be two emperors on earth." Regarding foreign monarchs and states as tributaries and thus causing obstacles to democratization.	Focusing on maximizing immediate gains and promoting checks and balances.

primarily to the dynamism of Islam and asserts that "the rise of China is the potential source of a big inter-civilizational war of core states" (p. 209). From his point of view, the opposition between Sinic and Western civilizations is a fundamental one. He has made a comparison between the two civilizations, shown in Table 1.1.

Huntington remarks that the two models, China's hierarchy of authority and the European balance of power, form a sharp contrast and China hardly ever shares common objectives with the United States on major policy issues, meaning that the differences between the two nations are diverse. China is driven by its culture, history, traditions, size, economic dynamism, and self-image to seek a hegemonic position in East Asia, which will undeniably threaten the core interests of the United States. The only possible primary balancer of China is Japan, but it is improbable that Japan will play such a role. In a 1994 survey in Japan on public speculations about the most influential nation in Asia in the twenty-first century, 44, 30 and 16 percent voted in favor of China, the United States, and Japan, respectively. Mu'ammar al-Qadhafi proposed to build a "Tehran–Islamabad–Beijing axis" and he declared, "So, we as Muslims, will support China in its fight against our common enemy... We wish China victory" (as cited in Huntington, 1996, p. 143). Huntington (1996) argues, "If Chinese economic development continues, this could be the single most serious security issue American policymakers confront in the early twenty-first century" (p. 232).

5   Crucial to the survival of the West is that Westerners should admit the uniqueness of their civilization rather than deem it as universal and they should unite to guard against challenges from non-Western societies. To prevent global inter-civilizational wars, world leaders should accept and

6   The Context of the Times

work together to maintain the multicivilizational nature of politics. It is unlikely, but not impossible, for the world to see a global war among the core states of major civilizations.

The Western "universal civilization", as Huntington sees it, will never replace multiculturality. The Davos World Economic Forum (Switzerland) with Western values at its core is rejected by the World Social Forum (held in Seattle, Genoa, and Brazil). Western consumption patterns and popular culture have spread around the world, but in some cases, ironically, it only enables people to blow up American aircraft while drinking Coca-Cola. The millions of Japanese cars imported to the United States have not "Japanized" the country. The prevalence of global communications has not led to the convergence of attitudes and beliefs, but the opposite.

While the disintegration of mankind caused by the Cold War has ended, the fundamental divides in ethnicities, religions and civilizations remain, which requires the maintenance of multiculturality. A conclusion can be drawn that the West has been declining in a gradual and irregular manner since the early twentieth century, and that either the decline could last for several more decades, or the West could enter a stage of revival as an example for other civilizations to follow and copy. The West is intent on developing a system equivalent to a universal empire. Huntington (1996) diverges from neoconservatives in the twenty-first century in his observation that "the prudent course for the West is not to attempt to stop the shift in power but to learn to navigate the shallows, endure the miseries, moderate its ventures, and safeguard its culture" (p. 311).

Huntington fears the challenge from immigrants and their theoretical perspectives. He (1996) writes in explicit terms that a "more immediate and dangerous challenge exists in the United States." "In the name of multi-culturalism, they [intellectuals and publicists] have attacked the identification of the United States with Western civilization, denied the existence of a common American culture, and promoted racial, ethnic, and other subnational cultural identities and groupings" (p. 305). In his paper, Huntington (1997) argues that "American popular culture and consumer products have swept the world, permeating the most distant and resistant societies. American economic, ideological, military, technological, and cultural primacy is, in short, overwhelming" (p. 40). He further points out that Americans have to begin "countering the cults of diversity and multiculturalism", and then draws a conclusion: "If multiculturalism prevails and if the consensus on liberal democracy disintegrates, the United States could join the Soviet Union on the ash heap of history" (p. 40). Therefore, if the nation is to enhance the "consensus" and "cohesion among people", it must stay alert and construct an "opposing other".

In brief, Huntington contends that the United States should promote multiculturalism abroad but not at home because multiculturalism at home will lead to the retrogression and disintegration of unique American culture and threaten the nation and the West in general. In contrast, if multiculturalism is not practiced internationally and other cultures are subjected to American culture, there will be rebellions involving ethnic groups, which will pose a threat to the West and to the world. In fact, while universalists want to "Americanize" the world, multiculturalists want the United States to resemble the world. He believes that neither is possible. For him, a non-Western America is not American, and it is impossible to build a culturally generalized global empire totally covered by American culture. Huntington (1996) states, "The preservation of the United States and the West requires the renewal of Western identity. The security of the world requires acceptance of global multiculturality" (p. 318). His arguments have given way to neoconservatism in the new era but the impact of his theory remains.

1.1.2 The Development of the "Clash of Civilizations" Theory: The Publication of Empire

The 2000 book *Empire*, co-authored by Michael Hardt and Antonio Negri, is a critical involvement in the discussion of empire. Hardt is currently a professor of Literature at Duke University, and Negri a political philosophy professor at the University of Padua and a member of Red Brigades. Accused of leading a terrorist organization, Negri was apprehended in 1979. While imprisoned awaiting trial, he was given a temporary release in 1983 upon his election to the Italian legislature as a member for the Radical Party and then fled to France. After his 14 years' exile in France, he returned to Italy where he was put into prison again and released in the spring of 2003. The basic standpoint of *Empire*, as is concluded in the Chinese translation of the book, is that right before our eyes is an empire growing and taking shape, unbounded and endless, and that a global political order, a new form of sovereignty, is emerging.

Throughout the drastically transforming contemporary times, while political controls, state functions, and regulatory mechanisms have retained their ruling role in economic and social production and exchange, a new form of sovereignty has taken shape, where national and supranational organizations are integrated under the single logic of rule. This emerging form of global sovereignty is called "Empire". It is an apparatus characterized by decentered structure and de-territorializing, where culture and economy retain unimpeded mobility. The concept of nation-states has been ebbing and the supranational imperial regime takes over the task of global rule. In short, out there is emerging "a new form of sovereignty. Empire is the political subject that effectively regulates [these] global exchanges, the sovereign power that governs the world" (Negri & Hardt, 2001, p. xi).

Hardt and Negri argue that with the destabilization of the Cold War regime, barriers to the capitalist market and globalization of production are eliminated and a new world order has presented itself. The political subject in this new world regime takes the form of "Empire" whose inside and outside are indistinguishable, and it operates in omnipresent virtual space not partitioned by territorial boundaries of conventional nation-states.

8 *The Context of the Times*

The formation of Empire is the transformation from the European model to the American model, from imperialism based on nation-states where spaces are attributed to an Empire, to an Empire with open spaces.

Differences between the new Empire and the old include:

1 While the old Empire is characterized by an obvious geography of territorial boundaries, the new Empire is composed of multilayered networks across unbounded territories. Without boundaries, the new Empire can expand without limit.
2 The old Empire regards colonies as under the authority of sovereign affairs. Dominant sovereign countries substantially rule over their colonies and exhibit aggressiveness and destructiveness against other cultures. The new Empire makes renewals and adjustments via economic and political means, thus exercising control imperceptibly.
3 The old Empire practices regional regulation and monopoly while the new Empire has no demarcated domain for productivity, and new technologies can spread all over the world rapidly, forming a network. Only a new Empire can have exclusive global control.
4 The old Empire is bound to produce racial differences to exert differential regulation. The new Empire imposes rule through networks and can be more inclusive in cultural terms.

In short, the new Empire is not a decadent stage of monopolized capitalism, as in Lenin's terminology, but a phase of development and revival of capitalism; it is the only sovereignty beyond national borders and multinational negotiation. Quite a few Americans trust and favor a "mild imperialism" where world affairs are conducted on equal terms, evil is brought to justice and good is praised, and disparities in social classes, labor types and urban–rural statuses are presented in a totally different way. The new Empire deterritorializes the world and will rule over the whole globe in peace, and in the meantime, unite underprivileged groups, which will act as the major agent to restrain the Empire. On the cover page of the Chinese translation of *Empire*, it reads: "From modernity to post-modernity, from imperialism to Empire, what will become of this new era, universal harmony and order, or oppression and constraint? The future hinges on the interaction between the Empire and its offsetting forces" (Negri & Hardt, 2003, Cover).

1.1.3 The Theory of "New Empire": The Emergence of Postmodern Neo-imperialism

The "New Empire" Theory serves the unilateral American hegemony. It holds that humans are entering a transformative period of divergence and disorder, a period of great uncertainty and nebulous historical trends. International authorities no longer strive to safeguard the existing system and they make policies based on the judgment of the disintegration of the current system, seeking to maximize their profits.

The Context of the Times 9

John Mearsheimer, professor at the University of Chicago, points out, in his 2002 book *The Tragedy of Great Power Politics*, that every state seeks to maximize its power, and a check-and-balance mechanism is hence unlikely to be implemented. For him, the best defense is a good offense.

According to Philip Bobbitt and Robert Cooper, the nation-state has developed into the market-state, which internally does not deliver social welfare but instead provides legislation and opportunities, leaving citizens free to pursue profits in the market, and externally uses every means possible to ensure that its institution is applied globally. Nation-states continue to promote the concept of "new imperialism" which means that postmodern states exert their national power to control modern states (that is, nation-states such as China, India and Brazil) and to deter onslaughts among pre-modern states.

Neoconservatism in the twenty-first century, represented by Donald Rumsfeld, Dick Cheney and Paul Wolfowitz, has three core components: (1) readiness to use military force; (2) proposition to establish the "benevolent global hegemony" of the United States; and (3) an emphasis on the spreading of American democracy and values. Since the year 2000, neoconservatives have been at the core in the United States' international affairs and in control of its national political power. They all believe that "today's international system is built not around a balance of power but around American hegemony" and that with any lessening of the American hegemony will emerge countries shaping the world according to their own needs (Kagan & Kristol, 2000, pp. 57–69). In their point of view, countries such as China and Russia, if given the chance, will configure an international system significantly different from the present one. Consequently, they have a firm conviction that it is of necessity to avoid the emergence of great regional powers in Europe, East Asia and the Middle East because these powers will threaten the predominance of the United States.

The Project for the New American Century (PNAC), founded by William Kristol and Robert Kagan, is intended to maintain a "unipolar twenty-first century". It aims to "deter the rise of a new great-power competitor", "defend key regions of Europe, East Asia and the Middle East", advance the transformation of the U.S. armed forces and war itself, maintain dominance in cyberspace and space, and spread the American principles of liberty, democracy and freedom around the globe (Kagan et al., 2000, pp. 2–3). Their neo-imperial grand strategy is to take the initiative, conceive an imaginary enemy as the object of attack, redefine "sovereignty", and promote the concept of "limited sovereignty". They show contempt for and intend to revise international norms and advocate the advent of an "era of post-nationalism".

1.2 New Trends Resisting Imperial Homogeneity

1.2.1 Edgar Morin and His "Beyond Globalization and Development"

Edgar Morin is a French philosopher and now researcher emeritus at the National Centre for Scientific Research in France. His works include *Le Paradigme Perdu: La Nature Humaine* (*The Lost Paradigm: Human Nature*),

10 *The Context of the Times*

La Méthode (6 volumes) and *Science Avec Conscience* (*Science with Conscience*). Morin's recent article, "Au-delà de la globalisation et du développement, société-monde ou empire-monde?" ("Beyond Globalization and Development: World Society or World Empire?"), has attracted considerable attention. His major arguments are summarized as follows:

1   Globalization in the 1990s, as Morin sees it, has advanced not only in technological and economic terms, but also in humanitarian and democratic ones. It is unfinished, insufficient and fragile, but has introduced peoples under oppression to the notion of liberty, and subsequently triggered decolonization in most regions around the globe. People have come to realize that Western values could only be adopted through competing with Western imperialism. Globalization in this period is a part of the dual process of "rule-liberation" and has wrought new characteristics for this process.

2   Cultural globalization has not led to cultural homogeneity. Innovation occurs in the process of cross-cultural communication, and cross-cultural encounters, in turn, incentivize national cultures to display ingenious expressions internally. Cultural blending is bound to result in growing diversities within cultures and it facilitates exchanges. For example, after rhythm and blues encountered each other, rock and roll music spread among the white market in America and later prevailed throughout the world. People in different regions began to perform the music in their own languages and have formed their own distinctive characteristics. Today, people are seen dancing to rock music, celebrating with rock music and communicating with each other by means of rock music in, for instance, Beijing, Guangdong, Tokyo, Paris and Moscow. To the same rhythm, young adults all over the world can truly spread their wings and fly on this planet.

3   Morin views development with suspicion. There have been considerable misunderstandings of cultural globalization, among which the most serious one is development regardless of costs. The concept of "development" inevitably contains economic and technological components and can be measured by income figures or growth index, in other words, can be "quantified". The assumption underlying this concept is that economic and technological development is naturally the engine of "human development" and the successful model is the so-called highly-developed Western countries.

The concept of "development" has left out those existences that deny calculation or measurement such as living, sorrow, happiness and love. The only dimension of development is growth (say, of products, labor productivity and monetary income). With quantity as the only measure, this concept ignores quality, such as that of reason for existence, benevolence, social environment, and the quality of life.

The logic of "development" neglects the moral and psychological lethargy generated in humans by economic and technological growth. Excessive specialization, the disconnectedness of domains, extreme individualism, and obsession with a lust for gain, all result in people losing their sense of solidarity and reciprocity.

Specialization of knowledge resulting from "development" leaves people no way out of plights and complex problems. Specialized education in developed countries can admittedly help people learn enormously, but meanwhile it constrains intellectual abilities and renders people almost blind to fundamental and global problems.

"Development" also overlooks mental wealth, which cannot be calculated or traded, such as dedication, nobility, credibility and conscience. Unfortunately, wherever it goes, "development" undermines cultural treasures and the wisdom in ancient traditions and even civilizations themselves.

"Development", for sure, has brought about scientific, technological, medical and social progress; however, it has also caused environmental degradation, cultural decline, new inequalities, and, consequently, a new form of slavery replacing the conventional one.

Finally, the logic held by "development", with reference to the model, ideal and purposes of Western civilization, does not consider that Western civilization *per se* is shrouded by crisis. The blessing of Western civilization carries with it the seed of its curse; its individualism contains the isolation and loneliness of egocentricity and its achievements in urban technology and industry have brought anxiety and detriment to people. The force caused by "development", especially by scientific ignorance and urban pollution, will lead people towards nuclear apocalypse and ecological death.

1.2.2 Efforts Against Unilateralism and Towards European Renaissance

On May 31, 2003, the article "Unsere Erneuerung. Nach dem Krieg: Die Wiedergeburt Europas" ("Our Renovation. After the War: The Renaissance of Europe"), co-written by Jürgen Habermas and Jacques Derrida, was published in many leading European newspapers. Many other well-known philosophers, artists and litterateurs also had their own articles published during the same period. Their major opinions are summarized as follows:

1   Secularization in European societies is far advanced. Citizens oppose the transgression of political and religious borders.
2   In comparison, Europeans tend to have more faith in national organizational and steering capacities, and harbor deep skepticism about the regulatory capacities of the market.
3   Europeans are not blindly optimistic about technological progress.
4   Europeans maintain a preference for regulations based on communal solidarity, respect the integrity of individual dignity, advocate the strengthening of the role of the United Nations based on military violence control and abatement, and favor the establishment of effective global domestic politics.

12   *The Context of the Times*

The first step to counterbalance the United States, according to the authors, is to rejuvenate Europe, since China and Russia are not yet powerful enough, and to construct a "core Europe" is the grand historical mission assigned to intellectuals. Richard Rorty, a famed American philosopher, also joined this discussion. He published an article titled "Humiliation or Solidarity?" in the newspaper *Süddeutsche Zeitung*. Rorty (2005) writes:

> Such an upsurge of [European] idealistic self-redefinition would be responded to around the world, in the US and China as well as in Brazil and Russia... Both Europe and America contain many millions of people who see clearly that, despite all that America has done for the cause of human freedom, its assertion of a right to permanent hegemony is a terrible mistake. Americans who realize this need all the help they can get to persuade their fellow-citizens that Bush has been taking their country down the wrong path.
>
> (p. 40)

Europe has experienced two world wars, and all the great European nations witnessed the pinnacle of imperial power. They must learn some lessons from the imperial fall. Gone are the imperial governance and the history of colonization, and "the European powers also got the chance to assume a reflexive distance from themselves" (Habermas & Derrida, 2005, p. 34). This may contribute to the abolition of Eurocentrism and expedite the realization of the Kantian hope for global domestic politics.

Admittedly, there has been much controversy about European integration, but the recent adoption of the European Constitution is a good sign.

1.2.3 The Conception of Global Civil Society

Since the 1970s, many intellectuals have sensed the current crisis and then conceived the idea of a "global civil society". Pioneers have established such organizations as Médecins Sans Frontières, known in English as Doctors Without Borders (a humanitarian medical organization), and Greenpeace. Organizations of a similar nature have been successively formed since then.

1   The building of a global civil society took its first substantive leap in late 1999, when protests, against economic and technological globalization, broke out in Seattle. The event demonstrated an anticipation of another type of globalization under the slogan of "Our world is not for sale". People became aware that whilst they had to come up with global solutions to global issues, they also had to exert pressure at the global scale and propose motions. The "Battle of Seattle", as the protests became known, triggered a few gatherings, out of which the Global Citizen Forum emerged. Thereafter, those involved in the demonstrations are termed as "Seattle people".

The Context of the Times   13

2   In 2001, the first World Social Forum was held in Brazil, involving 4,700 delegates from 117 countries and thousands of non-officially invited attendees. People attended the forum with piles of now seemingly Utopian appeals. Non-governmental organizations all over the world expressed their support for those appeals and aspirations by peaceful or unpeaceful means (for example, a French peasant leader, Joseph Bové, played a significant role in activities to dismantle a McDonald's franchise, incinerate imported genetically modified crops and rip up an experimental genetically modified crop field during the 2001 Forum). After the Forum, while a plane was hovering in the sky, demonstrating a flying banner reading, "Our world is not for sale", people marched on the ground, singing and dancing. The delegates made a mosaic of a stone book with rocks they brought with them and set the mosaic book at the venue of the Forum to record the development of a global civil society, and the rock from China bears these words: "天下为公" ("The world is for all."). The 2002 Forum was held in the same place, drawing 60,000 participants from 123 countries, including around 1,000 politicians, 6 incumbent ministers of France, the mayor of Paris, and representatives from the French Prime Minister's Office and French President's Office. The Forum had about 700 workshops and talks on themes such as world trade, world bank, transgenics, social exclusion, the role of nations, economic development and agricultural protection, and the additional theme of diversifying culture and language. The 2003 Forum, which took place still on the same spot, expanded in scale and was held under the slogan of "Another world is possible". It was determined that the 2004 event would be organized in India.

3   The first World Assembly of Citizens was held in Lille in December, 2001. The ten-day-long conference convened over 700 citizens from different continents, who entered into discussions over and over again with great zeal and brought forth the draft Charter of Human Responsibilities (2001), proposing:

Facing the radically new situation of humankind, a third ethical pillar, common to all societies and all social spheres, is needed to serve as a complement to the two existing pillars which underpin international life: the Universal Declaration of Human Rights and the Charter of the United Nations.

The main dimensions of the Charter (2001) are: "accepting responsibility for the direct and indirect consequences of our actions; uniting with one another to escape from powerlessness; acknowledging that our responsibility is proportional to the knowledge and power which each of us holds."

To conclude, the global trend towards a unified empire has, on the one hand, inspired the imagination of a global civil society, and, on the other, incurred resistance from nation-states, races and religions. The elimination of such resistance calls for more brutal rule, which, at its extreme, takes the form

14 *The Context of the Times*

of sharp collisions between cultural fundamentalism and cultural hegemonism. The two are advancing side by side worldwide, becoming the chief culprits of estrangement among people. If mankind is to get rid of this entanglement, people must make a leap in their spirit, this requiring an essential elevation in terms of the inner mental aspects rather than technological and scientific capacities or cognitive abilities to understand complexity. To build a global civil world is not to erect a perfect, flawless hegemonic empire, but to lay the foundation for civil alliance. What is lacking is not planning or designing, but theoretical foundations and the principles to guide us. The most important underlying principle is to rediscover the "other" and the East through interactive cognition.

1.3 The Thought Pattern of Interactive Cognition and the Oriental Turn

1.3.1 The Transformation of Cognitive Style

Bertrand Russell (1945) states, in his *A History of Western Philosophy*, that "the Cartesian system presents two parallel but independent worlds, that of mind and that of matter, each of which can be studied without reference to the other" (p. 567). As the system denotes, Western philosophy had treated the spiritual and material worlds as mutually independent and irrelevant, and, consequently, it had been premised on an external relationship between the "mind" and "matter", and its thought patterns had long been characterized by the "mind–body duality".

In the second half of the twentieth century, there emerged a significant epistemological and methodological shift from the logistical paradigm to a phenomenological one. The logistical paradigm falls under the category of content analysis whereby, through inspissation, concrete contents are drained and the most concise generalized forms are derived, and it finally boils down to the metaphysical Logos or absolute spirit in Hegel's thought. Proceeding from the logistical paradigm, every concept can be simplified into a pure ideal form void of body, substance and time, and every narrative can be reduced into a clearly-defined, closed space where all processes merely express a fundamental structural form. For instance, narratives in many works can be reduced into this structure: preexistent "deficiency" and then "deficiency remedied" or "deficiency predestined to be irremediable". A multiplicity of such narratives combines to form a "meta-narrative" or "meta-text" of the same structure, demonstrating some laws, essence, and inevitability.

Unlike the logistical paradigm, the phenomenological one does not take form as its object of inquiry. Instead, it takes the "body" as its primary concern; a living body that has its existence and acts, and one that can feel pain and joy. Everything surrounding the body is fixed, but its effect changes according to the emotions and perspectives of the body. Hence, the space in phenomenological inquiries is an open topological space that constantly changes with the passion, desire and will of the subject.

In the phenomenological paradigm, the depth model that many are accustomed to is deconstructed: phenomena do not necessarily have an essence beneath, contingency is not always predicated on inevitability, and a "signifier" does not necessarily correspond to a fixed "signified". Similarly, the center is also deconstructed and everything that has been rendered marginal, fragmentary, dormant, and obscure now unleashes new energy. History disintegrates into two layers, namely, the "history of events" and the "narrated history". The former refers to the history that is happening and lived or witnessed. Since the scope of living or witnessing is rather limited, for the most part we can only get to know history via narratives, and therefore that history is called "narrated history". However, what to narrate, how detailed the narration is, and from which angle or perspective to narrate, are all inevitably affected by subjective constraints. Thus, all history is essentially contemporary history, or, in other words, history transcribed and interpreted by contemporaries. In fact, these two history layers usually coexist and are applied in different domains in the same way that Newtonian mechanics and quantum mechanics are employed in different areas of inquiry. In cultural studies, the phenomenological paradigm serves to dismantle the center, emancipate the mind, escape from authorities, and maximize creativity, but it has also caused the discreteness and irrelevance of human cognition.

1.3.2 Interactive Cognition

Proceeding from the phenomenological paradigm, it is of great significance to understand the subject. The exorcism of rigidity and fixedness in self-cognition entails the involvement of the "other"; in other words, cognition is generated through the interaction between the subject and the object; it is not a one-sided activity; neither is it an understanding imposed on the latter by the former nor intrinsic features of the latter *per se*. In the conventional thought pattern, cognition starts from formula, definition, classification and deduction and what it describes is how a reliable subject "gets acquainted with" a relatively established object, thereby defining, delineating and classifying it into our epistemological frame. By contrast, the pattern of interactive cognition emphasizes the changes and the subsequent result or development experienced by the subject and the "other" during cognitive interaction. It underlines the "principle of the other", which is the opposite of the "principle of the subject", and highlights the indeterminate "principle of interaction", the opposite of determinacy and the "principle of general applicability". In a nutshell, it emphasizes that an immutable subject does not suffice to form a deep knowledge of things, which can only be achieved through observation and reflection from the viewpoint of the "other", and that the significance of all things is by no means immutable and there is not necessarily any predetermined answer, but instead, amidst all the variable interactions and the infinity of uncertain possibilities, only one possibility becomes the reality as a consequence of all occurrences and chances.

16　*The Context of the Times*

1.3.3 *François Jullien and His "Why We Westerners Cannot Avoid China in Our Study of Philosophy"*

Considering the situations mentioned above, Chinese culture will surely become a significant "other" for the rest of the world. François Jullien, a French philosopher, states (as cited in Wong, 2012, p. 142):

> The Chinese language, which is outside the enormous Indo-European language system, explores another possibility of writing. The Chinese civilization is one that has the longest history and had evolved independently without being influenced by European culture... All in all, China is an ideal image contrasted with which we will be able to free ourselves from some preconceived ideas and gaze at our own thoughts from the outside.

Some Western philosophers have begun their inquiries of interactive cognition and have broken encouragingly new ground in this area. Many people have come to realize that if they are to gain comprehensive self-awareness, or knowledge about themselves, they have to become detached from the closed self and examine it from various external angles. In his paper "Why We Westerners Cannot Avoid China in Our Study of Philosophy", Jullien writes (as cited in Wong, 2012, p. 130):

> When we choose to start, we actually choose to depart so that we can have a broader view for our meditation. In the remotest reaches of the exotic world, such activities are carried out all the time. We navigate China to know Greece better. Despite some gaps in our knowledge, we are still too close to and familiar with the Greek thought, which is part of our own heritage. In order to understand it and make new discoveries, we have to cut ourselves off from this familiarity so that we can form a fresh perspective from the outside.

From the "space for perspective-taking" and the "external point of view of the other", we can form a new understanding of ourselves. The Chinese version of Jullien's *Fonder la Morale: Dialogue de Mencius avec un Philosophe des Lumières* (*Grounding Morals: Mencius' Dialogue with an Enlightenment Philosopher*), published recently by Peking University Press, investigates this issue. In the preface, Jullien (2002) states:

> The author has set out from such a distant perspective, and the motivation is not the pursuit of exotic charm, nor the alluring delight in comparison, but the mere longing to retrieve some room for a theoretical detour: in virtue of a new starting point, I want to liberate myself from theoretical arguments that I have failed to disentangle because of my position in the heart of them.

(p. 6)

The Context of the Times   17

In fact, Chinese philosophers developed such awareness long ago. Su Shi (1037–1101), a distinguished poet in the Song dynasty, composed the following poem:

> From the side, a whole range; from the end, a single peak;
> far, near, high, low, no two parts alike.
> Why can't I tell the true shape of Lu-shan?
> Because I myself am in the mountain.[6]

Essentially, Su Shi epitomizes the effort to create a "space for perspective-taking" and an "external point of view". To truly understand ourselves, we should not only view the self as the subject but also hold an "external point of view", including reference to other subjects (the "other") and opinions on the self from different angles or cultural contexts. Sometimes, we, when reminded or inspired by the "other", may gain an unexpected, renewed understanding of things around that we have failed to notice.

1.3.4 Roger T. Ames and David L. Hall and Their Thinking Through Confucius, among Others

In fact, quite a few scholars hold opinions akin to Jullien's, and publications of a similar nature have generated a wave of heated discussion. In America, three books in this area co-authored by the renowned sinologist Roger Ames and the eminent philosopher David Hall have been published successively and become somewhat sensational. The first book, *Thinking Through Confucius*, re-explores Confucius' thinking by new concepts in contemporary philosophy. The second one, *Anticipating China: Thinking Through the Narrations of Chinese and Western Culture*, emphasizes that the Western way of thinking values transcendence, order, and durability, while the Chinese way values practicality, fuzziness, and variation. The third book, *Thinking from the Han: Self, Truth and Transcendence in Chinese and Western Culture*, focuses on the exploration of self, truth and transcendence. In his 2000 book *The Siren and the Sage: Knowledge and Wisdom in Ancient Greece and China*, Stephan Shankman makes a bidirectional interpretation of cognition in Ancient Greece and China, with either serving as the other's frame of reference. Incidentally, his edited book *Early China/Ancient Greece: Thinking Through Comparisons* published in 2002 includes a collection of celebrated works from over two years' study of Chinese and Ancient Greek traditional cultures from their roots and through interaction.

Ames points out that Western philosophy is undergoing radical changes. Philosophers and philosophical movements alike have been challenging, in many respects, the established idea of well-acquainted theoretical and methodological objectivity. Criticism is gaining momentum within Western societies, bearing various names or banners such as neo-pragmatism, post-structuralism, hermeneutics, neo-Marxism, deconstruction, feminist philosophy, environmental philosophy, and post-modernism. This general

18   *The Context of the Times*

trend urges us to forsake assumptions about certainty without analysis, and about the hegemonic notion of the priority of science over literature, of rationality over language, of cognition over emotion, and of males over females. This multi-perspective, multi-dimensional criticism of both positivism and scientism represents a true revolution in Western ideology.

What Ames stresses is not merely knowledge of the self through the "other" but also the development of the self that is made possible by new conclusions drawn from dialogue. For instance, Ames contends that "Confucian democracy" is derived from the dialogue between Dewey and Confucius. The major obstacle to democracy, as John Dewey has argued, is the confusion of democratic ideals with political institutions, especially when the latter hypocritically claims to embody such democratic ideals. The foundation of democracy, in Dewey's view, is the communication between human communities, the unity of which can help establish personal values. Confucius and Dewey emphasize the identity of the individual as a "person-in-concrete-context" and reject the notion of the anarchistic, unrestricted individual. The cultural values that they both espouse are accomplishments of human communities accumulated over a fairly long period. Dewey has shown his "insistence that democracy is expressed in attitudes rather than institutions, and that the sort of democratic attitudes entailed by his vision of democracy are both gradually formed by and reinforced through education" (Ames & Hall, 1999, p. 142). He points out that the mere pursuit of the independent and liberated self has not benefited the United States, but in fact, has impeded the progress of American society. All these ideas can be corroborated, justified and carried forward by Confucius's teachings.

1.3.5 The Eastern Ideal in E. F. Schumacher's Small Is Beautiful

Jean-François Revel, a contemporary philosopher and member of the Académie Française, along with his Buddhist son Matthieu Ricard, have proposed the argument in their dialogue that the failure of the West, if any, has little to do with science but much to do with philosophy. Philosophy has two fundamental functions: wisdom and science. During the last three centuries, Western philosophy has abandoned its function of wisdom, and meanwhile, been deprived of the function of science by science itself. To conclude the discussion, Ricard (1999) states:

> Over the last twenty years, after centuries of mutual ignorance, a real dialogue between Buddhism and the main currents of Western thought has started. Buddhism can now take its rightful place in the history of ideas and the sciences... Behind what might initially look like its exotic forms, the Buddhist path, like all the great spiritual traditions, is designed to help us become better human beings. Science has neither the design nor the means to help us attain that goal.
>
> (p. 308)

This represents a sober-minded, reflective understanding of modern Western culture.

In his *Small Is Beautiful* published in the early 1970s (the Chinese version came out in 1984), E. F. Schumacher, a German-born British economist, introduces a highly impressive Buddhist economics as opposed to modern economics. Schumacher (1973) argues:

> Buddhist economics must be very different from the economics of modem materialism, since the Buddhist sees the essence of civilization not in a multiplication of wants but in the purification of human character. From a Buddhist point of view, the economics of modem materialism is standing the truth on its head by considering goods as more important than people and consumption as more important than creative activity. For the modern economist this is very difficult to understand. He is used to measuring the "standard of living" by the amount of annual consumption, assuming all the time that a man who consumes more is "better off" than a man who consumes less. A Buddhist economist would consider this approach excessively irrational, since as consumption is merely a means to realize human well-being, the aim should be to obtain the maximum amount of well-being with the minimum amount of consumption.
>
> (p. 42)

This is the enlightenment Schumacher obtained from oriental philosophy. Buddhist observations, among other things, have brought him remarkable insights, which enabled him to break away from the fetishism or superstition of Western science. In the Buddhist tradition, what science reveals is but one aspect of the truth about the physical world, and observations merely in the physical dimension will surely fail to attain the possible whole truth about existences and their being.

The renowned Swiss psychiatrist and psychoanalyst Carl Gustav Jung (1875–1961) confesses that the super wisdom that he had been trying in vain to seek in Western classics for decades has been discovered in a Chinese Taoist classic which was translated into German and later from German to English, titled *The Secret of the Golden Flower*.[7] Jung regards the *neidan* (内丹, inner alchemy) meditation as a product of "high culture", and, by contrast, Western intellectualism becomes "a mark of barbarism". Jung suggests that Westerners should abstain from the arrogance of science and rationality and draw on the oriental wisdom of comprehending the world in its entirety. He expresses his concern: the most urgent question today is... how can we alter the mind of Western man so that he would renounce his terrible skill? It is infinitely more important to strip him of the illusion of his power than to strengthen him still further in the mistaken idea that he can do everything he wills. The slogan one hears so often in Germany, "Where there's a will there's a way," has cost the lives of millions of human beings (Jung, 1978, pp. 82–83).

20   *The Context of the Times*

In his *Modernity and the Holocaust*, Zygmunt Bauman, a representative of mainstream sociology, also argues that high level of civilization and high level of barbarity are, in fact, interconnected and hardly distinguishable. His book is exceedingly vivid and straightforward testimony to the thought-provoking argument that some of the essential factors of modernity combined, for example, cold and unduly precise rational calculation, self-perpetuating technology with its morally neutral façade fueling the engine of self-destruction of human beings, and social management leaning to an inhuman engineering approach, have made the dehumanizing tragedy of persecution and slaughter of human beings a collective activity of society with the designer, executor, and victim cooperating closely together. Modernity originates from rationality, and now it seems that extreme rationality leads to extreme irrationality. Modernity results from modern civilization, the extensive development of which has gone beyond the human grip, leading to the high stage of barbarity.

These plights urge the West to introspect and seek from the East, which is an "other", a different lifestyle and a different thought pattern, which serve as an opposite frame of reference.

To conclude, personages of broad vision all over the world are exploring how to rescue mankind from the "clash of civilizations" that has already caused enormous calamities. To this end, an important way is to enable cultural reflections, consciousness and dialogue through multi-dimensional, multi-directional reference and interactive cognition.

Notes

1 If religion is defined as a system of belief in a god or gods, Confucianism, which has no transcendental god, is not a religion, but moral and social philosophy.
2 See: Spengler, O. (1928). *The decline of the West* (Two Vols.) (C. F. Atkinson, Trans.). New York: Alfred A. Knopf. p. 21.
3 See: Toynbee, A. J. (1946). *A study of history* (Abridgement of Vols. I–VI). New York: Oxford University Press. p. 39.
4 See: Huntington, S. P. (1996). *The clash of civilizations and the remaking of world order*. New York: Simon & Schuster. p. 55.
5 See: Braudel, F. (1980). *On history*. Chicago: The University of Chicago Press. p. xxxiii.
6 Translated by Watson. See: Su, S. (1084). Written on the Wall at West Forest Temple. In *Selected poems of Su Tung-P'o*. (1994). (B. Watson, Trans.). Port Townsend, WA: Copper Canyon Press. p. 108.
7 The Chinese title of the original book is "太乙金华宗旨" (*Taiyi Jinhua Zongzhi*, cited as *T'ai I Chin Hua Tsung Chin* in *The Secret of the Golden Flower*).

References

Ames, R. T., & Hall, D. L. (1999). *The democracy of the dead: Dewey, Confucius, and the hope for democracy in China*. Chicago: Carus Publishing Company.
Habermas, J., & Derrida, J. (2005). February 15, or what binds Europeans together: A plea for a common foreign policy, beginning in the core of Europe. In M. Pensky (Ed.), *Globalizing critical theory*. Lanham: Rowman & Littlefield Publishers. Inc.

Huntington, S. P. (1996). *The clash of civilizations and the remaking of world order.* New York: Simon & Schuster.

Huntington, S. P. (1997). The erosion of American national interests. *Foreign Affairs, 76*(5), 28–49.

Jaspers, K. (1953). *The origin and goal of history* (M. Bullock, Trans.). New Haven and London: Yale University Press.

Jullien, F. (2002). *Grounding morals: Mencius' dialogue with an enlightenment philosopher* (G. Song, Trans.). Beijing: Peking University Press.

Jung, C. G. (1978). *Psychology and the East* (R. F. C. Hull, Trans.). Princeton, NJ: Princeton University Press.

Kagan, D., Schmitt, G., & Donnelly, T. (2000). *Rebuilding America's defenses: Strategy, forces and resources for a new century. A report of the Project for The New American Century.* New American Century. Retrieved from http://www.newamericancentury.org/RebuildingAmericasDefenses.pdf

Kagan, R., & Kristol, W. (2000). The present danger. *The National Interest, 59*(Spring), 57–69.

Negri, A., & Hardt, M. (2001). *Empire.* Cambridge, MA: Harvard University Press.

Negri, A., & Hardt, M. (2003). *Empire: A globalized political order* (J. G. Yang, & Y. T. Fan, Trans.). Nanjing: Jiangsu People's Publishing House.

Revel, J. F., & Ricard, M. (1999). *The monk and the philosopher: A father and son discuss the meaning of life* (J. Canti, Trans.). New York: Schocken Books.

Rorty, R. (2005). Humiliation or solidarity? In D. Levy, M. Pensky & J. Torpey (Eds.), *Old Europe, new Europe, core Europe: Transatlantic relations after the Iraq War.* London: Verso.

Russell, B. (1945). *A history of Western philosophy.* New York: Simon & Schuster.

Schumacher, E. F. (1973). *Small is beautiful: A study of economics as if people mattered.* London: Blond & Briggs.

Wong, S. K. (Ed.). (2012). *Confucianism, Chinese history and society.* Singapore: World Scientific Publishing Company.

World Citizens Assembly. (2001). *Charter of human responsibilities.* Retrieved from http://www.alliance21.org/lille/en/resultats/charte.html

2 The Neo-Humanism for the Twenty-first Century

Exploring the form of neo-humanism that is suitable for the twenty-first century can be broken down into asking a few key questions. What is humanism? Why should we propose neo-humanism today? What are its fundamental contents and what contribution can Chinese culture make to it in this multi-cultural world?

2.1 What Is Humanism?

Derived from Latin, the term "humanism" has been widely used since the fifteenth century. After the European Renaissance, especially after the sixteenth and seventeenth centuries, it began to have broader, more diversified applications and meanings, of which the most fundamental ones include: (1) "humanity" (human nature) that is made up of one or more qualities which determine what it is to be a human being and distinguishes human beings from other species; (2) "humanitarianism", highlighting compassion, sympathy, and kinship, and different from humanism in many ways; and (3) "human-centeredness" and the idea of "people first and foremost".

In the Western sense of the word, humanism, whether used in the broad sense of humanitarianism or human-centeredness, emphasizes the understanding of, and respect for, human nature, dignity, value, and the elevation of human status and wellbeing in general. Part of its concern focuses on the free development and actualization of the individual to resist the theocracy of the Middle Ages and the tyranny of authoritarian regimes.

In the Chinese context, the focus of *renwen*, as in *renwenism*,[1] is more inclined toward human relationships and the nexus between man and nature, and is the most fundamental point of departure and the most distinctive feature that make humans genuinely human. The term *renwen* first appeared in the Hexagram Bi of *The Book of Changes*, reading:

> The entwinement of the tough and courageous with the gentle constitutes the order (*wen*) of the cosmos. Human (*ren*) order emerges and shines from understanding and following the order of the cosmos and knowing when and where to stop. By observing the order of the cosmos,

DOI: 10.4324/9781003356240-2

we detect changes of the times, and by observing human order or culture, we help to nurture the world in its entirety.

(Ma, 2017, p. 193)

Therefore, *renwen* in this case emphasizes social order, cultural nurturing and ethnicity, as opposed to the natural world *per se*. If the overarching law of the cosmos is the entwinement of *yin* and *yang*, then the fundamental law of *renwen* is "knowing the limit" (knowing when and where to stop). In fact, from its very beginning, Chinese culture has always emphasized that the fundamental value by which the world and society can be nurtured is none other than "knowing the limit". Admittedly, human nature can be encouraged and elevated, but humans should know where and when, if carried too far, it will become indulgence or promiscuity. In other words, there should be self-restraint and self-discipline; one should not give rein to one's "freedom" as one wills. This idea is also clearly conveyed by a host of expressions about traditional Chinese values such as "Benevolence means the suppression of the self and the restoration of propriety", "The superior man attains his greatest height and brilliancy and follows the path of the golden mean", "Never overdo anything (since a little wind kindles, but much puts out the fire)", and "Refrain from going to extremes". Only if people realize the limit of human agency and know when and where to stop is a harmonious society possible. Though they both proceed from respect for mankind and have developed out of similar concerns, Chinese *renwenism* and Western humanism have markedly different expressions and foci.

2.2 Why Is Neo-Humanism Relevant Today?

Human beings are now undergoing unprecedented dramatic spatial and temporal changes as embodied by the Internet, mobile communications, drastically reduced time-space distances due to computer storage technology, bewilderment with regard to human nature and its future aroused by life sciences, and the prospect of the revelation of a once-unknown micro world thanks to nanotechnology. These have brought profound, far-reaching changes to almost all aspects of life, the enormity of which can only be matched by the significant social changes that mirror the historic transition from hunting and fishing to farming societies or from agriculture to mechanical industrial production. Today, the economic, technological and information revolution sweeping the world has enabled dehumanized mechanical laws such as the law of the market to exercise greater control over mankind and thus steadily diminished most people's power to influence society. Cyberspace, created by the digital revolution, epitomizes the emergence of a new continent to which most human activities gravitate. This continent has become an integral part of human activity. The revolution in genetics means that humans now can copy, alter and selectively improve the corporeal body by means of genetic modification, stem cell therapy, cloning and in vitro fertilization. In short, both the meaning of being and the definition of human nature have been

24   *The Neo-Humanism for the Twenty-first Century*

fundamentally challenged, leading to a drastic, all-round impact on everything that was believed to belong to the domains of "meaning" and "norm".

In addition, after centuries of development, modern society, whilst it has created progress and wealth never seen before, has clearly demonstrated its weaknesses. The prime features of modernity, such as the negative impacts of concepts such as "almighty economic growth," "absolute individual freedom", "anthropocentrism" and "scientism", are increasingly called into question.

First of all, let's put "almighty economic growth" into perspective. In fact, boundless economic growth is not only far from "almighty", but also unprecedentedly detrimental to mankind. Economic growth implies increases in both production and profit. If it is from the increase of armaments, then, as a result, wars will be unleashed. If it is from the increase of regular products, then high consumption must be advocated, and, somewhat paradoxically, consumption means currently useful resources or goods are rendered useless. The Bible relates an allegory of consumption: when the Israelites were leaving Egypt, God prepared food called "manna" for them during their forty years in the desert. Every day, they could take what they needed for the day. Some decided to hoard it, but it all decayed. Today, considerably large quantities of useful goods are meaninglessly rendered useless, and people regard material wealth accumulation as the most desirable pursuit in life, ignoring more spiritually-inclined pursuits. A life lived this way is not necessarily a life of happiness. The United States takes a clear lead in material wealth, but the percentage of Americans believing themselves to be happy to the total population ranks 16th in the world. The American population, which accounts for less than 5% of the world's total population, consumes up to one-third of the world's energy, showing that excessive consumption and desire for gratification are a big drain on Mother Earth's plentitude and generosity.

The social damage, among other things, of absolute individual freedom is grave. As is pointed out by Edgar Morin, a French thinker and advanced social science academician, individualism in Western civilization contains isolation and loneliness born out of self-centeredness; it has caused moral and psychological lethargy and disconnectedness in all its realms, thus restricting human capacity for wisdom, and rendering its people powerless when confronted with complex issues or blind to fundamental or global problems (Morin, 2002, pp. 43–53). Similarly, Zygmunt Bauman (2002) emphasizes, in his *Modernity and the Holocaust*, that modernity has arisen as a result of modern civilization, but the development of the latter has gone beyond human's control and thus moved toward barbarity (pp. 5–6).

Blind, arrogant "human-centrism" has pushed the Earth we shelter and feed from to the verge of crises that cannot be undone, and this evil consequence is the direct result of centuries of development of Western civilization. The "conquest of nature" and "reshaping nature", serving as the foundation of Western Enlightenment science, apparently satisfies human needs, but they have also caused today's various environmental disasters. Indisputably, science, whilst promoting social progress, has led human beings closer to nuclear or ecological death.

Traditional Chinese culture rarely endorses the idea of man's selfish manipulation of the environment; it values instead the philosophy of the "unity of heaven and man"[2] which, in turn, indicates that humans need to readjust themselves in accordance with the environment. Unfortunately, however, after a half-century of modernization, China also has to pay an extremely high price for the damage it has wrought on its natural environment. As one of the most rapidly developing economies in the world, China has 16 of the world's most heavily polluted cities. Immediate comprehensive eco-protection is truly the primary requirement of today's pursuit of "sustainable development".

A core concept of modernity, "scientism" holds that only a scientific cognitive style conforms to reason. However, cognitive patterns and styles should be diversified since religion, music, art, poetry, etc. can generate wisdom and therefore be synthesized into humanity's intellectual legacy. Traditional Chinese culture has accepted *qing*[3] as its core, and helped numerous sages create their spiritual worlds through "sudden enlightenment." However, such cognition and spiritual worlds are unexceptionally labeled "unscientific" or "pseudo-scientific" and thus dismissed from the domain of human cognition. The situation of the theory and practice of traditional Chinese medicine in China is a good case in point.

Confronted with such damaging realities as the dramatic temporal-spatial changes driven by scientific and technological advances mentioned earlier, the grave problems generated by centuries of modernization, the catastrophic memories of the two world wars, and ideological disasters as represented by the Nazi Jewish concentration camps, the "Gulag Archipelago", and the "Cultural Revolution", we are compelled to rethink what kind of material and spiritual worldview of life humans should establish in the twenty-first century so that they can address new global-scale complexities, redefine the human situation, and reflect upon human existence and its meaning. It is in exactly this context that the neo-humanism for the twenty-first century is advanced.

2.3 Fundamentals of Neo-humanism

In the 1930s, Irving Babbitt, the first dean of the Department of Comparative Literature at Harvard University, put forward the notion of "neo-humanism" and tried to explore its meaning by drawing on the Chinese notion of "knowing when and where to stop". As discussed earlier, the statement that "human society and order should know when and where to stop" means civilization should not go beyond its limits, rather than try every possible means to pursue absolute individual freedom or extreme individualism. Babbitt opposes romanticism without restrictions and Baconian objective scientism, which seeks to transcend morality. Instead, he argues that a life lived in a scientistic way does not work. He states in explicit terms that, as a great humanist, Confucius surpasses many of his Western counterparts, expressing his sincere hope to synthesize Western humanism and Chinese *renwenisn* into

26   *The Neo-Humanism for the Twenty-first Century*

a single entity. He argues to the effect that if humans are to become truly human, they should not indulge themselves by following the regular "self", but should discipline and regulate themselves because self-discipline enables the ordinary self[4] to have more in-depth cognition, a better sense of proportion, and a more conscious notion of the norm of "being a human being" as opposed to a wild beast that can freely let is savagery develop. In fact, self-suppression, as in Confucius' advocacy of "benevolence as the suppression of the self and the restoration of propriety", means self-discipline or the willing imposition of norms on oneself, and it is believed to be the highest ideal of humanism. Babbitt's Chinese followers such as Wu Mi and Mei Guangdi believe that Confucian "golden mean" and self-suppression reflect precisely the fundamental spirit of Babbitt's neo-humanism. They tried in vain to save society by a neo-humanism that blended Western and Chinese humanism. Their endeavor, though rendered futile then, represented a good beginning.

You may ask then: what is the neo-humanism for the twenty-first century? To this question, there is perhaps no single essential answer, but we may contemplate it from the following perspectives or dimensions.

Firstly, neo-humanism is a new type of view of history. According to this view of history, the modern outlook on development relying on accruing material wealth, ecological destruction, and unrestrained consumption will be corrected. In fact, neo-humanism transcends human-centrism and elevates ecological consciousness. It argues that man is one of the many species and is by no means better or worse than any other species; he has his due place in the ecological system and only when he is conducive to the system can he be deemed as having value of his own. The famous ecologist Thomas Berry believes the Chinese have a better definition of human as the *xin*[5] of heaven and earth, and it is man's mission to have consciousness of the world and care for heaven and earth. Zhu Xi's explanation may serve as a good footnote. He argues that "Heaven is Man and Man Heaven. Man rests on Heaven and Heaven dwells in Man". In other words, Heaven is to be manifested by man. In fact, only free, creative, autonomous "man" who maintains communion with "Heaven" can help demonstrate Heaven's vitality. If "remolding nature" to satisfy human needs and expectations was the foundation of the Western Enlightenment science, then the Chinese way is to reject the idea of man's control of the environment and to regulate and readjust oneself according to needs of the environment so that nature and man can form a "community of life". In brief, mutually generative Western and Chinese ecological thought and the conception of sustainable development are important components of the neo-humanism for the twenty-first century.

Secondly, neo-humanism emphasizes "sustainable civilization", which is based on the quality of life rather than on unlimited wealth accumulation and material enjoyment. The quality of life refers to "real life conditions" and "individual citizens' subjective feelings of happiness" such as health, joy, harmonious social relationships, and a green natural environment. A "sustainable civilization" built on this basis particularly values universal and natural human rights rather than simply private property rights; it highlights global cooperation and not unilateral power abuse; and it emphasizes interdependence within the community rather than absolute individual independence. In a community of this kind, freedom does not mean the individual's right to do whatever he pleases, but rather the capacity to enter into numerous mutually dependent relationships with others; and the more communities in which one is involved, the greater one's power of choice, or the greater freedom one enjoys. In such a community, the individual will end up weakening himself if he uses his "freedom" to weaken the social community. In the Confucian tradition, no "self" can exist in isolation, or be contemplated in the abstract. In fact, the Confucian "self" is the sum of the roles played in one's interactions with others, and the Taoist "self", like all things, exists in relationships of opposing nature or force, both contradicting and complementing each other.

Thirdly, neo-humanism rejects the concept of abstract freedom and inclines toward responsible, profound freedom. It reveals the intrinsic relationship between freedom and obligation by introducing the notions of responsibility and duty into the concept of freedom. What neo-humanism pursues is not a broadened scope of power, but an extended mutual understanding; it strives to rectify materialism, as wrongly advocated by the first Enlightenment, unbridled progressivism, characterized by linear, immediate, and unrestrained pursuit of "novelty", and individualism carried out to extremes. Its ultimate goal is to liberate human nature from the yoke of materialism primarily by transcending instrumental reason, elevating value rationality, and evoking aesthetic wisdom. Instrumental reason has brought great progress and wealth; however, it has also rendered people powerless to discard their utilitarian motivations. Therefore, it must be aided by value rationality and aesthetic wisdom. Aesthetic wisdom is an integrated wisdom based on the concept of organic interconnectedness, in a quest for the harmonious integration of the true, the good, and the beautiful, and of cognition, affect, and will. In aesthetic wisdom, scientific, rational, emotional, religious, and artistic thinking complement and enrich each other. Influenced by dualistic thinking, modern instrumental reason is premised on the rejection of sensibility, emotional value, and beauty; aesthetic wisdom, however, emphasizes a harmonious both-this-and-that thinking. Traditional Chinese culture is centered around such fundamental concepts as *qing*, harmony, and the value of natural beauty, and therefore will surely develop a brand new system of thought, vastly different from that of the West in a global context.

Fourthly, if the first Enlightenment of the eighteenth century focused on "the liberation of the self" and "the pursuit of universality", then the neo-humanism for the twenty-first century focuses on the promotion of respect for the other, difference, and multi-cultural complementarity, especially between Western and Eastern cultures. By the 1960s, the post-modernist deconstructionist movement had rendered all authoritative and tyrannical unity of thinking shaped by modernity powerless, and it had also rendered everything discrete, broken, and superficial, thus leaving us fragmentary thought and a

28 *The Neo-Humanism for the Twenty-first Century*

disintegrated world of heteroglossia. Consequently, in an uncharted, chaotic and disintegrated world, humans have become existentialist tribes, ceaselessly wandering in desperation. As Rifkin (2004) observes in his *The European Dream*, the two "crosscutting currents" are: (1) the longing for some higher personal calling in an increasingly materialistically oriented world; and (2) the demand for some sense of shared community in a society growing increasingly remote and indifferent (p. 2). Therefore, humans should develop new ideas and philosophies and try to establish a more and deeper sense of community, so as to co-exist in an increasingly closely connected world. The "shared sense of community" in question and commensurabilities hinge on the refashioning of neo-humanism for the twenty-first century.

In a nutshell, judging from the natural environment, the development of science and technology, and changing social needs, humans are confronted with an unprecedented transformation. If humans are to fare well in this transformation, they should change their view of life and of the world and reconstruct their intellectual, cultural, and spiritual world, which is in fact the core value of the neo-humanism in question. Chinese culture has great capacity for thought generation and it has been honoring the well-established traditions of pursuing a spiritual life and prioritizing morality. For its enormous potential and possibilities, Chinese culture can facilitate mankind's reconciliation with nature, and fix the rifts between rationality and faith, material pursuit and aesthetic perception, natural sciences and humanistic care. If these cultural genes are combined with modern interpretations and directed at this multi-cultural world, new conceptual, discourse and epistemological systems can be created. In this way, Chinese culture, along with other cultures, can help to construct a neo-humanism for the twenty-first century and usher in a brand new historical era for all mankind.

Notes

1 The term *renwenism*, the translator's coinage, corresponds to humanism. *Ren* (人) means "human" and *wen* (文) order or culture. When combined, *renwenism*, as its name suggests, can be roughly understood as the "ism of human order and/or culture".

2 "The unity of heaven and man" is a world outlook and a way of thinking in which heaven and earth and man are interconnected, emphasizing the integration and inherent relationship between them. Historically, this idea has multiple expressions such as "heaven and man are of the same category, sharing the same vital energy, or sharing the same principles." Laozi maintains that "man's law is earthly, the earth's law is natural, and heaven's law is Dao." The term may have different meanings, depending on the situations and interpretations of "heaven" and "man".

3 *Qing* literally means affect, feelings, emotions, or sentiment. Primarily, it means human emotions and desires, referring to the natural and instinctive reaction to external circumstances, not a learned response. Secondly, it refers to specific human emotions and desires, commonly known as the six human emotions, namely, love, hatred, happiness, anger, sadness, and joy. Some scholars advocate that emotions should be restrained or controlled, while others believe that emotions and desires are natural and should be properly guided. According to "the

origination of *xing* from *ming*" of the bamboo slip records of Chu excavated in Guodian, Tao originates in *qing*, which originates from *xing* (human nature or what-is-so-of-itself), which, in turn, descends from Heaven.

4 Babbitt argues, "As against expansionists of every kind, I do not hesitate to affirm what is specifically human in man and ultimately divine is a certain quality of will, a will that is felt in relation to his ordinary self as a will to refrain."

5 Or *hsin* in Thomas Berry's spelling, literally meaning "the heart of the universe", or in Berry's terms, "the consciousness of the world" or "the psyche of the universe". Refer to Thomas Berry's *The Dream of the Earth* and *The Ecozoic Era*.

References

Bauman, Z. (2002). *Modernity and the holocaust* (Y. D. Yang, & J. H. Shi, Trans.). Nanjing: Yilin Press.

Ma, H. J. (Ed.). (2017). *Book of changes* (Full edition annotated). Beijing: Huaxia Publishing House.

Morin, E. (2002). Au–delà de la globalisation et du développement, société–monde ou empire–monde? [Beyond globalization and development: World society or world empire?] *Revue du MAUSS, 20*(2), 43–53.

Rifkin, J. (2004). *The European dream: How Europe's vision of the future is quietly eclipsing the American dream.* New York: Jeremy P. Tarcher/Penguin.

3 The Transformation of the Post-Modernist Ethos and a New Platform for Literary Studies

3.1 The Transformation of the Post-modernist Ethos

As mentioned earlier, in the 1960s, the modern deconstructive movement, informed by post-modernism, eclipsed the authoritative and tyrannical unity of thinking, and at the same time rendered almost everything discrete, superficial and fragmentary, thus leaving us nothing but fragmentary thought and a world of heteroglossia. Those deconstructionists succeeded in conjuring up a grand narrative aimed at subverting authority and modernism but failed to map out a new era.

In the late twentieth and early twenty-first centuries, some scholars, now having realized the danger of the rampaging post-modernist ethos more than ever, proposed a shift from deconstructive post-modernism to constructive modernism. The core of constructive post-modernism is the conception of organic, systematic holism, meaning due attention to harmony, wholeness, and interconnectedness between things; thus, it attempts to serve as the rationale for the peaceful coexistence of cultures. For instance, John Cobb, one of the champions of this idea, believes that the organic holism theory points to the fact that all cultures contain some sort of universalism and unique value and under some circumstances such unique value may become universal value that benefits other cultures. He explains with an example that modern Western thought started with differentiation and classification: modern medicine identifies and differentiates pathogens and healthy cells; it separates the pure from the impure and kills the latter, pathogens included. Traditional Chinese culture, of which traditional Chinese medicine is part, follows a different thought pattern. It does not separate or refine; it balances the part and the whole, and the many forces within the body. Cobb believes that though contemporary Western thought and traditional Chinese thought seem vastly different, yet they are profoundly commensurable and any rich culture can have common values beneficial to other cultures. He is convinced that future philosophy will depend heavily on the complementarity and integration between Western culture and Eastern culture.

Like Cobb, some other Western scholars are also trying to discover universal values in Chinese culture to solve global issues they have encountered. Some of those who are recently involved in the discussion on "aesthetic order

DOI: 10.4324/9781003356240-3

and rational order" in Europe argue that a return to a possibly re-interpreted *qing*, the most natural and fundamental point of departure of Chinese culture, may help to change the Western overemphasis on instrumental and technological rationality and thus usher in a new aesthetic perception-centered entity that can elevate humans' mental and spiritual realm. An October 2012 article in *The New York Times* emphasized that reliance on reason and inference alone is not sufficient to create a beautiful existence and it praised Chinese "reasonability" as compensation for inadequacies in pure rationality. The article's recognition and exploration of the value of other cultures without the subjection of one culture to another is a brand new, unbiased and reciprocal cross-cultural dialogue that transcends "identity" and "difference".

In short, from a post-modernist point of view, the world has entered into an era of pluralism and volatility. History ceases to be an object of inquiry that is predeterminedly linear, orderly, structurally stable, and thus ultimately meaningful. Rather, it has become an open text displaying unlimited difference and plurality, or, in Foucault's (1998) words, "a network that connects points and weaves its skein" (p. 175). This notion lays a foundation for resistance to cultural homogenization and unipolarization and for the construction of the ideal of the development of a multi-cultural world. At the same time, it offers fresh insight into literary scholarship.

3.2 Contemplations on Literary Studies of the New Era

This notion of change mentioned above first finds expression in heated discussions on world literature. *Comparative Literature in China*, a quarterly journal edited by Professor Xie Tianzhen, has organized very fruitful special columns on world literature over the past few years. Traditionally, Chinese definitions of world literature have largely been derived from either Goethe or Marx. The former's summation theory highlights that world literature is the "sum total" of excellent literary works of all nations, and the latter stressed: "National one-sidedness and narrow-mindedness become more and more impossible, and from the numerous national and local literatures, there arises a world literature" (Marx & Engels, 2009, pp. 45–46). As capitalism expands, the "many" have contributed to the "one", this being a totally brand new world literature. As time progressed, going from a Goethean to a Marxist definition, world literature experienced the phases of "sum total of excellent literary works" to "market interconnectedness" and is now moving toward a "plural dialogue". This latest type of world literature should not be an aggregation of isolated works or an alloy of many literatures, but rather a complementary, reciprocal, and mutually definitive entity or sum total within which different literatures draw on and contribute to each other.

Some Chinese scholars adopted this different approach from the beginning, as represented by Lu Xun's 1907 article "On the Power of the Satanic School of Poetry," in which he proposed that a scholar should "know thyself and then others". To know thyself is of paramount significance. For instance, in his discussion of the influence of the Satanic School as represented by

32 Post-Modernism and a New Platform for Literary Studies

Byron and Shelley on Russia and Eastern Europe, his primary focus was that "since the thought of the Slavic peoples is different from that of Europe", "Pushkin's affections gradually turned away from the Byronic hero to the ordinary people of his motherland" as a result of "different national characters" (Lu, 1907, p. 86). Lu Xun noted that the Satanic School was influential in Eastern Europe: "As it found acceptance in Russia, it was transformed into Pushkin the national poet; in Poland, it created Mickiewics the poet of vengeance; and in Hungary, it awakened the patriotic Petöfi" (ibid. pp. 100–101). However, Lu Xun's remarks are not a simple summation, and even less are they a simple "reduction of all literatures to one"; rather, he advocated the preservation of the difference between different national literatures and at the same time empowerment by drawing on each other.

In the same vein, Yang Zhouhan, the first chairperson of the Chinese Comparative Literature Association, argued that Chinese scholarship on foreign literature should not be without a Chinese soul, meaning that such scholarship should be preceded by a deep understanding of Chinese culture and the Chinese people; therefore, the scholarship may have Chinese characteristics and Chinese literature created in this way may find global acceptance.

Chen Sihe, a professor at Fudan University, also offered his own contemplations in this regard. As early as 1991, he proposed the notion of the "global elements in Chinese literature". He (2003) stressed:

> Chinese literature, for its distinctive features, becomes part of world culture and thereby can enrich the latter. Such a perspective and paradigm implies that a complex pattern of world literature can be constructed by the totality of Chinese literature and other literatures on an equal footing.
>
> (pp. 159–170)

He argued that "when Chinese literature is integrated into the general background of world or comparative literature, the entire world view defined by Westerners should change accordingly" (Chen, 2003). Chen's focus is the construction of a complex pattern of world literature on the basis of all literatures, which in turn are each rooted in their uniqueness. His opinions resonate in many aspects with current discussions on world literature. In fact, he was engaged not only in theoretical exploration, but also in pursuing the global elements in question in literature, such as the consciousnesses of "remorsefulness", "satanicity", and "survival". In short, Chen's ideas have drawn on those of Kant and Marx but diverged from their definitions of world literature.

I am also reminded of the recent achievements in this field that some young scholars have made at Peking University. They strongly emphasize the mindset of dynamism and openness. For instance, in his latest work "The Liberation of Literature", Zhang Pei states that in this globalized world of ours, "literature" is necessarily of the "world" since both the objective corresponding being and the intentional object are none other than the "world".

Post-Modernism and a New Platform for Literary Studies   33

For him, the world is an entity in time and its being possesses the property of "becoming". In other words, the world is worlding: it is in a continuous process of self-presentation and *différance*, to use Derrida's term. Zhang emphasizes that everything is undetermined, ever-changing and in the process of becoming. Similarly, in his monograph "What Kind of World and How to Define Literature", Chen Yuehong reveals that both the world and literature are in constant change. His argument draws on Bakhtin's wisdom:

> It is only in the eyes of another culture that foreign culture reveals itself fully and profoundly (but not maximally fully, because there will be cultures that see and understand even more.) A meaning only reveals its depth once it has encountered and come into contact with another, foreign meaning.
>
> (Bakhtin, 2010, p. 7)

What has been discussed above can be encapsulated in three arguments. Firstly, world literature does not occur or exist in isolation. A literature is likely to become part of world literature only through its reception, interpretation, and even transformation by another literature; therefore, what matters here is the type of culture or literature that serves as the point of departure. Professor Zhang Hui of Peking University argues that only by virtue of cross-cultural, translingual, and cross-disciplinary translation and research can national literature, originally in relative isolation, become an important part of other literatures or world literature. He cites this example: for Chinese readers who do not understand Spanish, *Don Quixote* will remain "non-existent" since it cannot become part of Chinese literature, nor therefore part of world literature. In the Chinese translation, the work then has Chinese culture infused or imbued, and this partly explains David Damrosch's argument that there are as many world literatures as there are ethnic literatures. Likewise, it is safe to say that comparative literature with cross-cultural literature study at its core is the precondition for the existent scholarship of world literature.

Secondly, world literature, as Chinese scholars view it, is not some sort of fixed object, but rather, a process occurring in an ever-changing world where different peoples interpret, appreciate, absorb, and alter different literatures. What plays a predominant role in this process is the subject's in-depth experience of his accumulated culture, while it also demonstrates his understanding of or passion for other cultures. In this regard, I truly agree with David Damrosch's idea that world literature is "not a set canon of texts but a mode of reading" (Damrosch, 2003, p. 281). Zhang Jin, a young editor of *Foreign Literature Review*, states that as modern concepts, literature and comparative literature are mutually definitive and generative, in that they are in a dynamic, mutually constructive relationship, and that comparative literature is no longer absolutely rooted in the comparison or relationship between different national literatures, while national literatures always dwell within a context of world literature. Among the questions we may ask here are: is world

34 *Post-Modernism and a New Platform for Literary Studies*

literature not literature of the world, and is its worlding not merely derived from the *différance* of the world *per se*? A further question is: do world literature and comparative literature at this stage converge on plural dialogue and heterogeneous interaction? Indeed, can we say that if world literature is viewed as a process, comparative literature is the path leading to the process?

In brief, on this platform initiated by a constructive post-modern ethos, national literature study, which was originally comparatively isolated, is infused with fresh, organic elements of world literature, and approaches originating from comparative literature such as mutual objectivity, mutual reference, and mutual elucidation, which have inevitably severed the self-imposed restraints of national literatures. Chen Yuehong argues that

> discussions on world literature are essentially about trying to find a way of international literary ecological construction with comparative literature as the precondition and basis in order to promote plural literary values and criteria in the ecology of world literature.

In China, such a cosmopolitan spirit of world literature and comparative literature has found its way into many fields and areas such as literary theory, literature criticism, literary history, classical literature study, modern and contemporary literature study. Such penetration entails and enables the reconstruction and upgrading of literary scholarship in general. These are the precise purposes for which we promote comparative literature and world literature.

In a post-modern context that transcends essentialism, I do not deem it to be completely necessary or highly likely to be able to define comparative literature, world literature, and the relationship between them, because we should first face some deeper problems from which we have no escape.

3.3 Issues to be Addressed

In this great era of development and transformation, we are inevitably and continuously confronted with unsettled and emerging theoretical issues. The primary questions in my mind are whether cultural communication and assimilation results in the narrowing or even disappearance of cultural differences; whether one culture's exposure to and reception of other cultures will change its original fundamental features; and whether cultural communication is hardly possible because of the incommensurability that arises from engrained cultural differences.

Another question concerns the issue of the "self" and the "other" in dialogue across cultural boundaries. Since the "other" is what the self is not, attention should be paid first of all to the difference in its own right. Only when such face-to-face heterogeneity is revealed, can the "other" become a frame of reference for helping introspection or self-examination. However, if heterogeneity is solely or unduly emphasized, disengagement of the self and the other may occur, and thus communication and understanding would hardly be possible. In the same vein, if heterogeneity is not emphasized, the distinctive features of the "other" may be sacrificed and an inauthentic identity may arise as a result. How can this paradox be settled?

Thirdly, there exists an even more important question, namely, the question of discourse in dialogue between cultures. The primary condition for equal dialogue is the existence of a discourse both parties find understandable and acceptable. However, at present, developing countries encounter an entire set of discourse and as a result a conceptual system that has already been established by the developed world due to its overwhelming political, economic, and cultural strengths, this being a system that is already widely accepted. This established set of discourse has been enriched and carried forward because of centuries of intellectual accumulation and input from countless sages, especially in term of contemplations on issues regarding humanity. Life as it is now can hardly go on without such discourse. Nevertheless, if native or local culture is interpreted and treated solely by this discourse and the various paradigms this discourse has generated, many distinctive, original, and living cultures will be excluded simply because of their lack of compliance with such discourse and paradigms. Should this be the case, the so-called dialogue between cultures will end up a cultural monologue, with other cultures humbly providing outlandish materials or exoticism, and therefore real cultural dialogue will be rendered impossible. Therefore, here arises the question: how can a new discourse conducive to equal dialogue be created?

These long-discussed and yet unsettled questions above aside, some new issues also keep looming. How can a newly independent culture break away from the cultural or spiritual tyranny inflicted by strong cultures because of the latter's random "borrowing"? How can a history of writing and reading across cultural, spatial, and temporal boundaries be written? How should we understand the shift of culture, originally with printed texts as the major carrier, in light of the rise of image media culture, and the dynamic interaction between them?

In brief, human beings are experiencing a period of transformation never seen before; the wiser among them are ever-increasingly aware of the growing role of literature, especially comparative literature and world literature, in constructing an ideal world of global cultural coexistence. Literature scholars the world over should work together to rethink the value of human existence and to remold a new spiritual domain that acknowledges and encompasses the entire world.

References

Bakhtin, M. M. (2010). Response to a question from the *Novy Mir* editorial staff. In C. Emerson & M. Holquist (Eds.), *Speech genres and other late essays* (V. W. McGee, Trans.). Austin: University of Texas Press.

Chen, S. H. (2003). Dialogue on satanic factors. *The Yellow River*, *2003*(4), 159–170.

36 *Post-Modernism and a New Platform for Literary Studies*

Damrosch, D. (2003). *What is world literature?* Princeton & Oxford: Princeton University Press.

Foucault, M. (1998). Different spaces. In J. D. Faubion (Ed.), *Aesthetics, method, and epistemology: The essential works of Foucault, 1954–1984* (Vol. 2) (R. Hurley, et al. Trans.). New York: The New Press.

Lu, X. (1907). On the power of Mara Poetry. In *Collected works of Lu Xun* (Vol. 1). Beijing: People's Literature Publishing House.

Marx, K., & Engels, F. (2009). *Manifesto of the communist party.* New York: Cosimo, Inc.

Zhang, Pei. (2012). The Liberation of Literature. *Dialogue Transculturel, 29,* 360–368.

4 The American, European, and Chinese Dreams

An Example of Cultural Transformation

Humankind is facing unprecedented temporal-spatial changes, which are incomparable with the previous shifts from hunting to farming, to mechanical production, and then to the early information age. First of all, the software and computer revolution, the global Internet, and the rise of mobile communications have essentially made the general public their own sovereigns who can freely express their opinions. Hence, the new generation is free to a certain extent from the intergenerational inheritance from the past; instead, they grow up within the context of the interactive influence of the Internet. Without a sound understanding of our next generation, or, better still, generations, a clear view of humanity's future would be hardly possible. Secondly, the development and application of bioengineering technologies such as genetic modification, stem cells, and cloning, have even baffled human beings about the prospect of their own flesh-and-blood existence. Life was originally the natural creation of the universe over millions of years, but it is now subject to copying, adaptation, and selection by some artificial means. What's more, nanotechnology will eventually enable human beings to study and employ to their own wishes to the laws and characteristics of the movement of electrons, atoms, and molecules on the scale of one billionth of a meter. As a result, humans are literally in charge of the entire micro-world. Revolutionary new knowledge and new technologies permeate every aspect of human life, leading to fundamental changes in the way humans view time and space.

Also, written in human history are brutal experiences such as sufferings in the twentieth century that include the two world wars, the fascist anti-Semitic concentration camps, the Gulag Archipelago, the Cultural Revolution in China, and critical challenges concerning the two main characteristics of modernity, which are "omnipotent economic growth" and "absolute individual freedom". These unprecedented changes urge us to redefine the human condition, reconsider the meaning and manner of human existence, and contemplate what kind of world we need to shape, and what kind of outlook on life and the world we need to build to respond to this new, complex situation that affects our entire planet.

Jeremy Rifkin attempts to illustrate in his *The European Dream* this complexity with the concepts of the "American Dream" and the "European Dream". The two dreams Rifkin deals with are not so much divided by

DOI: 10.4324/9781003356240-4

38 *The American, European, and Chinese Dreams*

geographical differences, but refer to two completely different historical stages, and different ways of thinking and survival in separate time and space.

4.1 What Is the American Dream?

The so-called "American Dream" mainly means that everyone has unlimited opportunities to seek and accumulate wealth. As Rifkin sees it, it includes the following three aspects:

1 In the pursuit of the "American Dream", private property is seen as a passport to personal freedom. The more property a person owns, the greater autonomy and mobility one has, and the less dependent on or receiving from others a person is, the less one is subject to the environment: more wealth means greater freedom and independence.
2 Wealth brings exclusivity and security. With wealth being the boundary between the self and the other, the achievement of individuals in amassing huge wealth is regarded as the sole or main criterion of success. Therefore, with the amassing of more wealth, individuals become more distinctive and rise in social status, and thus become more secure.
3 Under the American Dream, people pursue autonomy whatever it takes, overconsuming, indulging every desire, and squandering the resources of the earth. Such a society encourages unrestricted economic growth, rewards the strong and marginalizes the weak. Americans regard themselves as the chosen people of God, and thus that their presumed entitlement to a wealth on Earth that exceeds their fair share. Today, Americans consume as much as one-third of the world's energy, as well as a staggering amount of other resources, even though they only account for less than 5 percent of the world's population. Supposing everyone in China reached the same level of the middle class in America today, we would need 7 Earths!
4 All major activities in American society revolve around the possession and distribution of capital and the protection of private property rights. Civil rights, political rights, and social rights are all designed in certain ways to boost property interests. As a country, America is fully committed to protecting its own interests and has built the most powerful military machine in history to obtain and defend what it wants and it believes this is what it deserves.

In short, the American Dream is to "make the most money with the greatest freedom." To a large extent, the American Dream was once a dream shared by the whole world. It created unprecedented wealth and brought unparalleled material progress. Even today, it is still the most influential dream so that few people even come to dream their own dreams. The American Dream represents personal freedom, advanced material progress, rich and especially equal opportunity for success: all to the maximum. From a philosophical point of view, the spiritual principles of the American Dream are liberalism, individualism, populism, pragmatism, competition, and conquest. Altogether, it means that everyone has access to personal success, that is, making a fortune, through his or her own hard work. In fact, the reality of America did provide such opportunities. Just as Boorstin (1958) describes in *The Americans: The Colonial Experience*, the early days of American exploitation and development abounded with unlimited land, endless resources, and countless opportunities, and unlike Europe, America is said to be "a crowded society, where every place is over-stocked" (p. 30). As long as one works hard, everyone can succeed. Such success has nothing to do with the interests won from unscrupulously defeating opponents in competition, but is a justified gain in proportion to hard work (of course, Americans often forget their oppression and exploitation of native American Indians). However, this kind of positive local experience in America has deteriorated due to aggressive development. With excessive development, America has not only fully developed its own land, but also needs to open up the entire world to satisfy its desire for lasting development. The two world wars created an unprecedented opportunity for America to succeed, establishing the situation of the American people by collectively exploiting the people of the world, which has sustained the resplendent and even enchanted myth of the American Dream. Established on the suffering, poverty, and hopelessness of the people across the world, the American Dream is not a dream of the world, nor a dream "for the world". Today, people have realized that if we must adhere to the modern principle of unlimited development our finite world is far from able to sustain a global American Dream, and not even America's own American Dream.

America has finally shaped itself into a new empire trying to rule the world. It distinguishes America from "the rest of the world" and makes its existence a mission. Yet, as it fabricates itself a political theological mission to save the world, it in actual fact stands as the enemy of the world in a sense.

Obviously, as long as the American Dream adheres to the principle of maximizing personal interests, it cannot be a universally effective one, because there is insufficient social space to provide for everyone's success. "Everyone's success" is the least possible of all possibilities, unless there is an entirely different interpretation of the connotation of "success". In this sense, logically speaking, the American Dream can only be the dream of "some" but not the dream of "all". Such a dream is wonderful for some but a nightmare for others. Therefore, the American Dream in its deepest meaning is one that crushes the dreams of others. The American Dream unconditionally affirms personal freedom and success so that anything or anyone that hinders personal freedom is an opposing party, and even all societies and cultures that differ from America are regarded as potential threats to freedom and are all defined *a priori* as enemies of America. Nevertheless, the ironclad fact is that only when people surrender certain freedoms can they form friendly relations that are cooperative and coordinated and which reap more factual gains. If the absoluteness of freedom is exaggerated, friendliness would be nowhere to be found. For this reason, Hu Shi argues: "Tolerance is more important than freedom." Dreams that only emphasize freedom are bound to be based on

40 *The American, European, and Chinese Dreams*

the consciousness of hostility to others. America claims that the country is a free "paradise" for its native people and an "ark" for the unfree in the world, and that it is a model for the free world and a savior for the rest. As mentioned above, when America constructed such a political theology, it finally shaped itself into a new empire trying to rule the world. It draws an absolute demarcation between America and "the rest of the world" and makes its particular existence a mission. While fabricating its political theological mission to save the world, it also turns itself into an enemy of the world. In essence, the American Dream is not a dream for the world, but a dream for the happiness of its own, a dream that alienates itself from the world, and a dream that divides rather than unites the world.

4.2 What Is the European Dream?

What does the "European Dream" mean? According to J. Rifkin, the "European Dream" is a new historical view and from such a view, the material-based "modern development view" itself will be revised. This is a "sustainable civilization" based on the "quality of life" rather than "unlimited individual accumulation of wealth". The so-called "quality of life" includes the "actual living conditions" and the "subjective well-being of individual citizens" such as health, social relations, and the natural environment. The goal of a sustainable global economy is to connect human production and consumption with the capabilities of the natural world, and to continuously reproduce a high-quality life through waste recycling and resource replenishment. In such a sustainable and stable economic state, it is not the material accumulation of the individual that matters, but self-cultivation; not the amassing of material wealth, but the elevation of the spirit; not the expansion of territory, but the expansion of empathy. In brief, a life of high quality refers to a life featuring universal wealth, social security and "taste" in the sense of aesthetic discrimination. It is established on a welfare society which is, in turn, based on high levels of material production, thus freeing people from worries about food, clothing, housing, travelling and ensuring the security of life; meanwhile, it also ensures that people have full freedom, time, and conditions to pursue diversified and enriched spiritual lives. As the two pillars of the European Dream, multiculturalism and global ecological consciousness liberate human nature from rampant materialism, thus generating or contributing to a new human nature.

As is indicated in the European Dream, the attainment of freedom means being able to enter into numerous interdependent relationships with others. The more access a person has to communities, the more choices one has. With connections comes inclusiveness, and, with inclusiveness, security. The European Dream emphasizes mutual dependence in communities rather than absolute independence of the individual; emphasizes cultural diversity rather than likeness; emphasizes the quality of life rather than wealth accumulation; emphasizes sustainable development rather than unlimited material growth; emphasizes dedication and enjoyment combined rather than

The American, European, and Chinese Dreams 41

crazy hard work; emphasizes universal human rights and natural rights rather than private property rights; and emphasizes global cooperation rather than unilateral abuse of power. In short, what the European Dream seeks is not to desperately expand wealth but to improve the spiritual level; not to expand the scope of power but to extend mutual understanding. The European Dream is considered to be a close "second Enlightenment"; one that uses a new "idealism" to offset the "materialism" wrongly advocated by the first Enlightenment and to offset unlimited progressivism (straight, rapid, infinite pursuit of the new) and absolute individualism. More specifically, the European Dream and the American Dream differ remarkably in the following aspects.

1   The difference between a market economy and a network economy

In order to further explore the above two different historical states as well as the different ways of thinking and survival they have produced, J. Rifkin analyzes the difference between the market economy and the network economy as the two bases of the two stages of economy. He believes that in the scope of market economy, the enhancement of common interests is achieved through the results of everyone's pursuit of their own interests, while in a network economy it is achieved through everyone's contribution to others, maximization of the interests of the wider community, and thus the improvement of the wellbeing of all individuals is made possible, which is now often referred to as "mutual benefit or win–win situation". To take this explanation a step further, the market is based on the pursuit of self-interests while the network pursues a larger range of common interests; the former is based on distrust and the latter on a certain amount of trust; the former maintains distanced transactions, but the latter entails closer relationships; the former secures property by competition with others in a hostile market framework, and the latter secures by belonging rather than belongings. For the network economy, the most important thing is the path (access to certain relationships) and attribution, and success comes as a result of shared relationships rather than isolated struggles. In conclusion, the market is competitive while the network embraces both competition and cooperation.

2   Societal, political, and cultural differences

Accordingly, the above economic difference also brings about differences in society, politics, and culture. According to J. Rifkin, in the capitalist market economy era, the struggle is centered on the possession and distribution of wealth and the protection of private property rights, with civil rights, political rights, and social rights designed in one way or another to increase the value of property interests. Freedom is defined as independence from others, and with enough property, people can do almost whatever they want. However, in today's networked age of globalization, the struggle is pluralistic, and more about preserving cultural identity and gaining rights in a world where all depend on each other; where cultural identity establishes the demarcation between individuals

42 *The American, European, and Chinese Dreams*

and the outside world and can be availed upon to protect the rights of individuals to enter the surrounding worldwide exchanges. To gain freedom means to be more deeply involved in the network of relationships where people are mutually dependent on each other. Inclusion in a network of relationships requires one to find paths, and the more paths one has, the more relationships one can enter, and hence more freedom can be experienced.

3 Different theoretical bases

The "American Dream" and the "European Dream" have different theoretical bases. The "American Dream" has Locke's theory at its core in that the protection of private property is the primary foundation of the protection of the right to individual freedom. This theory has been popular in America. On the other hand, the "European Dream" takes Kant's thought on human rights as its theoretical basis, and his perpetual peace has become the theoretical basis of Europe's politics today. If both Europe and America regard the absoluteness of the individual as a principle of supremacy, Europe is more concerned with spiritual individualism, while America advocates material individualism. This difference, though not sufficient to form a significant difference in terms of "political modernity", determines the considerable diversity in the style and taste of daily life, as well as the perception of the environment.

4 Different historical reasons

The difference between the "American Dream" and the "European Dream" can be attributed to historical reasons. World War II can be said to be a watershed in Western experience, from which Europe and America learned completely different lessons. Europe experienced the pain of destruction caused by the aggressive efforts of modernization and development, and has moved towards pacifism, rationality in dialogue, and cooperative strategies. America experienced glory and dreams, success and splendor, leadership and domination, thus becoming more inclined to strengthen hegemonism, unilateralism, and competitive strategies. It is safe to conclude that, from World War II, Europe suffered a series of negative experiences, and thus began a profound reflection on modernity, forming a post-modern trend of thought. In contrast, America, with all the positive experiences from the war, was determined to push modernity to its utmost. Although there were also some negative thoughts in postwar America, it was clear that those thoughts lacked social influence considering the astonishing material and political success of the nation.

J. Rifkin summarizes the major changes in human life in the late twentieth and early twenty-first centuries along with the subsequent series of changes in the way of thinking and living. His conclusion is thought-provoking, and although the "American Dream" he describes is a long-standing historical state, the "European Dream" is still an imaginary or developing historical trend. Rifkin (2004) calls it a "new historical framework", and that "[if] the

European Dream represents the end of one history, it also suggests the beginning of another" (p. 8).

In general, he believes that what the American Dream can create is not a good life, but a costly bad life (an expensive life does not mean a quality life). Now most people in the world are aware that the American path to modernization is beyond the capability of the world's resources and its people. Simply put, the world cannot afford it. America itself has already advanced too much through its excessive exploitation of the world. Rifkin believes that American unilateralism will get tougher and become a dangerous yet inefficient strategy, one that is not even favorable to America itself because globalization is a polycentric trend. Although it is likely that no one can cause a radical shake-up to the leadership of America, globalization is bringing about a global "conjugation" of interests, and the maximization of unilateral interests has become impractical, which, in addition to causing resistance and conflict, has no positive significance. The world cannot afford the American Dream, and for the world, the American Dream may not necessarily be a good dream. In this regard, the American Dream is indeed "outdated".

It can be seen that the European Dream is actually a dream of regional protectionism; it is a strategy to protect vested interests, but not a universal dream worldwide. On the one hand, the European Dream protects the European quality and tries to resist "bad" lifestyles and values embraced by America; on the other hand, it aims to resist the "bad" manners of competition and unfair approaches to immigration issues in developing countries so as to protect the European welfare system and vested interests.

The immigration issues are a fundamental test of the "European Dream". First of all, Europe cannot do without immigrants. "[R]esearchers conclude that Europe would have to take in more than a million immigrants a year to be equivalent to European women having, on average, one more child" (Rifkin, 2004, p. 255) Research also suggests that "Germany alone would have to welcome 500,000 young immigrants every year for the next thirty years, or double its birthrate, to avoid a steep demographic decline" (ibid., p. 255). Mixed cultural marriages have raised more complex issues. "In 1960, only 1.3 percent of births had a foreign mother or father. By 1994, 18.8 percent of newborns had a foreign mother, father or both" (ibid., p. 252) This trend is sure to accelerate. As J. Rifkin puts it, although mixed cultural marriages have opened up new channels of cross-cultural communication and bridged certain cultural gaps, they have also deepened the sense of decline of German culture and led to cultural suppression and the revenge of deeper hostility towards foreigners. Europeans find themselves in a dilemma to some extent: without a flood of immigrants into Europe over the next few decades, Europe would have to face an aging population and a decline in their economic programs; on the other hand, the immigration flow will threaten, and may even overwhelm, the already tight government budget for welfare, as well

44　The American, European, and Chinese Dreams

as diminish people's sense of cultural identity. Rifkin (2004) has to ask the following questions:

> Absent of unswerving loyalty to a territorially anchored nation-state, and bound by a commonly accepted meta-narrative and ideology to live by, how do disparate peoples get along? What unites them, if not a shared territory, loyalty to a state, and a common ideology?
>
> (p. 264)

Whether the emerging European Dream can be a success largely depends on how contemporary Europeans deal with immigration issues and how they truly realize their dream of multicultural symbiosis. Moreover, whether or not immigration issues can develop in the direction that people expect is still uncertain.

4.3　Can "the Chinese Dream" Define a New Historical Era?

If the American Dream and the European Dream each represent a historical stage, is it also possible that the Chinese Dream represents a new historical period?

J. Rifkin attaches great importance to China's position in the construction of the future world. He is not a China expert, but he agrees with Richard Nisbett's opinion, in his *The Geography of Thought*, that Asian peoples and countries may be more suitable than Westerners to create network governance, transnational space, and global consciousness. Rifkin quotes Henry Rosemount, a sinologist and philosopher, as saying that in Confucianism, there is no "me" that can exist in isolation or be considered abstract and that "I" is the sum of various roles played in the relationship with others. Taoism otherwise holds that the whole exists in the relationship between opposite forces, and they complement each other. Rifkin also agrees with Nisbett's statement that the continuous attention to relationships makes Asians more sensitive to feelings and emotions. While American parents adopt a "self-and-other" way of thinking in educating their children to think in terms of encroachment, seizure, and property relations, traditional Asian parents pay more regard to emotional and social relations, helping their children interact with others and to coordinate their behavior. Similarly, he believes that Asians have always emphasized harmony between man and nature due to their holistic tendency. As Rifkin puts it, the foundation of Western Enlightenment-based science is to reshape nature to conform to human perception while the East abandons the idea that humans can manipulate the environment and instead focuses on adjusting themselves according to the needs of the environment. In short, Rifkin admits that traditional Chinese thought pays more attention to harmony, integrity, and the mutual influence of all things rather than isolated phenomena.

Furthermore, he also explored the recent situation in China. To overcome poverty, China's President Deng Xiaoping re-adjusted the country's century-old modernization dream back to the direction of material modernization, and brought about a change in China's strategy, advancing his proposal that "development is the only hard truth" and that it is of necessity to "let some people get rich first". When the issue of poverty was initially relieved, the problem was concentrated in the disparity between the rich and the poor, and consequently further development of modernization had to depend on the proposal of a "harmonious society". From a perspective of over twenty years' development, we can tell that China's dream of modernization is a comprehensive re-creation of Western experience, drawing both on American competition as well as trying to learn from European equality, as if to combine a part of the American Dream with a part of the European Dream. With its long history and culture, China is expected to make a positive contribution to the world dream of humankind and to have a profound impact on the future of the human species as a whole.

In fact, China is a country of dreams. In traditional Chinese culture, the earliest Chinese Dream is Laozi's dream of non-doing and Confucius' dream of Great Unity. Laozi declares:

> Let the country be small,
> And the inhabitants few.
> Although there are weapons
> For tens and hundreds of soldiers,
> They will not be used.
> Let people take death seriously,
> And not travel far.
> Although they have boats and carriages,
> There's no occasion to use them.
> Although they have armor and weapons,
> There's no occasion to wear them.
> Let people return to making knots on ropes,
> Instead of writing.
> Their food will be tasty.
> Their clothes will be comfortable.
> Their homes will be tranquil.
> They will rejoice in their daily life.
> They can see their neighbors.
> Roosters and dogs can be heard from there.
> Still, they will age and die
> Without visiting one another.
> (Tao Te Ching: Chapter 80)

Confucius states (as cited in Cooper, 1981, p. 28):

> When the Great Tao prevailed the whole world was one community. Men of talent and virtue were chosen to lead the people, their words were sincere and they cultivated harmony. Men treated the parents of others as their own and cherished the children of others as their own. Proper provision was made for the aged until their death, work was provided for the able-bodied and education for the young; kindness and compassion

46 *The American, European, and Chinese Dreams*

were shown to widows, orphans, childless men and those disabled by disease, so that all were looked after. For every male there was a division of land; for every female a home. The people disliked to have wealth wasted but they did not hoard it up for themselves; they disliked to have their talents unemployed, but they did not work solely for themselves; hence all cunning designs became useless and theft and banditry did not exist. The outer doors of houses remained open and were never shut... this was called "the Age of Great Universality".

This is a dream of peace (the relationship between man and nature and the world), amity (the relationship between man and man), and harmony (the relationship between the inside and outside the mind and body of man), to be "in concord" ("和" *he*, a concept embodied in the above three states) is at the heart of traditional Chinese thinking.

However, neither Laozi's dream of non-doing nor Confucius' dream of Great Unity has benefited modern China; rather, they have made the country both poorer and more vulnerable. Hence, it is inevitable that those dreams be replaced by another dream, founded upon the century-old dream of building a strong nation, namely, the dream of modernization. As China conceives the "Chinese Dream of modernization", it often hopes to combine the advantages of various modernization models worldwide, and those of Chinese and Western cultures, but to also avoid the disadvantages of pure Western capitalism. If the condition for Western, including Japanese, modernization is colonial plunder and endless wars, then China's modernization must be sought elsewhere.

Zhao Tingyang at the Chinese Academy of Social Sciences (CASS) has put forward some significant ideas about China's dream of modernization, arguing that Mao Zedong, in pursuit of the dream of building a modern power, conceived a dream of purity with extraordinary imagination, a dream that is "the freshest and the most beautiful" (Zhao, 2006, pp. 143–164). The ideal society Mao Zedong conceived is a society that would "break completely" from all the previous social models, and would be an absolutely new society, neither Chinese nor Western, so Mao proposed that "a blank sheet" shall be best suited to draw "the freshest and the most beautiful of pictures" and that being "poor and blank" was the starting point of the new Chinese Dream. He gives credence to the potential of a brand new social operation mode to promote brand new experiences, and thus brand new lifestyles. The "new society" should be a pure society that sweeps away all the ugly phenomena that all societies have failed to avoid, and, astonishingly, Mao Zedong made it. At the beginning of China's liberation in 1949, the whole country eliminated pornography, gambling, drugs, and other dirty crimes to a certain extent. A new social order was established gradually, and some places even attained a situation that the moral standard was such that people left the door unbolted at night and no one would pick up and pocket anything lost on the street. The "new society" embraced significant enthusiasm in the "new" and "continuous renewal" in abandoning the old model, welcoming new experience,

The American, European, and Chinese Dreams   47

exploring a new system, etc. Mao's dream of purity still inspires the Chinese people and many others in third world countries.

It is hard to imagine whether this dream of purity would have a chance to develop if it had been moving in the direction pointed out in Mao's "On New Democracy" and "On Coalition Government", but for various reasons Chinese society in the late 1970s was on the verge of collapse so that Deng Xiaoping had to reorient China's dream of modernization towards material modernization, proposing that "development is the only hard truth". This strategic shift was first manifested in "getting some people rich first", which led to great economic development and the initial relief of poverty. However, the problem then became the widening gap between the rich and the poor and the AFR (rural area, agriculture and farmers) issue. Therefore, the dream of modernization is further manifested in the pursuit of balanced "sustainable development" and "harmonious society". It can be seen that China's comprehensive reconstruction of the Western experience in its dream of modernization not only draws on American material competition, but also tries to learn from the European pursuit of the quality of life and equality, attempting to combine some parts of the American Dream and the European Dream, and linking with China's thousands of years of "dream of harmony".

To be brief, the core of the Chinese Dream is to build a modern New China that is different from both the West and ancient China; a New China that is endowed with a new Chinese ethos. Margaret Thatcher once asserted that China was unlikely to become a world power because it did not have an independent ideology that would suffice to influence the world. Zhao Tingyang (2005) argues,

> If China's knowledge system fails to participate in the construction of the world's knowledge system from which a new universal world knowledge system arises, it cannot become a major knowledge producer. And if so, even though the country manages to achieve a huge economic scale, it can be a power in material production but still a minor country.
>
> (p. 2)

According to Zhao's analysis, the systems of concepts, discourse, and knowledge currently available in our reflections on all kinds of things are defined mainly by the West. In particular, such decisive concepts as human rights, democracy, freedom, justice, and truth primarily mean and refer to what has been determined by the West. Moreover, these Western-defined concepts themselves are problematic in many ways, and, in particular, not entirely suited to Chinese experience. The new Chinese ethos should mean that China must establish the image of a social ideology, a living attitude, a set of values, and a Chinese concept about the world in the Chinese way, because China must become a great power responsible for the world. If China fails to develop its own set of systems of concepts, discourse, and knowledge, we will not be able to participate in the reconstruction of the ever-developing world

48 *The American, European, and Chinese Dreams*

culture with a new Chinese ethos infused. China should not be satisfied with Chinese culture of local characteristics, and nor should we be enclosed merely in traditional culture; instead we must reinterpret and empower Chinese legacy and enable it to make a contribution to global culture. Without "world-ness", the Chinese Dream will be literally a daydream. I very much agree with him.

According to Zhao's reflections, the Chinese Dream needs to consider the following questions: (1) What kind of thought/knowledge system can enable effective thinking concerning the fundamental questions of the contemporary world? Without strong intellectual powers, it would be impossible to create the ideas needed by society, or, better still, a strong culture and society itself. This has long been overlooked in China. (2) What kind of social system can make a man of virtue willing to live in this society? This requires a design for a just society, a design so tough that all societies known today fail to meet its standards, since all societies have been designed either for economic men and petty people or for the mediocre and the vulnerable, with not one society designed to be most beneficial to persons of virtue. (3) What kind of lifestyle can ensure that people always feel the meaningfulness of life? This requires a society that must be conducive to the development of a high level of spiritual life. Apparently, material life is charming in a way that is monotonous, simple and poor, and, in the long run, no society can rely solely on a high level of material life to maintain people's feeling of meaningfulness and interest in life. People will eventually pursue a spiritual life, which is the only way of life to have unlimited space for development. (Zhao, 2006)

These are the fundamental problems of human society, and the various dreams of the world are not yet able to provide a fine solution. History has proven that Chinese culture is a culture with strong mind powers, and that it has a far-reaching tradition of pursuing spiritual life and exalting morality. Chinese culture retains an extremely large space for reconciliation between man and nature and accommodation of the break between rational thinking and spiritual belief, material pursuit and aesthetic taste, natural science and humanistic care. If these cultural genes inherent in Chinese culture are combined with modern interpretations in this contemporary multicultural world, a new Chinese Dream which can represent a new historical stage will surely emerge to benefit the world.

As noted above, *The European Dream* raises many profound and forward-looking questions, a number of which have not yet been tested by facts, and therefore not yet finally resolved, or not even currently solvable. However, Rifkin's book shows great foresight, as it points out the gravity of the issues and the direction for thinking. What's more, it is worthy of praise that Rifkin, in contrast to the former norm of Western centrism, has always placed China in an important position in his vision as he looks ahead and well into the future of society. In many ways, he argues, Europe and China are fighting side by side. Europe, for example, is trying to strike a balance between a social structure that emphasizes security and stability, and a market system that values independent entrepreneurship; to balance the two systems is exactly what China is aspiring after and its similar efforts are becoming a key topic of discussion across China. As he puts it:

> At the eye of the storm were two crosscutting currents: the first, a restless yearning for some kind of higher personal calling in what was perceived to be an increasingly materialistically oriented world; the second, the need to find some sense of shared community in a society grown remote and uncaring.
>
> (Rifkin, 2004, p. 2)

According to Rifkin, this is also what European and Chinese people of vision have been after. In his point of view, Europe and China both dream of a new era when everyone's rights are respected and cultural differences welcomed, and everyone enjoys a quality (not luxurious) life that is within the limits of the Earth's sustainability so that human beings can live in peace and harmony. Rifkin argues that in order to coexist in an increasingly connected world, humanity needs to constantly create new ideas, and that China and Europe will find more and deeper commonalities in this regard. At present, as the American Dream fades from its former glory in the twenty-first century, the world is turning its attention to the European Union and China. From Rifkin's perspective, while it is too early to assert what combined effect the European Dream and the awakening Chinese Dream will have, it is far from overblown to predict that the emerging European Dream and the Chinese Dream will have a profound impact on the future of humankind as a whole.

In his letter to Chinese readers upon the publication of the Chinese version of his book, Rifkin (2006) indicates that when looking back on our lives in old age, we will come to a clear awareness that all the critical moments have nothing to do with material accumulation but are closely related to our love for our fellow human beings, to our connection as individuals with the human species as a whole, and to our connection with the planet we live on (p. ii). As he sees it, the European Dream unfolding in front of us is an attempt to open a gate towards questions of higher gravity; those on the significance of life *per se*. He then poses the question: inhabiting this planet, what indeed is the true meaning and purpose of our existence in the twenty-first century? That is precisely the question that each of us should ask ourselves and truly try to find answers to.

References

Boorstin, D. J. (1958). *The Americans: The colonial experience*. New York: Vintage Books.

J. C. Cooper. (1981). *Yin & Yang: The Taoist harmony of opposites*. Wellingborough, Northamptonshire: Aquarian Press.

Rifkin, J. (2004). *The European dream: How Europe's vision of the future is quietly eclipsing the American dream*. New York: Jeremy P. Tarcher/Penguin.

Rifkin, J. (2006). To Chinese readers. In *The European Dream* (Z. Y. Yang, Trans.). Chongqing: Chongqing Publishing House.

Tao Te Ching: Chapter 80 (S. Stenudd, Trans.). Retrieved from https://www.taoistic. com/taoteching-laotzu/taoteching-80.htm

Zhao, T. Y. (2005). *The Tianxia system: An introduction to the philosophy of the world institution*. Nanjing: Jiangsu Education Publishing House.

Zhao, T. Y. (2006). American dream, European dream and China's dream. *Dialogue Transculturel*, *18*, 143–164.

5 Thoughts on Comparative Literature and World Literature

5.1 Fresh Insights into Evolving Comparative Literature and World Literature

In the face of such a major change, many far-sighted Western scholars, reflecting on history and examining reality, have responded by putting forward new theories. Here are some examples:

1 New complex thinking. Edgar Morin, a well-known French thinker, points out that behind the wellbeing of Western civilization is precisely the root of its evils: its individualism encompasses self-centered insularity and loneliness; its blind economic development has brought moral and psychological trauma to humankind, resulting in isolation in various fields, limiting people's intellectual ability, and making people helpless in the face of complex questions, causing them to turn a blind eye to fundamental questions and those of global significance; science and technology have promoted social progress, but also brought about the destruction of the environment and culture and led to new inequalities, replacing the conventional form of slavery with a new one. Particularly, urban pollution and scientific blindness cause tension and danger for people, leading them to risk nuclear or ecological death (Morin, 2002). He deems that new complex situations must be approached with new complexity thinking.

2 Mutually subjective cognitive approaches. Some French philosophers, as represented by François Jullien, believe that in the current situation, the priority is to return to the origin of our own cultures, re-examine history and find a new starting point. This requires a new "other" as a frame of reference for the introspection of our own history and culture. In his "Why We Westerners Cannot Avoid China in Our Study of Philosophy", Jullien (2000) emphasizes that for a sound self-understanding, one must get detached from the closed self and examine it from external views, as he points out, "China presents a case study through which to contemplate Western thought from the outside" (p. 9). At the International Conference on Esthetique du Divers (Diverse Esthetics) held by the Institute of Comparative Literature and Culture, Peking University,

DOI: 10.4324/9781003356240-5

52 Thoughts on Comparative Literature and World Literature

Professor Daniel-Henri Pageaux, a French comparative literature leader, singled out Jullien's study of Greek and Chinese cultures as an excellent example of the benefits of a "detour" through the "other".

3   Constructive postmodernism. After reviewing the maladies of the fragmentation, superficiality, and alienation of the postmodern society during the late twentieth century, constructive postmodernism posed a new proposition based on Whitehead's process philosophy at the beginning of the twenty-first century. The core idea of Whitehead's process philosophy follows an organic, holistic and systematic approach, which holds that there is no such thing as a never-changing entity but only relationships that are constantly evolving; humans should not be regarded as the center of everything, but man and nature should be seen as a closely connected "community of shared futures". John Cobb, an advocate of "constructive postmodernism", believes that this organic-holistic philosophy is profoundly commensurable with many traditional Chinese thoughts. As he puts it, traditional Chinese culture has always been organically holist. To illustrate this point of view, he explains that modern Western thinking starts with separation and classification; modern medicine distinguishes pathogens and healthy cells, separating the pure from the impure and then eliminating the latter. The Chinese philosophy of *yin* and *yang*, on the contrary, stems from the unity of opposites, so traditional Chinese medicine seeks balance instead of separation and purity. The treatment in Western medicine aims to destroy the pathogenic actors, while Chinese medicine is about the coordination between parts and the whole so as to strike a balance of power within the body. Cobb believes that the continued growth and perpetual change underlined in *The Book of Changes* and the "process" emphasized by Whitehead accord with each other, which leads him to a firm belief that philosophy is heading towards complementation and integration of Western and Eastern cultures.

4   Redefining literature and humanism. Professor Armando Gnisci, of the University of Rome, Italy, points out in "Comparative Literature as a Discipline of Decolonization" that we have to redefine literature and humanism through the lens of an evolving world, or, to be precise, a postcolonial world with which we are all involved. This may call forth a global, multi-level new humanistic formula, which would no longer be imposed by European civilization on the pretext of its so-called universality of reason, but would be established by way of dialogue between cultures, that is, "to talk together", or "colloquium" in Latin. Gnisci (1996) further asserts:

If we say that to those countries having shaken off Western colonialism, comparative literature introduces a way of comprehending, researching, and realizing post-colonialism, then for all European scholars, it represents a kind of reflection, a kind of self-criticism and learning, what we might see as a way to extricate ourselves from our colonialist mindset.

Thoughts on Comparative Literature and World Literature   53

This will not be empty words given that we admit to the fact that we belong to a "post-colonial world where ex-colonizers and the ex-colonized live the same way and coexist". The "discipline" I am talking about has nothing to do with the academic institutions in the West: it amounts to an educating experience of the self and the other. It is "askesis" of some sort.

To varying degrees, the development of the above ideas constitutes an important frame of reference for the study of literature today, especially comparative literature and world literature.

5.2 What Is World Literature?

At present, the heated discussion among many scholars regarding world literature is a reaction to the new vision as introduced above. Over the past two years, the quarterly journal *Comparative Literature in China*, published in Shanghai, has devoted several columns to world literature and as a result brought together brilliant insights and opinions.

As I see it, the concept of world literature commonly adopted by Chinese scholars in the past has mostly been an extension of what has been defined by Goethe and Marx. The former emphasizes that world literature is an aggregation of the outstanding literature of all peoples, while the latter points out that "from the numerous national and local literatures, there arises a world literature" (Marx & Engels, 2009, p. 46), that is, in the context of the development of capitalism, the "many" in the past come to be "one single sort", a new world literature of generality that is distinct from previous forms. Yet, with the changing times, both definitions seem to have certain flaws. Some Chinese scholars consider world literature in these senses to be not so much a literary reality as a beautiful ideal and a valuable utopia. They believe that world literature is not merely an aggregation of a variety of unrelated excellent works as Goethe thought, but one that features mutual understanding, mutual authentication, and mutual complementation, and that which is an organic combination with a certain sense of comparative literature; it is not what Marx and Engels deemed "a compound integrating a variety of literatures" but is, rather, a community of diverse literatures where they maintain and develop their own characteristics, derive nourishment from other literatures, and make their unique contributions to other literatures.

Chinese scholars have been going along different paths in their exploration of world literature from the very beginning, with the first step taken by Lu Xun's "On the Power of Mara Poetry" (1907). In his article, Lu Xun proposes to know the self first and then others, thus putting self-understanding in a primary position. For example, when discussing the influence of the Satanic school of poetry represented by Byron and Shelley on Russia and Eastern Europe, his focus is firstly on the discrepancy between the Slavic people and Western Europe in thinking and he further points out that Pushkin's gradual inclination towards the ordinary people of his motherland instead of Byron's praise for warriors is attributed to the difference of their national characters.

54 *Thoughts on Comparative Literature and World Literature*

Lu Xun highlights the far-reaching influence of Byron and Shelley in Eastern Europe, taking as examples, Russian poet Pushkin, the Polish poet Adam Mickiewicz, and the Hungarian poet Sándor Petőfi. Lu Xun's exposition of these influences is not a simple narrative; much less than simply combining them into one, in actual fact, it goes much further and advocates maintaining the differences between national literatures when they converge and at the same time indicates how literatures can benefit from their relationship with others.

Succeeding Lu Xun, Yang Zhouhan, the first president of the Chinese Comparative Literature Association (CCLA), suggests that when Chinese scholars study foreign literature, one prerequisite is that they must have a Chinese soul, that is, to understand themselves and to base their scholarship on their profound cultural heritage, so that their study of foreign literatures can have Chinese characteristics, and thus those persistent theories, approaches to, and appreciations of Chinese literature can find their way into the world via this unique Chinese soul interpretation.

Professor Chen Sihe at Fudan University has also provided his own unique opinions on world literature. As early as 1991, he proposed that there are global factors in Chinese literature. As Chen (2000) puts it, Chinese literature

> has made its way into world literature in its distinctive posture, and has enriched world literature. From this research perspective, Chinese literature and other national literatures have constructed a complex model of world literature, with all literatures in equal positions.
>
> (pp. 31–32)

His claims are very much compatible with the current discussion of world literature. Furthermore, Chen has not only provided in-depth theoretical discussion, but also devoted himself to seeking these "global factors in Chinese literature". The "penitent conscience", "awareness of inner demons", "survival consciousness" and so forth that he mentions repeatedly have all shown to varying degrees the universal values of different cultures, which are manifested through their own cultural characteristics and which experience new development along the path of comparative literature, that is, through mutual understanding, mutual authentication, and mutual complementation. In August 2011, at the 10th Annual Conference and International Symposium of Chinese Comparative Literature held in Shanghai, some scholars questioned the term "global factor". Under the premise of emphasizing differences, variability, and networking, the existence of "global factors" is beyond doubt, as I see it, if not understood in an essentialist way. However, this issue is open to further discussion, as follows.

Some young scholars in Beijing have also offered many new insights in their study of world literature. They particularly value the dynamic and open mind. One example is the article "The Liberation of Literature" by Zhang Pei, which highlights that in today's globalized context, "literature" is bound to be "of the world". The world is both the "objective counterpart" and "intentional object" of "literature". On the other hand, the world is a "tangible existence in time", and "the existence of the world is characterized by its occurring". In other words, the world is always worlding: its exposure and *différance* never stop. Such scholars hold that the rigid habitual mindset of the past, characterized by a subjective–objective dichotomy, should be altered, emphasizing that nothing is fully determined or unchangeable, but is always in the process of formation. Another paper, "What Kind of World and How to Define Literature?" by Chen Yuehong, more explicitly stresses that the world and literature are constantly changing. Chen's argument is valid, just as Bakhtin (2010) writes, "It is only in the eyes of another culture that foreign culture reveals itself fully and profoundly (but not maximally fully, because there will be cultures that see and understand even more)" (p. 7). Only after one connotation encounters another, will it reveal its deep foundation. Therefore, the discussion of world literature is essentially about finding a path for the construction of an international literary ecology in a diversified context, and to promote the formation of pluralistic literary values and standards in this ecology. In other words, world literature is literature that is constantly evolving and changing in and along with the ever-changing world.

5.3 Comparative Literature and World Literature

The world features diversity, and so does culture. Identifying differences, allowing them to be manifested in collisions between cultures, and bringing about new developments through mutual learning and benefit; this is the original intention of comparative literature. As two modern concepts, comparative literature and world literature determine and generate each other, and constitute the object of research for each other, existing in a dynamic constructive relationship. In the present-day globalization, national literatures can no longer be studied with a relatively closed and isolated approach as before, since new elements such as comparative literature and world literature inevitably make their way into such studies; that is to say, the epistemological and methodological principles, for instance, intersubjectivity, mutual reference and mutual illumination, have irresistibly broken through the self-limitation of national literatures, opening up a new path of integrating national literature research with comparative literature and world literature studies. On the other hand, comparative literature is no longer limited to its previous framework; instead, it focuses on the theories, relationships and dynamics between the ever-changing literatures of various countries, namely, to stress new issues including changeable literary and cultural intertextuality, and heterogeneous space.

In this sense, it can be said that the dynamic world literature is the object of comparative literature and without such a world literature as its object, there would be no need for comparative literature, and that, equally, comparative literature is also the forerunner of world literature and promotes the

56 *Thoughts on Comparative Literature and World Literature*

aggregation and variation of literatures around the globe, and without comparative literature as an epistemology (interactive cognition) and methodology (mutual understanding, mutual authentication and mutual complementation), it would be difficult for world literature to develop, or, even worse, world literature could be merely an accumulation of irrelevant materials or scattered grains of sand.

As already proven, comparative literature does provide possibilities for world literature: with cross-cultural, cross-lingual, and cross-disciplinary literary research as the core, comparative literature, especially translation, makes national literatures that used to be to some extent isolated truly cosmopolitan and thus become an important part of the literature and culture of other nations; creating a special form of national literature. As pointed out by Professor Zhang Hui at Peking University, if it were not for Ms. Yang Jiang's translation, *Don Quixote* would always be alien or even nonexistent to a person in China who does not understand Spanish, and, moreover, it was only thanks to Kumarajiva, Xuanzang, Ji Xianlin, Jin Kemu, etc. that Buddhist scriptures and Sanskrit literature have practically become part of Chinese literature, indeed an indispensable part. It is also the case with the translation of the Bible, Shakespeare's works, and so on. What many of these outstanding translators and researchers have been up to is in fact comparative literature. In other words, comparative literature adds new contents to original national literatures, endowing them with new global characteristics. Conversely, comparative literature also brings additional global elements into one certain literature when it acknowledges another literature, to which a new interpretation is made through the lens of comparative literature. This is what some scholars have highlighted; that world literature must depart from a specific kind of culture and hence produce a new and special understanding of another literature.

It is worth noting that since the beginning of the twenty-first century, with this new vogue embedded in and entailed by globalization, world literature and comparative literature have found their way into all aspects of literary research, including literary theory, literary criticism, literary history, classical literature research, and modern literature research. This will undoubtedly lead to the reconstruction and updating of the entire literary scholarship.

5.4 Emerging Theoretical Questions

As mentioned in earlier chapters, in this era of transformation, many theoretical questions have emerged. The primary one is whether cultural exchange will result in the gradual shrinking of cultural discrepancies or even their disappearance due to cultural blending. Consequently, will the acceptance of external influences change the fundamental characteristics of the original culture? Are cultures "incommensurable" because of differences, such that they cannot totally communicate? In addition to these problems, there is the issue of the "self" and the "other" in such dialogue. Since the "other" is what I "am not," we should first pay attention to the dissimilarity *per se*. Only by way of fully demonstrating this "face-to-face" dissimilarity of the "other" can it become a frame of reference for the reflection of the "self". Nevertheless, mere emphasis on dissimilarities tends to end up with the two becoming "unrelated" and thus unlikely to reach mutual understanding, and yet, no emphasis on dissimilarities at all will sacrifice the characteristics of each so that the other and the self eventually converge. How are we supposed to deal with this paradox? Another even more important issue regards discourse in the dialogue between cultures. The principal prerequisite for equal dialogue is to have discourse that both parties can understand and accept and that they can use such to communicate. At present, developing countries are faced with a whole set of well-established systems of concept that the developed world has formulated, due to its strong political and economic strength over centuries. After hundreds of years of accumulation, this "set" of discourse has brought together millions of intellectuals' reflections on various human issues, and has been enriched and developed via cultural interactions. Should such discourse be abandoned, life as it is now could hardly continue. However, if local culture is interpreted and intercepted only with this set of discourse and the pattern it constitutes, many local, original, and vital cultures will be excluded due to their inability to fit within the pattern. Should this be the case, the so-called dialogue would, in fact, only be a monologue of the same culture, and it will achieve nothing more than replenishing the culture itself with some foreign materials; therefore, it cannot form a truly interactive dialogue. How can we establish a new set of discourse that has something new to present and that is truly conducive to equal dialogue?

Apart from these unsettled issues, many new ones keep arising. One example is the arbitrary "appropriation" of new independent cultures by powerful ones, that is, American global multiculturalism, wherein the hegemonic interpretation of various cultures is taken as the only acceptable interpretation of global multiculturalism. In essence, this is still colonization, albeit in the spiritual sense. Moreover, day-to-day real-life colonization is likely to continue to flow from such a dominant spirit. A significant number of people in the West cannot treat other cultures equally, as exemplified by the right-wing mass murder in Norway. Another issue is how the people of former colonized countries can finally obtain thorough liberation from spiritual colonization. Other problems include the outlining of the history of writing and reading beyond cultural, temporal, and spatial boundaries, the happening of a shift in printed text culture, and the rise of digital image culture. All the above questions should be properly solved.

All in all, we are in an unprecedented period of transition. People increasingly feel that in the building of an ideal world of cultural diversity and symbiosis, that literature, especially comparative literature and world literature as the object of comparative literature, plays an increasingly significant role. All literary researchers worldwide should move forward together, redefine literature and humanism, reconsider the meaning and pattern of human survival, and reshape the new spiritual world for us all.

58 *Thoughts on Comparative Literature and World Literature*

References

Bakhtin, M. M. (2010). Response to a question from the *Novy Mir* editorial staff. In C. Emerson & M. Holquist (Eds.), *Speech genres and other late essays* (V. W. McGee, Trans.). Austin: University of Texas Press.

Chen, S. H. (2000). On the global elements of twentieth-century Chinese literature. *Comparative Literature in China*, *38*(1), 31–32.

Foucault, M. (1967). Of other spaces: Utopias and heterotopias (J. Miskowiec, Trans.). *Diacritics*, *16*(1), 22–27.

Gnisci, A. (1996). Comparative literature as a discipline of decolonialization. *Chinese Comparative Literature Bulletin*, *1996*(04), 113–120.

Jullien, F. (2000). *Detour and access: Strategies of meaning in China and Greece* (S. Hawkes, Trans.). New York: Zone.

Marx, K., & Engels, F. (2009). *Manifesto of the communist party*. New York: Cosimo, Inc.

Morin, E. (2002). Au-delà de la globalisation et du développement, société-monde ou empire-monde? [Beyond globalization and development: World society or world empire?] *Revue du MAUSS*, *20*(2), 43–53.

6 Interactive Cognition
The Case of Literature–Science Interaction

Neo-humanism for the twenty-first century features interactive cognition, or bidirectional epistemology, with mutual reference, mutual authentication, mutual understanding and mutual complementation as its core.

6.1 Two Patterns of Cognition

The second half of the twentieth century witnessed a significant epistemological and methodological shift. The past's logical paradigm of cognition, which fell under the category of content analysis, whereby, through inspissation, concrete contents are drained and the most concise generalized forms are derived, and it finally boils down to the metaphysical Logos, or absolute spirit according to Hegel. By applying the logical paradigm, every concept can be simplified into a pure ideal form that is devoid of body, substance and time, and every narrative can be reduced into a clearly defined, closed space where all processes merely express a fundamental structural form and all contents can be generalized in this form, while, by the reverse procedure, the form can accommodate diverse contents. For instance, narratives in many works can be reduced into this structure: preexistent "deficiency" and then "deficiency remedied" or "deficiency predestined to be irremediable". *The Dream of Red Mansions*, for example, tells a story of a piece of hard rock that was discontent with its "deficiency" of being left behind by the goddess while she was amending the sky and then experienced the earthly world but ended up in a void. *Journey to the West* is another example of this; Sun Wukong, dissatisfied with the "deficiency" of his life as the Monkey King in Mount Huaguo, wreaked havoc in Heaven, and, after suffering eighty-one tribulations, reaped his final Buddhist merit. A multiplicity of such narratives combines to form a "meta-narrative" or "meta-text" of the same structure, demonstrating some laws, essence, and inevitability.

In modern days, there is another prevailing paradigm of cognition, one that does not take form as its object of inquiry but takes the "body" instead as its primary concern; a living body that has its existence and acts, and that can feel pain and joy. Everything surrounding the body is fixed, but changes with the emotions and perspectives of the body. Hence, the space this paradigm inquires within is an open topological space that constantly changes

DOI: 10.4324/9781003356240-6

60 *Interactive Cognition*

with the passion, desire and will of the subject. In this paradigm, the depth model that people are accustomed to is deconstructed: the center no longer exists and any concrete or devoid entity may become a center; everything that has been rendered marginal, fragmentary, dormant, and obscure now unleashes new energy; phenomena do not necessarily have an essence beneath, contingency is not always predicated on inevitability, and a "signifier" does not necessarily correspond to a fixed "signified". History, for instance, disintegrates into two layers: namely, the "history of events" and the "narrated history". However, the scope of witnessing is rather limited. For the most part we can only get to know history via narratives, and what to narrate, how detailed the narration is, and from which angle or perspective to narrate, are all inevitably affected by subjective constraints; thus, all history is contemporary history, that is, history transcribed and interpreted by contemporaries.

With the originally fixed "meta-narrative" framework deconstructed, each individual strives to give full play to their own characteristics and creativity, and the need to emphasize differences overwhelms the interest in seeking common ground. It has been found that the more differences that are acknowledged and respected, the better individuals can get along in an atmosphere of mutual understanding. In fact, it is far from enough to merely admit "differences". What we need are not isolated, unrelated individuals, but communities of diverse individuals connected through mutual understanding and respect, with their initial differences retained. This is what Chinese tradition cherishes as "*he*" (harmony). Confucius long ago proposed: "A man of virtue pursues harmony but does not seek uniformity; a petty man seeks uniformity but does not pursue harmony." Repetition of the same thing can never produce anything new. Only when different individuals exert influence on each other, namely, to interact, can new development be possible. As *Discourses on Governance of the States*: *Discourses of Zheng* explicitly points out: "Harmony begets new things; while uniformity does not lead to continuation".

Hence, the "principle of the other" is now highlighted. It is the opposite of the former principle in which the subject observes and determines everything. The indeterminate "principle of interaction" is underlined, and its opposite stresses determinacy and the "principle of general applicability". In brief, this new pattern of cognition highlights that a deep knowledge of both the subject and the object can only be achieved through observation and reflection from the viewpoint of the "other". Su Shi (1037–1101), a distinguished poet in the Song dynasty, composed the following poem:

> From the side, a whole range; from the end, a single peak;
> far, near, high, low, no two parts alike.
> Why can't I tell the true shape of Lu-shan?
> Because I myself am in the mountain.[1]

Simply put, due to the different statuses and positions of observers, the subjective worlds and the objective worlds alter. Hence, for a sound understanding of the world (including the subject), we should hold an "external point of view", including reference to others (other cultures included) in viewing things from different angles. Sometimes, when reminded or inspired by the "other", we may gain an unexpected, renewed understanding of things around that we had previously failed to notice. This "space for perspective-taking" constituted by "external points of views" provides vast possibilities for the development of cognition.

Since everything varies with the change of space, time, status, and perspective, nothing can ever have static meanings. In fact, everything in the world is condensed into a reality due to multitudinous coincidences in the ever-changing interactive relationships and in uncertain, endless possibilities. Taoism refers to this state of chaos that contains abundant possibilities and is subject to constant changes as "a consistent mix of everything", which is what Taoism defines as the "*Dao*" (the "Way"). Chapter 21 of *Tao Te Ching* reads:

> Its [the Way] nature is utterly vague and evasive.
> How evasive and vague!
> Yet its center has form.
> How vague and evasive!
> Yet its center has substance.

Here, the "form" (*xiang*) and the "substance" (*wu*) are the possibility that does not yet exist but is bound to happen. This possibility will become a reality in the wake of the interaction of various factors and the dynamic evolution of the subjective and the objective. To put it another way, the understanding of things cannot be immutable, but instead will inevitably present different forms according to the different understandings of the "individuals" (subjects). Therefore, the process of understanding is also a process of interaction and reconstruction.

6.2 Natural Sciences and the Humanities

Generally speaking, natural sciences focus on the study of natural objects. Natural objects are generated naturally: they cannot be created artificially, no matter how advanced science is today. Even the most advanced cloning technology is unlikely to produce a living thing out of thin air, since it must rely on stem cells from a certain existing organism. Natural sciences, with nature as the research object, and social sciences and the humanities, with society and human cultures created by human beings as the research object, significantly differ from each other in their way of thinking. First of all, changes in nature mostly follow some laws within a certain range, and those laws can be repeated over and over again. For example, when water is heated to 100°C, it boils and evaporates; when it is cooled under 0°C, it freezes into ice. This process can have infinite replications and can stand tests. In contrast, while social and humanistic phenomena can be simulated, they cannot be replicated and thus fail to endure tests in conventionally scientific terms. For example, in examining the victory or defeat in a war, no matter what theory is applied, the war

62 *Interactive Cognition*

cannot be repeated for analysis purposes. Secondly, while the laws of nature are independent of human will, the same conditions and the same processes always produce the same results, and the development of social and human phenomena as well as their results vary with timing, geographical conditions and human relations and are restricted by a multitude of incidental factors.

Therefore, in the scope of natural sciences, people mainly rely on the methods of formal logic, mathematical descriptions and specific experiments, which fall into the first paradigm of cognition mentioned above, one that is based on classification and generalization, induction and deduction, while, in contrast, social sciences and the humanities are mainly dependent on the second paradigm, which is a comparative paradigm. As Marx (1904) summarizes, the human brain processes the world in four ways: in addition to natural sciences, it also approaches the world by way of art, religions, and practical-and-spiritual modes, and the four elucidate each other, but not as a replacement for each other (pp. 292–293).

Yet the aforementioned epistemology and methodology of natural sciences have limited applicability and, beyond the range of applicability, it will be a different thing altogether. The case of water boiling at 100°C and freezing at 0°C no longer works if not at one atmosphere of pressure. The laws applicable within the scope of Newtonian mechanics also vary under the conditions of quantum mechanics. Furthermore, what is known to humankind is rather limited while the unknown is endless. If the "unknowns" are to become "knowns", we must first rely on the experimental frameworks designed by humans, through which the unknowns are verified and hence become knowns. Then, how about the vast uncharted territory that has not been verified or where no experimental framework is available? It is practically impossible to employ known laws to generalize unknown fields. The knowledge of natural sciences must, above all, rest on experimental propositions conceived by humans, which in turn can only be established after verification by experiments. It can thus be seen that the knowledge and laws of natural sciences are not absolute either, nor can they be separated from the interaction between natural objects and between natural objects and humans, not to mention that the purpose of natural sciences *per se* is to put people first and to benefit humankind as a whole.

However, in modern times, the "scientific" and "humanistic" realms seem to have been split into two distinct worlds. In the twentieth century, people cannot help but suffer the harm to human society caused by the misuse or abuse of scientific achievements, and feel the gloom and threat from the predictions of future scientific development, such as a series of societal and ethical issues brought by the deciphering of genes and the cloning of organisms. Needless to say, the advance of science has jeopardized the human body itself some ways. Moreover, the human ability to form mental images through imagination and words is damaged to a considerable extent, not to mention the already serious air pollution, ecological imbalance, atomic weapons, and depleted uranium bombs, to name but a few. In the past, when children read a fairytale book, an imaginary world would naturally unfold in their minds. Nowadays, due to the excessive reliance on the visual images provided by televisions, computers and game consoles, children's capacity to create their own images through texts has been greatly weakened. Overwhelmed by all the images visualized in comics and cartoons, which have been created by others and are circulated through the media, children are gradually losing their own imagination. Thus, the emergence in the West of an anti-intellectual strain of wishing to return to innocence and flee modern civilization is of no surprise.

Nonetheless, it is obviously not science itself that imperils humankind, but the people who hold and utilize its power. The problem is how to control this power and involve the broad masses of the people. The global environmental movement is a successful example of this type of endeavor. Human beings are striving for a power mechanism with a wider community involved. This may also standardize the control and use of the power of science and avoid the potential harms it may inflict.

Although the sciences and humanities adopt different ways of cognition and thinking, they are far from being in absolute opposition; rather, they can communicate, understand, and utilize each other. This is because "mankind" as a part of nature is essentially consistent with nature *per se*. For instance, when scientists term the "harmony in mathematics", they believe that this "harmony" is common across all disciplines. Another example would be the "golden ratio" of 1.618, which has been recognized by painters as the ideal and which is not only a principle of composition created by painters, but also an optimal measure of natural visual selection. The distribution of leaf veins, the colors and patterns on animals, the ratio of shoulder width to waist width and the head-to-waist over waist-to-floor ratio of dancers, and the optimization method formulated by mathematicians for industrial and agricultural production, as well as the best proportion of ingredients determined, are all approximations of the golden ratio. Countless other examples can be cited to prove this unity of diversity and commonality between man and nature. In fact, as modern science progresses, people constantly discover common attributes in diverse fields, which had not been noticed before, and modern science provides means (such as computers) to make it possible to study these common attributes and relationships. As Marx (1975) foresaw long ago, "Natural science will in time incorporate into itself the science of man, just as the science of man will incorporate into itself natural science: there will be one science" (p. 47). The second half of the twentieth century saw the emergence of a wide range of interdisciplinary research: isolated and fragmented categories are rejoined again and all parts, facets, and factors of a certain matter are considered together so that an encompassing conclusion can be produced out of commonalities and regularities as well as the framework, functions, and manners of their interactions. On the other hand, various things and movements in the world are no longer regarded as incidental and isolated or as a mechanical totality of certain phenomena or processes. It turns out that certain attributes and characteristics are nowhere to be found in isolated individuals; they only exist in their interconnection within given wholes, that is, as mentioned above, interactive relationships. In this sense, it is unfeasible to segment the interactive, organic wholes into static, dead parts

64   *Interactive Cognition*

in research, but instead the characteristics of the matters in question can only be revealed when all parts are considered in the dynamic process of interdependence and mutual restraint. The following part will take the interaction between literature and natural sciences, which are seemingly vastly different from each other, as an example.

6.3 Literature and Natural Sciences

In the early 1950s, when discussing the definition and function of comparative literature, American scholar Henry Remak (1961) stated:

> We must have syntheses unless the study of literature wants to condemn itself to eternal fragmentation and isolation. If we have any ambitions of participating in the intellectual and emotional life of the world, we must, now and then, pull together the insights and results achieved by research in literature and make meaningful conclusions available to other disciplines, to the nation and to the world at large.
>
> (p. 5)

Comparative literature, in addition to its role as a bond linking literatures of various regions, is supposed to be a "bridge between organically related but physically separated areas of human creativeness". Remak (1961) invites us to understand the definition of comparative literature as follows:

> Comparative literature is the study of literature beyond the confines of one particular country, and the study of the relationships between literature on the one hand and other areas of knowledge and belief, such as the arts (e.g., painting, sculpture, architecture, music), philosophy, history, the social sciences (e.g., politics, economics, sociology), the sciences, religion, etc., on the other. In brief, it is the comparison of one culture's literature with another or others, and the comparison of literature with other spheres of human expression.
>
> (p. 3)

Then, the study of the relationship between literature and other disciplines has always been a vital part of comparative literature, and considerable progress has been made, especially in the interactive relationships between literature and the natural sciences.

In the first half of the twentieth century, the theory of evolution and Freud's psychology completely renewed the fields of literary theory, literary criticism, literary history, and even literary creation and notions. In the second half of the same century, systems theory, information theory, cybernetics, and the concept of entropy in the second law of thermodynamics had no less impact on literature. Since the "three theories" (systems theory, information theory, and cybernetics) have been much discussed, I will focus on how the notion of entropy has been influencing literature.

The concepts of dissipative structure and entropy derived from the second law of thermodynamics have gradually found their way into social science and literary research since the second half of the twentieth century. The second law states that in a closed system, with work being done, higher-level and orderly energy is dissipated, producing lower-level and more disorderly energy. For example, when hot water and cold water are poured into a container simultaneously, they cannot exist separately, but quickly mix into becoming warm water, which cannot then be restored to the original two states. In this irreversible process, during which orderly energy decreases and eventually becomes exhausted, the "entropy", a net measure of order and disorder, increases. Entropy measures the degree of disorder, and when it increases, orders are broken, that is, the differences and characteristics of all the individual matters involved are submerged, leading to a monotonous, unified, and chaotic state. In the preface to his 1988 book *The Human Use of Human Beings*, scientist Robert Wiener (1988) indicates:

> As entropy increases, the universe, and all closed systems in the universe, tend naturally to deteriorate and lose their distinctiveness; moving from the least to the most probable state, from a state of organization and differentiation in which distinctions and forms exist, to a state of chaos and sameness. In Gibbs' universe order is least probable, and chaos most probable.
>
> (p. 12)

This means, viewed from the development trend of the whole world, with energy dispersal the total energy that can be used to perform work continue to decrease, during which everything becomes old, known and disordered and in turn things that are fresh, incidental and that are arranged in particular orders and thus have their own particularities, become rare; such is what Weiner described as "to move from the least to the most probable state, from a state of organization and differentiation in which distinctions and forms exist, to a state of chaos and sameness"; in other words, the overwhelming tendency of the entropy to increase. Supposing that one is cut off from the outside world and thus becomes a closed system, consuming no food, absorbing no external information through the sensory organs, having no exchanges or reactions with the external world, like "*Hun Dun*" (Chaos), a fabled character (conceived by Taoist Zhuangzi), who has no "seven apertures" (*qiqiao*) (in the head, eyes, ears, nostrils and mouth) and thus cannot see, hear, eat, or breath; thus, the entropy in this person would grow ever greater and eventually lead to disorder and chaos, and then non-doing, immobility, balance, perpetual decay, and deadly stillness.

The concept of "entropy" has aroused significant reactions in American literature, especially fiction. Some of the most renowned contemporary American writers, such as Saul Bellow, John Updike and Norman Mailer, have all written about entropy in their works, and one of the earliest short stories by postmodernist writer Thomas Pynchon was "Entropy", which is in

66   *Interactive Cognition*

fact a preface to many of his later works. His works, such as *Gravity's Rainbow*, invariably have the notion of entropy beneath them. In her masterpiece *Death Kit*, Susan Sontag describes everything moving their way towards collapse and exhaustion, and heading for ultimate homogeneity and death. This kind of worry and fear is found in many of contemporary American writers' works. Notably, they are keen on elaborating such a course that something or someone, originally alive and spirited, full of activity, gradually heads towards meaningless, repetitive movements of powerlessness and death. Such accounts are indeed startling. Thus, in America, writers are seen as "anti-entropy" heroes who are likely to stop this tendency. As social operations incline towards unification, creative thinking, breakthrough thinking, and developmental thinking, which are crucial to social progress, are doomed to extinction. The "five unities" proposed by the Gang of Four (a political faction composed of four Chinese Communist Party officials) during the Cultural Revolution period, namely, to unify thoughts, wills, actions, language, and lifestyles, are extreme examples of ideological numbness and social stagnation. Artists are heroes against such "unified operations" because they deem such unification the ultimate paralysis of life. Paralysis occurs as things wear away. So long as their works are not hackneyed, artists will always introduce a certain amount of new information, and information is "negative entropy"; information breaks the old unity and stillness, reduces the degree of chaos, and thus decreases entropy. As such, artists play the role of "anti-entropy". It is artists' inclination to deliberately innovate, never stop overcoming familiarity, and to pursue "strangeness" that makes them "anti-entropy" heroes.

To prevent the increase of entropy, the closed, isolated systems shall be opened up to include more information, constantly exchange energy with the outside world and unceasingly alter the structure of the subject to adapt to new situations. Belgian physicist and Nobel Prize winner Ilya Prigogine introduced the concept of time irreversibility to physics and chemistry, investigated the state of non-equilibrium, and proposed a new notion of dissipative structure. Classical mechanics regards the laws of physics as reversible, with the past and the future undistinguished, and being independent of the factor of time, the result is always the same. For example, hydrogen and oxygen in a 2:1 ratio will always combine into water as long as certain conditions are met, and vice versa. This is a reversible equilibrium state. As Prigogine points out, such equilibrium is not what is abundant in nature, but instead the time-involving, irreversible non-equilibrium is. The diffusion of a drop of ink in water, mixing of hot water with cold water, and preserved eggs (food); all of these are unlikely to be reversed. The earlier instance, the synthesis and decomposition of water, is a stationary state which is objectively not dependent on time, but the example of ink diffusion in water is a dynamic, time-varying state which cannot return to its earlier conditions. The former case represents stable equilibriums while the latter example is an open non-equilibrium system. The latter system has great potential to exchange matter and energy with the outside world and it will increasingly deviate from its original

Interactive Cognition   67

state, acquiring new elements. With such acquisition, the system is gradually renewed and impossible to be restored, since the new elements have become its integral parts. Such a structure can take in new elements at any time, releasing energy and forming new matters.

The research object of comparative literature is not the linear evolutionary history serving as an A-B-C since such literature is a lively, open system. It studies not only the mutual penetration of literatures of different cultures, but also the "non-equilibriums" of literature created by natural sciences, social sciences, other forms of art, and even the influence of the environment and times. Therefore, whether it is the creative subject or the aesthetic subject, they should strive to break through their own enclosure and become an open system of originality, which is adept at taking in new elements, releasing energy and forming new matters. Natural sciences and literary research *per se* are a form of human thinking so they naturally have certain commonalities. Therefore, studying the new achievements and new methods of natural sciences and applying them to literature will undoubtedly open up a new stage and make new contributions to literary research and literary creation.

Note

1 Translated by Watson. See: Su, S. (1084). Written on the Wall at West Forest Temple. In *Selected poems of Su Tung-P'o*. (1994). (B. Watson, Trans.). Port Townsend, WA: Copper Canyon Press. p. 108.

References

Tao Te Ching: Chapter 21. (S. Stenudd, Trans.). https://www.taoistic.com/taoteching-laotzu/taoteching-21.htm

Marx, K. (1904). *A contribution to the critique of political economy* (N. I. Stone, Trans.). Chicago: Charles H. Kerr. & Co.

Marx, K. (1975). Economic and philosophic manuscripts of 1844: Private property and communism. In D. J. Struik, et al. (Eds.), *K. Marx & F. Engels: Collected works* (Vol. 3) (M. Milligan, & D. J. Struik, Trans.). London: Lawrence & Wishart.

Remak, H. (1961). Comparative literature, its definition and function. In N. P. Stallknecht & H. Frenz (Eds.), *Comparative literature: Method and perspective*. Carbondale: Southern Illinois University Press.

Wiener, N. (1988). *The human use of human beings: Cybernetics and society*. New York: Da Capo Press.

7　Interactive Cognition and Mutual Interpretation

7.1 Logical Cognition and Cognition-in-Interaction

For a long time, the interpretation of literature has been performed largely in the fashion of logical cognition which prescribes a dichotomic way of perceiving by separating the cognized subject from the objective surroundings. Analysis done in this fashion tends to "condense" the content of the work to an inductive abstraction, reducing textual complexities to a shared formulation, and ultimately distilling from such minimal common grounds the metaphysical Logos or Hegelian ideas about absolute spirit. From there, one can pursue the opposite by "deducing" from the abstraction a variety of possible realizations. Together, these two analytical procedures allow each concept to be readily reduced to a pure idealization free from constraints of the body, the substance, or the time. Narrations of all types thus become subject to a concealed space, where all processes point to the fundamental formulation that underlies all processual realizations and the content of the work. One such popular formulation depicts the process from "deficiency" to "deficiency redressed" or "deficiency destined beyond redress" before the eventual success or failure. The household legend of the Monkey King's journey to the West, for example, can be reduced to such a formulation. As the rock was turned into a monkey and became bored with his mundane life, he fought his way down Mount Huaguo before soaring his way up to stir the Jade Palace. Eventually he achieved enlightenment through battling through eighty-one tribulations. Another tale narrates that a piece of stone left on Greenery Peak was meant for mending the broken sky[1]. Lonely as it felt, the stone dreamt about experiencing the earthly joys and pleasure before returning to Mother Earth. Narrative compositions as such come to form what we call the "macro-narrative" or "macro-textual" structure, from which we can readily derive the "rule", the "essence", and the causal relation between occurrences.

The interactive cognition (or cognition-in-interaction) approach I propose here, however, takes a different path. Instead of insisting on the divide between the subject and the object, it holds that the definiteness of the object is defined by the cognition of the subject. That is, both are subject to change in the process of interaction and as a result change and reconstruct themselves towards new recognition and understandings. Abstract as this idea

DOI: 10.4324/9781003356240-7

Interactive Cognition and Mutual Interpretation   69

seems, it is not difficult to understand how one's perception and interpretation of a certain object depends on many factors on the part of the subject, including his location and movement (both physical and mental). Hence, when studying the speech pattern and the dialogic structure of the interaction, we need to pay heed to the potential changes in the object which may arise due to the changes in the subject, the same as we need to examine the changes in the subjective cognition due to the changes in the object.

The interactive cognition approach differs from logical cognition, though in one way or another they might nevertheless be related. One obvious difference is that while logical cognition deals with formal constructions derived or reduced from concrete realities, cognition-in-interaction deals with the reality itself. The cognizing subject is a living existence, with the movements of the body and the pain and pleasure it is experiencing. The cognized object – the surroundings – is subject to the changes of this body, along with the emotion and perspective it carries. Hence, what is being scrutinized under this theoretical lens is an open and dynamic space, which is constantly changing with changes in a subject that excites, desires, and wills. Compared with other theoretical lenses, this approach holds the potential to deconstruct the underlying pattern of our habits of cognition. The idea of the center collapses as any substance can be made a center. The marginalized, the fragmented, the implicit, all previously subjugated to the overwhelming center, are brought back to life. As there could be a bias in subjecting observations to one stereotypical "nature", accidental occurrences should not be easily reduced to predictable scripts, and neither do "signifiers" point to a fixed "signified". For example, we used to take historical determinacy as a fact. With the new approach, however, two components can be identified in the making of history. One is "history of events" and the other "narrated history". The former denotes historical facts – what happened at a certain time in history – and they shall not change. As the opportunities for these facts to have been precisely observed and recorded are rather limited, we mostly approximate history via narratives. When it comes to narratives, however, much depends on the narrator: what to include, to what lengths should one go, and from which angle or perspective. Hence all are subject to subjective constraints. In this sense, one may contend that all the history that we have been exposed to is nothing but contemporary in it is at best transcriptions and interpretations by contemporaries (including "contemporaries" at a given time in the past).

7.2 Mutual Interpretation and China as the "Other"

With the established "macro-narrative" melting away, the individuality and creativity of each entity within the system are brought to light, lending an emphasis to differences that surpass the interest in seeking the common ground. In his keynote address at the 1999 commemorative conference of the 900th anniversary of the founding of Università di Bologna, Umberto Eco, a renowned Italian thinker and writer, described the third-millennium goal of continental Europe as "coexistence in diversity and mutual respect". He

70   *Interactive Cognition and Mutual Interpretation*

believes that the more differences among individuals and groups are recognized, the greater are the chances for acceptance and respect, and thus there is a better coexistence in mutual understanding.

A multiplicity of measures is available for seeking development with differences. Two prominent ones suggest themselves: the "principle of the Other" and the "principle of interaction". These principles intend to emphasize observations and reflections gained through examining the issue from the viewpoint of the "Other", which serves as a basis on which any deeper understanding of the subject and the object may develop. The reason for this is that as the observer changes where one stands (location- and opinion-wise), one's subjective world and the objective world one cognizes change with it. Therefore, a genuine understanding of the world and the cognizing subject can only be achieved if one takes the "outsider" view of the "Other" by drawing diversely from alternative perspectives in foreign cultures. With inspirations from the "Other", we may expect to gain unfamiliar understandings of things that we have not been much aware of. This collection of alternative perspectives forms a "thought vista" which opens broad possibilities for better understanding. The attempts at interpreting the other from the perspective of the self while interpreting the self from the perspective of the other constitute what might be called "mutual interpretation".

The meaning of every object is subject to change because it is conditioned by changes in space, time, status, and viewpoint. In this light, everything may find itself in a web of interactive relationships and an undetermined state amidst infinite possibilities, which, by one chance or another, has come to form a reality of their own. In Taoist philosophy, this nebula of changes and possibilities is referred to as the "Way" or "*Tao*". The term is defined in *Tao Te Ching* as "a thing (that is) impalpable and incommensurable. Incommensurable and impalpable, yet latent in it are forms. Impalpable and incommensurable, yet within it are entities" (ch. 21) (as cited in Wang & Lou, 2008, p. 52). The "forms" and "entities" are both possibilities that have no material existence yet have been established, hence a "non-being existence", the possibilities of which are subject to interactions between elements and changes in subjective and objective status. The subsequent reality is what Laozi termed "something formless yet complete". This idea is held to characterize Chinese philosophy and the Chinese way of thinking, which tend to put a premium on functionality, relationships, and chance. Objects are brought together to form a reality by the act of chance, as only one out of an array of many possibilities is realized. Thus, our knowledge of an object by no means remains immutable. Our state of knowing changes as the subject and the object change. Hence the process of understanding can also be seen as one of interactive and mutual reconstruction.

The influence of mutual interpretation on cultural and literary studies is huge. As discussed earlier, mutual interpretation denotes a process starting with understanding the other and ending with refreshed understandings of both the self and the other. In between are observations and attempts to understand the self from the viewpoint of the other. Ever since multiculturalism was brought to the fore by globalization in economy and technology, the question as to how to advance tolerance and understanding across cultures has become a major topic of scholarly concern. The endeavor to focus on self-reflection from the viewpoint of the other (with an emphasis on "mutual subjectivity", "mutual contextualization", "mutual reference" and "mutual illumination") has seen gradual acceptance among theorists and has established a strong foundation for the growth of multiculturalism.

As such, China, readily taken as the "Other", has caught increasing attention from theorists. As the French sinologist François Jullien explains (as cited in Wong, 2012, p. 142):

> The Chinese language, which is outside the enormous Indo-European language system, explores another possibility of writing. The Chinese civilization is one that has the longest history and had evolved independently without being influenced by European culture... All in all, China is an ideal image contrasted with which we will be able to free ourselves from some preconceived ideas and gaze at our own thoughts from the outside.

In the US, three books in this theoretical field have been published in quick succession and are making the rounds. These books are co-authored by the famed sinologist Roger Ames and the reputed philosopher David Hall. The first volume in the trilogy, *Thinking Through Confucius* (1987), reconceptualizes Confucius' philosophy with modern philosophical terminology. This was followed by a comparative discussion in *Anticipating China: Thinking Through the Narrations of Chinese and Western Culture* (1995), where the authors draw a distinction between Western and Chinese thinking with the observation that the Western way of thinking puts greater emphasis on transcendence, order, and permanence. The final volume in the trilogy, *Thinking from the Han: Self, Truth and Transcendence in Chinese and Western Culture* (1998), is devoted to a discussion on the exploration of the self, truth, and transcendence. In his 2000 book *The Siren and the Sage: Knowledge and Wisdom in Ancient Greece and China*, Stephen Shankman attempts to read the differences in understanding between ancient Greece and China from the perspective of mutual interpretation. It refrains from relying on a subject/object dichotomy, which places China and the West as fixed objects independent from the subject. Rather, François Jullien (2000) notes:

> I believe it would be hardly possible to divide one book leaf into two, with China on one side and Greece on the other... That is because the intended meaning can only be approached from within, and understanding can only occur when individual logic is appreciated.

A less metaphorical way to put this is that neither Chinese nor Western culture remains immutable. They would be read differently by different individuals as knowing subjects. Hence, the process of comprehension is also one of reconstruction.

72 *Interactive Cognition and Mutual Interpretation*

Multiculturalism has not only contributed significantly to the advances in Western sinology; it has also refreshed Western theoretical discussions outside the realm of sinology. In the past, representative works on mainstream culture, such as those by Hegel and Max Weber, did spare some space for non-Western cultures; however, these sparing mentions were included mainly as a backdrop with an obscure position within the theoretical construct. This dismal situation is changed, however, with the new multipolar take on multiculturalism, as a number of non-sinologist theorists begin to adopt the "mutual interpretation" approach explained above and develop a non-centralist attitude towards exploring Western and non-Western cultures, and, thereupon, towards building new theories. The well-known US theorist Frederic Jameson, for example, visited China several times during which he conducted a course entitled "Post-Modernism and Cultural Theory" at Peking University. Though unversed in Chinese, he has read widely the works of Lu Xun, Lao She, and many others by way of translation and has watched a great number of Chinese films. As such, he developed his theories based on reflections on his Chinese experience. His collection of essays entitled *The Geopolitical Aesthetic: Cinema and Space in the World System* (1992) throws a supra-cultural and interdisciplinary light on the topic by applying the mutual interpretation approach to analyzing the clash between the function and meaning of film narratives in the West and the Third World. Umberto Eco, during his 1995 visit to China, delivered a lecture at Peking University, in which he proposed: "To understand others does not necessarily entail the need for proving similarities between us and the other; rather, it is to understand and respect the differences." On this point, he explained that the purpose of his trip to Beijing was dissimilar to that of Marco Polo in his hunt for the Western "unicorn" in the East; rather he sought to learn something about the Chinese dragon. His belief that "the more differences among individuals and groups are recognized, the greater chances for acceptance and respect, thus a better coexistence in mutual understanding" shattered the foundation of Western centralism.

The new advances In these theories" have also profoundly influenced the paradigm of Western comparative literature studies. Despite its nearly century-long history, comparative literature used to confine itself to Western systems built on Greek and Hebrew culture, with a consistent dominance over and contempt against non-Western cultures. Thanks to the new era of globalization, with the rise of multiculturalism, significant changes have been brought about in the field. It did not take long for comparative literature and culture studies to break out of the confines of Western culture and to enter a space for mutual learning between Western and non-Western cultures. This change came too abruptly to be readily accepted, however. Some scholars in the West who fail to value, understand, or prepare for the change often get confused. It has even caused some teaching and research institutions that specialize in comparative literature revolving around the Western system to suspend their operations, leading to cries of a crisis in the domain of comparative literature. This trend, however, is experienced by the old-fashioned comparative paradigm within the self-enclosed Eurocentric model. The emerging comparative literature, as defined by its cross-cultural nature, is, by contrast, vibrantly flourishing across the world, the trend of which has been predicted by some of the more acute scholars, who have adjusted their focus of research towards topics concerning heterogeneous culture and literature. The renowned US scholar Earl Miner, who has been serving as president of the International Comparative Literature Association for two consecutive terms, is one of them. His well-read work *Comparative Poetics: An Intercultural Essay on Theories of Literature* (1990) adopts a mutual contextualization approach to examine Eastern and Western poetics. The nine-volume *A History of World Comparative Literature*, edited by the International Comparative Literature Association, originally equated "the word" with Euro-American culture. It then incorporated a volume titled *The History of Comparative Literature in East Asia*, along with the addition of content on modern and contemporary literature from China and other non-Western regions to the volume on modernism and post-modernism.

Although comparative literature studies in China used to depend heavily on theoretical borrowings from the West, they have not been without their great achievements despite the various limitations. Today, with such new approaches as interactive cognition and mutual interpretation continuing to gain broad acceptance, scholars in comparative literature have started to implement the immediacy of addressing the multicultural and interdisciplinary aspects of the issue, which promises to lead to unprecedented growth of the field. Consequently, the three previously disconnected academic communities of sinologists, theorists, and comparative literature scholars in the West are converging rapidly towards a complementary balance where recognition and affirmation are made mutual. This favorable situation creates opportunities for fruitful collaboration between Chinese scholars and the rest of the world. With these efforts, the emerging comparative literature research can contribute to the reconstruction of culture in the twenty-first century.

Note

1 One Chinese legend has it that while the Goddess Nv Wa was patching up the broken sky with five-colored stones she smelted, she scattered the remaining stones on the earth. Inspired by this ancient tale, the hero Jia Baoyu in the classic Chinese novel *A Dream of Red Mansions* is believed to be an incarnation of the stone left by Nv Wa.

References

Jullien, F. (2000). Why we Westerners cannot avoid China in our study of philosophy. *Dialogue Transculturel*, 5, 146–156.

Wang, B., & Lou, Y. L. (2008). *Interpretations to and revisions of the classic of the way and the virtue*. Beijing: Zhonghua Book Company.

Wong, S. K. (Ed.). (2012). *Confucianism, Chinese history and society*. Singapore: World Scientific Publishing Company.

8 Difference and Dialogue

8.1 The Three Encounters Between China and the West

The history of China's interaction with the West is marked by three encounters.

The first encounter took place in the sixteenth century when Western missionaries came to preach in China. That was the time when religious missionaries made efforts towards seeking common ground and possible integration between China and the West. This period produced writings such as Matteo Ricci's *The True Meaning of the Lord of Heaven*[1] and Yan Mo's *Tian Di Kao*. Yan Mo, a Confucian monk and converted Catholic, who searched in the ancient Chinese Confucian classics and identified 65 instances of "*tian* (heaven)" and "*di* (emperor)"; two concepts which he further explored and concluded as bearing resemblance to the Catholic God. Yan's endeavor was discouraged by the Roman Church's decree against Chinese Catholics' practice of offering sacrifices to ancestors and the more general "Rite Controversy". Thus, the initial attempts for dialogue were rendered futile.

The second encounter occurred in the mid-nineteenth century when the door to China was forced open by the Opium Wars. Such an encounter was not based on equal undertakings, as the West, at a time of expansion, was looking for the identifiable "self" elsewhere beyond its realm of power, while China was undergoing an identity crisis of its own, doubting its historical and cultural heritage. This unequal interaction led to an imposed identity on China, which peaked in the country's overall embracing of Sovietized ideals in the 1950s. The century-long identity imposition lasted until the 1960s when the country closed its door to the outside world. Despite the colonized history, Chinese culture has never comfortably sat with the idea of colonization. Thus, it would be more apt to say that Chinese culture has been deeply influenced by cultures of the Other than to say that it has succumbed itself to such influences and completely lost itself.

The failure of dialogue in the first two encounters is, to some extent, predictable since the clash between two circles of civilization tends to be magnified rather than reduced when one intends to assimilate the other into its system. The third encounter, however, was distinct from the first two. Initiated during the country's reform and its period of "opening up", it featured mutual respect and the intention to establish a relationship characterized by

DOI: 10.4324/9781003356240-8

mutual viewing, mutual contextualization, mutual reference, and mutual mirroring. Any attempt to impose one's self-image on the other by insisting on one's own standards and norms would lead to conflicts and even devastating catastrophes. Therefore, the key to making dialogue lies in establishing the relationship between self-identity and the different characteristics of the other. That is, how the subject maintains its subjectivity while recognizing the other in term of interactions, exchanges, and mutual learning. This ongoing third encounter between China and the West can be sustained only if this relationship can be managed properly.

Two major issues are worthy to note to avoid conflicts in this new encounter. One is the need for cross-cultural dialogue to unfold on an equal footing, ensuring due respect to the particularities of the culture of the other. The other need is the requirement for expanding the range and diversity of the dialogue by including the previously less valued cultures of Africa, Latin America, Asia, and Oceania. The underlying belief is that if human civilization holds elements of universality, these should come from its rich particularity. Any thought or practice which aims at domesticating or rejecting the other can only lead to the destruction of such particularity and thus, opportunities of revealing universality. The ultimate goal of coexistence, which does justice to the multiplicity of human culture, can only be obtained via cross-cultural dialogues entailing mutual understanding, interpretation, and recognition that are based on an appreciation of each other's particularities.

8.2 Why Are Differences Important?

Traditionally, Chinese culture places great emphasis on differences, which serve as the premise for understanding; in the words of the old saying, "Things are born to be different". During its celebration of the new millennium in 2000, the Institute of Comparative Literature and Culture of Peking University convened a symposium titled "The Beauty of Diversity", an allusion to the French writer Victor Segalen's *Essay on Exoticism: An Aesthetics of Diversity*. The intention conveyed in "an aesthetics of diversity" is to recognize that beauty lies in differences, and that aesthetics rests on an appreciation of such differences. One of the speakers at the symposium was Daniel-Henri Pageaux, a famous French scholar in comparative literature. He commented on this theme by saying,

> To me, the program of the symposium spoke of "harmony" and the idea that ultimate harmony enables all things to grow and develop; yet if all things are identical, their development shall be hindered. The Chinese philosophy of "harmony without homogeneity" can make an important ethical resource from which we can draw upon to achieve coexistence in diversity and mutual respect in the third millennium (since the birth of Christ).

In a similar note, Umberto Eco, in his keynote address at the 1999 commemorative conference of the 900th anniversary of the founding of Università di

76 *Difference and Dialogue*

Bologna, described the third-millennium goal of continental Europe as "coexistence in diversity and mutual respect". He believed that the more differences among individuals and groups are recognized, the greater the chances are for acceptance and respect, and thus there is a better coexistence in mutual understanding. Such comments from Western scholars are in line with the traditional concept of "harmony" in Chinese culture, which holds that differences lead to prosperity and coexistence, as interactions between the different civilizations give birth to the new, while growth is not possible for a system with no differences among its constituents, as the whole is merely a static collection of its parts.

One may wonder, therefore, why such a theme as "existence in diversity and mutual respect" would prevail in the twenty-first century. This question can be approached from four distinct aspects.

Firstly, with the sweeping influence of globalization, colonial systems are increasingly replaced by globalized postcolonial societies. After declaring its legal independence, the formerly colonized countries are faced with the challenge of restoring their damaged national identity, among which efforts towards reconnecting people to their cultural roots have been proven most effective. Language, in particular, has been working as a unifying force. After World War II, for example, the Malaysian government insisted on the use of Malay as the national language; similarly, the Israeli government decided to restore the status of Hebrew, which used to serve only religious purposes, to everyday language for all communicative purposes. To highlight the uniqueness of their Oriental cultural identity, some leading figures in government and academia have come up with concepts such as "Asian values". These all point to the somewhat unexpected conclusion that despite the converging trend brought about by the integration of the world economy and the advancement in science and technology, both economic globalization and postcolonial states have, at a deeper level, promoted disintegration, with various forms of emerging "centrism". As all corners of the world have been integrated as parts of the human community on earth, each part has gained its legitimacy. This emerging new order disrupts the old which was built on dominating beliefs including Logocentrism, the "universal law", and the extensively applied "meta-narrative". Thus, the postcolonial era prepares the ground for the growth of pluralistic cultures.

Secondly, the twentieth century saw a paradigm shift in epistemology and methodology from a logistical paradigm to a phenomenological one. Studies conducted in the former paradigm tend to "reduce" the content of the work to an inductive abstraction, reducing complexities of the texts to a shared formulation, and, ultimately, distilling from such minimal common grounds the metaphysical Logos or Hegelian ideas about absolute spirit. Narrative compositions as such come to form what we call the "macro-narrative" or "macro-textual" structure, from which we can readily derive the "rule", the "essence", and the causal relation in between occurrences. However, taking a concrete "body" as the object of enquiry, rather than a reduced abstraction, studies in the phenomenological paradigm recognize the subject as a living existence, with the movements of the body and the pain and pleasure it experiences. Accordingly, the surroundings are construed as being subjected to the changes of this body, along with the emotions and perspectives the body carries. Hence, the phenomenological paradigm explores an open and dynamic space, which is constantly changing with changes in a subject that moves, excites, desires, and wills. Traditionally, such cognition is held to depend on formula, definition, classification, and deduction. Its main narration is about how a definitive subject "comes to know" a relatively definite object, which can be defined, delineated, and sorted into existing epistemological frames. In contrast, cognition that occurs in interaction centralizes the changes, the consequences, or the development experienced by the subject and the "other" in the interaction. It operates on the "principle of the other", as opposed to the Logocentralistic emphasis on the subject. It follows the indeterminate "principle of interaction", being opposed to the deterministic "principle of universal applicability". Simply put, it defines the "other" based on its difference from the self. Meanwhile, a deep understanding of the subjective self can only be achieved by observation and reflection from the perspective of the "other", rather than arrogant self-affirmation or self-gratification.

Thirdly, the two world wars and their traumatic aftermaths in the twentieth century have led eventually to a general improvement in cultural consciousness, which continues to be heightened into the twenty-first century. Edgar Morin (2002), a well-known French thinker and researcher at the Higher Academy of Social Sciences of France, comments on Western civilization as such:

> The blessing of Western civilization carries with it the seed of its curse. Its individualism contains the isolation and loneness of egocentricity; its blind economic development causes moral and psychological lethargy and creates disconnectedness in all domains. It puts a limit on people's capacity for wisdom, rendering them helpless in dealing with complex issues, and blinding them from the basic or fundamental problems. While science and technology accelerate social progress, they cause damage to environment and culture, give rise to new forms of inequality, and replace the old-fashioned slavery with its modern version. Urban pollution and unchecked scientific development, in particular, have engendered a sense of anxiety and endangerment and have the potential to lead to our ecological demise or nuclear apocalypse.

In a similarly critical reflection, the Polish sociologist Zygmunt Bauman stresses, in his book *Modernity and the Holocaust*, that Western civilization and barbarism in their extreme forms are interrelated. Modernity has come as a result of modern civilization, but the development of the latter has gone beyond human control and moved towards barbarism. In this light, scholars in the West have proposed that rather than a unilateral ideologically ruled world empire, humans need the multipolar balance of a "social world"; an alliance of advanced civilizations and diverse development, which articulates the

78 *Difference and Dialogue*

expectation for yet another phase of globalization. That is, a global multipolar balance and coexistence in diversity, based on the recognition of differences.

Fourthly, thanks to the material and cultural richness brought about by globalization, material and spiritual cultures in the impoverished and backward regions have been allowed to flourish. The rapid growth in economic and technological power has also made the world a more connected place with increasing interactions and spreading tourism. Statistics show that in China alone, the number of people who traveled abroad during the nine-year span from 1949 to 1958 was 280,000; by contrast, the figure for overseas travel was 34 million in 2006 alone, with 22 million foreigners coming to visit China. Apart from increased mobility, surging tourism and media attention have promoted the influence of ethnic minority cultures in far-flung areas. Though unavoidably bothered by issues of "commercialization" of the local economy, such increased popularity helps attract overdue attention into the characteristics and the survival of a mostly unknown culture.

8.3 Coexistence Among Differences

The genius of the idea of "harmony without homogeneity" in Chinese philosophy, as implied in the ancient quote "Different things are put together to achieve harmony, and therefore enrich and nourish other things (以他平他谓之和,故能丰长物而归之)", emphasizes development as a dynamic process. The notion of "harmony" in the quote depicts a competing rather than a resting state. That is, coexistence among differences is not a static, passive "existing together" with little interaction among the individuals. To dig deeper, we can ask; what does "以他平他" (*yi ta ping ta*) mean? The character "平" (*ping*), a phonetic loan character for "辩" (*bian*) and "辨" (*bian*), means both discrimination and evaluation. The Counsellor-in-chief in the Tang Dynasty, for instance, is referred to as "平章" (*ping zhang*), namely, someone who is good at distinguishing and evaluating things. Thus, the phrase "以他平他" intends to capture the dynamic nature in the development of a system where individuals grow in evaluation, comparison, and competition against one another. In contemporary discourse, it suggests a way of mutual understanding, interaction, and subjectivity, hence leading to development through engaging differences in dialogue.

In light of *yi ta ping ta*, an enriching dialogue, one that may make things "grow" (丰长), does not expect individuals to "talk past each other", but to hold a "productive dialogue" that can generate new understandings and new development possibilities. For such a dialogue to happen, each interlocutor should keep his or her subjectivity, the kind of cultural consciousness expounded on by Fei Xiaotong. Fei (1999) notes:

> People who live in a certain culture would acquire some awareness of that culture, its origin, history, characteristics, and future... Such awareness would help strengthen self-reliance in the transformation of the culture to better fit the new growth environment in the new era with more autonomy.

Difference and Dialogue 79

The process of becoming culturally conscious, however, is demanding. One should first come to know one's own culture, as well as the various other cultures one has been exposed to. This serves as the precondition for locating one's position in the emerging multicultural world. It is through self-adaption, borrowing, and learning from each other to improve on one's weaknesses that one's culture shall grow along with other cultures. This would create a commonly adaptable order for all cultures to coexist in peace, capitalize on strength, and forge ahead together.

(pp. 195–196)

Hence, one may conclude that the purpose of the dialogue is by no means to combine and integrate, to shift from a state of being "different" to one of being "identical"; instead, it aims for individuals to develop their strengths based on shared understandings, thereby negotiating the "differences" to achieve new harmony and unity. In this process, individuals can acquire new qualities, make new improvements, and create something new. Hence, the sought-after ideal in traditional Chinese culture is not the integration of everything, but "coexistence of all in harmony". This ideal is variously expressed in ancient quotes such as "All living things are nurtured without harming one another; all roads run parallel without interfering with one another". While the nurturing of all living things and the parallel running of all roads are states of "being different", the absence of mutual harm or interference indicates the ideal state of "harmony". Yet central to approaching this harmony is the subject's self-awareness.

In a similar vein, the prospective goal of "coexistence in diversity" for the third millennium in continental Europe does not predict a passive "coexistence" of differences. Rather, it seeks mutual development through active dialogues in all areas. The idea of dialogue seems to be popular between countries. In 1998, Iranian President Khatami proposed that the United Nations designate 2001 the "Year of Dialogue among Civilizations" for humanity, an appeal which then received unanimous approval by the UN General Assembly. China India, and Vietnam followed suit and convened meetings themed "Dialogue Among Civilizations" in 2001, 2003, and 2004, respectively. To varying degrees, dialogues as such have helped promote consensus among different cultures. As a member of the UN "Dialogue Among Civilizations" Team, Tu Weiming once noted, "Dialogue among civilizations is not only a strategy used by Western hegemony to dominate the world but also a response of the Islamic civilization to the unilateralism and conflicts between civilizations brought about by Western hegemony" (Cai & Jing, 2006, p. 68). Though not the solution to all problems, dialogue works better than conflicts and confrontation. More importantly, for now, it seems to remain the primary means to avoid mass killings and wars.

8.4 The Paradox of Dialogue

Becoming aware of the value of dialogue is but the first step and we would also need to have the goodwill and open-mindedness for holding a dialogue.

80 *Difference and Dialogue*

As the dialogue unfolds, we may well find ourselves often puzzled by four paradoxes: that between the universal and the particularistic, that between the intent to remain pure and the willingness to seek mutual influence, that between the other and the self, and that between the accessible and the inaccessible discourse of communication.

Evidence for the paradox between the universal and the particularistic can be found in the narrow-minded nationalism persisting among some in the postcolonial era. These are disbelievers in universality, holding that what we refer to as "universal" is mostly arbitrary and rigid, and a violent imposition on people. They also fight against structural restrictions of all kinds. Instead of there being a unifying center or universal traits, they see only particularities that are completely disconnected. They would subscribe to the idea of postmodern superficiality, which tends to eliminate all possible connections between phenomena and essence, between the inevitable and the contingent, between the universal and the particularistic, as well as between the signifier and the signified (the so-called "floating signifier"), rendering everything isolated with no temporal continuity or spatial congruity. In denying such general connections, they emphasize only the differences, to sustain which they would oppose mutual influence and suppress efforts towards development and renewal. Cultural isolationism and cultural relativism are two representatives of this line of thought (Yue, 2002, pp. 5–15, 35–55, 81–90). The truth is that the discussion on topics of "the general and the specific" and "the universal and the particularistic" has been around for quite some time in history. The earliest discussions can be traced back to ancient Greek, as Aristotle profoundly addressed this topic in his *Metaphysics* and pointed out that the specific and the general are, in essence, inseparable. This observation was later developed by Hegel in his brilliant argumentation. In today's reality, however, the historically endorsed connection has been severed, which has eroded harmony in all areas and impeded the growth of society. Restoring a healthy connection between the universal and the particularistic is essential for the development of multiple cultures, the protection of cultural ecology, and the mitigation of cultural conflicts.

As a dialogue unfolds, the intent to remain pure and unaffected, and yet the willingness to have beneficial interactions also makes for a paradox. On the one hand, there is a need to keep the cultures pure and "authentic" to preserve diversity; on the other hand, there is an inevitable trend for cultures to penetrate each other's boundaries and to interact and affect each other. The questions then would be: Is this interaction and influence towards inseparable integrity running contrary to preserving the distinctiveness and originality of individual cultures? Would the tearing down of cultural boundaries help iron out the differences among diverse world cultures and lead to a stiff monolithic structure?

In its history of coming to terms with the other, a culture would naturally subject the other culture to its perspective and standards. That is, instead of open-minded learning, it would choose to absorb only those that fit closely with its standards and goals. For example, Buddhism has enjoyed a sound

Difference and Dialogue 81

development in China as its teachings go close to those valued in Chinese culture. In comparison, the acceptance of the doctrines of *Vijñapti-mātratāsiddhi*, popular Buddhist beliefs in India, was not as welcome in China due to the doctrine's glaring inconsistencies with traditional Chinese beliefs. As Chen Yinque (1980) explained, given its incompatibility with traditional Chinese ethical concepts, the part of the Buddhist teachings that concern "the basics of human sexual intercourse" would not be swallowed by "even the most pious followers". Hence, "on the whole, they are kept hidden and unaddressed", since "the scriptures are hidden to prevent their circulation" (p. 155). China's borrowing from French symbolistic poetry in the 1930s told a similar story. While the poems by Rimbaud and Verlaine were translated into Chinese with great enthusiasm, the works of Mallarme, an outstanding poet and representative of French symbolistic poetry, had little influence on Chinese readership. This illustrates the selective interaction initiated by local cultures at the early stage of cultural contact.

The acceptance by one culture does not often entail complete transplantation, however. After a culture is introduced to a new context, it rarely follows its original path of development but combines with the native culture, which often leads to new, even spectacular, results. For instance, the accepted Greek culture and Hebrew culture have come to form the foundation of Western European culture, a brand new culture, different from its origins. Likewise, the introduction of Indian Buddhism to China has produced Sinicized Buddhist thoughts, including Tiantai, Huayan, and Chanzong, which have provided important opportunities for the growth of Neo-Confucianism in the Song and Ming Dynasties. Throughout history, there is no shortage of such cases where the development of a transplanted culture in a foreign land gave birth to a new culture.

Yet this is not to say that the interaction and mutual influence between cultures are a form of "assimilation". Instead, it resembles the transformation one undergoes to mold into a new entity when adapting to new circumstances. Regardless of the various choices and conditions involved in the interaction, the new that emerges from the old remains no longer the "pure" of the past, but a new form of "purity" born out of the past. As such, the new-born has its unique "gene" with distinctive features that are identical neither to that of the old nor to those of others. Thus, the result of the interaction of diversification brought about by globalization is not "convergence" or, ultimately, "unification", but a host of new features and differences derived from the new. This does not deny, however, the fact that some common standards of value will develop in the process of interaction and development. Yet these shared standards are often understood and practiced differently in different regions and among different people, hence the residue of the original particularity in the otherwise universality.

The relationship between the other and the self in the dialogue is a particularly complicated one. By taking one's perspective as the starting point, one seeks to assimilate the other, subjecting it to one's design and ideas, which would create convergence at the cost of losing the distinctiveness of

82 *Difference and Dialogue*

the other. What such a dialogue would produce is not a growth-enabling new "harmony", but an imposed "uniformity" that suffocates. For a better dialogue, the French philosopher Levinas cautions that one should start from the other and pay attention to those parts of the other that appear least clear and approachable, as the other is in constant change: "it will choose to follow your desires at the crossroads and naturally lead you to reach the limit of thought". He holds that "everyone that I come in contact with is superior to me in all aspects and someone from whom I shall obtain different values – an 'other' that is not unconfined to any system of knowledge" (Du, 2001, pp. 23–35). Du (1994) indicates the reason for this:

> The other is everything that I am not; it is not for his temperament, appearance or mindset that is different from mine, but the mere fact of his being different... It is this difference that marks the relationship between me and the other different from the taken-for-granted "convergence", but a type of "face-to-face" interaction.
>
> (p. 42)

Yet emphasizing differences alone would fail to bring us close to the goal of understanding and communication, as ignoring differences would lead to convergence. This paradox in sorting out the relationship between the other and the self is the most meaningful yet the most challenging part of a "productive dialogue".

Furthermore, there remains another discourse issue in cross-cultural dialogue. One would take it as a precondition that discourse should be made accessible to, and accepted by, both sides in the communication. However, for a long time the developed world has been accustomed to the Western-centric model of thinking and behaving, and it would be no easy task for the alien discourses of other cultures to be willingly and properly understood on an equal footing. In the cross-cultural dialogue the developing systems need to deal with the well-established discourse of the developed systems – a full set of widely recognized discourses covering all fields, including politics, economy, and culture. This established discourse needs to be duly respected, as it is one that has been perfected over centuries, with contributions from pioneering intellectuals to address some of our fundamental questions. Yet there is a danger of subscribing to this discourse and the model that it has constructed for examining and interpreting one's native culture. That is, much of the lively and unique features of local cultures may be excluded for failing to fit into this model. Seeing the peril of this paradox, some have turned to advocate "discovering" a discourse that is purely local with zero "contamination". To their dismay, however, such discourse does not exist at all, as the development of culture relies on its interaction with other cultures. Moreover, a purely "native" discourse would fall short of the purpose of communication. As such, solving the paradox of discourse remains a crucial challenge in dialogue (Yue, 2002, pp. 81–90).

None of the four paradoxes mentioned above are inclined towards easy resolution, yet a realization of their existence is necessary to achieve a better dialogue.

8.5 Dialogue, Difference, and Comparative Literature

Comparative literature attempts inter-literature comparison across cultures, which itself is the product of a "cultural field" or cultural network comprised of different cultures. Though deep into the information age, we do not seem to have done away with the time-honored questions in history. These include questions about life and death, love and desire, or how to achieve harmony between one's physical and mental existence; questions about power and identity, or how to achieve harmony when co-existing with others; questions about one's relationship with the surroundings, or how to achieve harmony while co-existing with nature; questions about the relationship between the known and the unknown, as well as that between one's life and fate. Our relentless pursuit to answer these questions is a universal endeavor across cultures and time. The efforts humanity has made in different historical periods, geographical regions, and cultural contexts towards these common goals have given rise to the particularities of cultures. It can thus be said that various cultures have been striving to solve these shared concerns about human existence and survival since ancient times. Among these efforts, achievements in literature and art have been playing an active part, with contributions that are already formed or ongoing making a substantial difference. Any masterpiece of art deals with some aspects of a shared human experience that resonates with its admirer. Meanwhile, it tells something personal about the artist's experience, imagination, and beliefs. As the creation of a masterpiece is deeply situated in a specific cultural context, it is intertwined with practices and ideas that are more locally relevant than universally applied, hence the cultural barrier. Appreciating the work involves dissolving the barrier with a common perception of a shared experience. As literature deals more with sentimentalized human experience than utilitarian calculations, the common topics in literature are wide-ranging across cultures, inspiring readers to venture their answers to the fundamental questions based on their own life stories and ways of thinking.

It is through the multiple rounds of dialogues between cultures that we can expect to obtain the best answers to the questions in our time. Moreover, these efforts entail a liberating expansion of perspective as we free ourselves from the unidirectional, inadequate, and biased models of cultural hegemonism and isolationism, which have given rise to prejudice, hatred, and conflicts. The inspirations from literature and art provide us with better communication and understanding of our thoughts and feelings to obtain mutual recognition, respect, learning, and appreciation. The role comparative literature plays towards arriving at this much-anticipated new globalized world of cultural diversity cannot be dismissed as trivial.

84   *Difference and Dialogue*

Note

1 Matteo Ricci (1552–1610), known by his Chinese name Li-ma-dou, is an Italian Jesuit missionary who is well known for his efforts to introduce Christian teachings to China in the 16th century.

References

Cai, D. L., & Jing, H. F. (Eds.). (2006). *Dialogues between civilizations*. Beijing: Tsinghua University Press.

Chen, Y. Q. (1980). *Cold willow hall collection*. Shanghai: Shanghai Chinese Classic Publishing House.

Du, X. Z. (1994). *Lévinas*. Hong Kong: Joint Publishing.

Du, X. Z. (2001). The dialogue between Judaist and Levinas. *Dialogue Transculturel*, *7*, 23–35.

Fei, X. T. (1999). *Collected works of Fei Xiaotong* (Vol. 14). Beijing: Qunyuan Press.

Morin, E. (2002). Au–delà de la globalisation et du développement, société–monde ou empire–monde? [Beyond globalization and development: World society or world empire?] *Revue du MAUSS*, *20*(2), 43–53.

Yue, D. Y. (2002). *A bridge across cultures*. Beijing: Peking University Press.

9 Chinese Culture and the Reconstruction of World Culture

9.1 The Complex Situations of Today

The changes we are experiencing today are unprecedented and phenomenal. They stand out among the epoch-making changes we have been through in history: the shift from hunting to farming, from farming to machines and factories, and then to the early age of information. Today, we are hurled into a world of dazzling changes brought about by the revolution of software and computer science, the invention of the global Internet, and advances in tele-communication technologies. These changes displace us from occupying a space subject to space-time constraints. The younger generation, in particular, has been nurtured largely in a virtual space created by the Internet and as such have been detached from the lived experiences of their older generations. With little shared understanding with our children, we may feel equally detached from our future.

Not only are we baffled by the changes in the surroundings; we even start to get confused over our mere existence with the marvelous achievements made in biotechnology. As the once-unthinkable editing of the gene becomes an operational reality and cloning an intimidating yet tempting possibility, the very existence of humankind and the definition of humanness have been put into question. In a general sense, this amounts to an attack on all aspects of the realm of meaning. In a similar way, advances in nanotechnology, with its potential to extend human manipulation of particles to the molecular level, add new depths to our cognition of the world.

The all-pervasive influence of these new conclusions, brought about by the technological revolutions, reaches down to every detail of our life, leading to fundamental changes in our perceptions of time and space. Hegemony and terrorism, born into a time of materialistic plentifulness, pose a dangerous threat to the survival of mankind and the planet. More worryingly still, as the coming generation grows up, their perceptions of the world and the self will be fundamentally different from ours. Any attempt to convert them to the stereotypes we uphold would be futile at best.

Together with the earlier hardships of the twentieth century (e.g., the two world wars, the Nazi Jewish concentration camps, the Gulag labor camps), these significant changes have wrought reflections that have not only changed

DOI: 10.4324/9781003356240-9

86   *Chinese Culture and the Reconstruction of World Culture*

our perception of humanity but also urged us to redefine our situation, to reflect on what kind of world we need to shape, and what worldview and life view we need to establish to address the emerging complexities on a global scale.

9.2 The Western Understanding of the Current Cultural Crisis

In recent times, Western culture has been tacitly equated with a strong culture. However, it has only become culturally self-aware lately when it started to examine its weakness and the crises it suffers. Some of the initial efforts to reflect and self-criticize were made by Oswald Spengler in his *The Decline of the West: Perspectives of World-History* at the beginning of the twentieth century. Such efforts continue well into the twenty-first century, bringing deeper reflections and sharper insights. Edgar Morin (2002), a well-known French thinker and researcher at the Higher Academy of Social Sciences, comments on Western civilization in the following terms:

> The blessing of Western civilization carries with it the seed of its curse. Its individualism contains the isolation and loneness of egocentricity; its blind economic development causes moral and psychological lethargy and creates a disconnectedness in all domains. It puts a limit on people's capacity for wisdom, rendering them helpless in dealing with complex issues, and blinding them from the basic or fundamental problems. While science and technology accelerate social progress, they cause damage to environment and culture, gives rise to new forms of inequality, and replaces the old-fashioned slavery with its modern version. Urban pollution and unchecked scientific development, in particular, have engendered a sense of anxiety and endangerment, and have the potential to lead to our ecological demise or nuclear apocalypse.

In a similarly critical reflection, Polish sociologist Zygmunt Bauman stresses, in his book *Modernity and the Holocaust*, that Western civilization and barbarism in their extreme forms are interrelated. Modernity has come as a result of modern civilization, but the development of the latter has gone beyond human control and moved towards barbarism.

In short, what these pioneering intellectuals visualize for an improved human existence is not a unipolar imperial world, but a multipolar social world, a strong alliance blessed with civilization and diversity. To achieve this, "tremendous growth" needs to be fostered from within. This will lead us to embrace the vision of globalization of a different kind; a sustainable civilization where individuals focus on improving the quality of their existence rather than the restless pursuit of wealth.

To survive the impending crises and achieve the "tremendous growth", Western thinkers have suggested three areas of efforts to address the status quo and to seek future development. The first is to seek a new starting point in the origin of one's culture by re-examining its history and rediscovering oneself in the process. In doing so, one would need a new frame of reference, or the new "other", against whom one can re-examine and reinterpret one's culture. In his monograph "Why We Westerners Cannot Avoid China in Our Study of Philosophy", French sinologist François Jullien contends that a full understanding of the self cannot be achieved without abandoning the isolated self and exposing it to examinations from various perspectives of the other. He believes that we can refer to China to know Greece better as we are too familiar with the Greek philosophy; yet to understand it better and to make discoveries, we need to cut ourselves off from this familiarity and to adopt a fresh perspective from outside (Jullien, 2000). China can serve as the best frame of reference in this regard, he explains (as cited in Wong, 2012, p. 142):

> The Chinese language, which is outside the enormous Indo-European language system, explores another possibility of writing. The Chinese civilization is one that has the longest history and had evolved independently without being influenced by European culture... All in all, China is an ideal image contrasted with which we will be able to free ourselves from some preconceived ideas and gaze at our own thoughts from the outside.

He also notes:

> The author has set out from such a distant perspective. The motivation is not the pursuit of exotic charm, nor the alluring delight in comparison, but the mere longing to retrieve some room for a theoretical detour: by virtue of a new starting point, I want to liberate myself from theoretical arguments that I have failed to disentangle because of my position in the heart of them.
>
> (Jullien, 2002, p. 6)

Apart from a new frame of reference, there is also a need to learn from non-Western cultures. During his 2004 visit to the Department of Philosophy at Fudan University, Richard Rorty exclaimed, "This is my second visit to Shanghai after 20 years. The changes in China are miraculous. This miracle does not change what I believe but consolidate my belief that China is the hope of the world in the future." In the "The Beauty of Diversity" symposium held by the Institute of Comparative Literature and Comparative Culture of Peking University, Professor Daniel-Henri Pageaux, the great French scholar in comparative literature, hailed François Jullien's research on Greek and Chinese culture as a fitting example for what he argues as the gains in revisiting the self via the other. In commenting on the theme of the symposium, Pageaux (2001) said:

> To me, the program of the symposium spoke of "harmony" and the idea that ultimate harmony enables all things to grow and develop; yet if all things are identical, the development shall be hindered. The Chinese

88　*Chinese Culture and the Reconstruction of World Culture*

philosophy of "harmony without homogeneity" will make an important ethical resource from which we can draw upon to achieve coexistence in diversity and mutual respect in the third millennium.

(p. 133)

This overall change of viewpoint can also be found in the works by some American sinologists, such as *Thinking Through Confucius*, written by Roger Ames and David Hall, and *Early China/Ancient Greece: Thinking Through Comparisons*, edited by Stephen Shankman.

Equally needed is a change of mentality, from that of a centralist colonizer to that of one willing to embrace the non-Western cultural diversity without exclusion or contempt. Professor Gnisci, from the University of Rome in Italy, refers to the process of overcoming West-centrism as "askesis". In his *Comparative Literature as a Discipline of Decolonialization*, he states:

> If we say that to those countries having shaken off Western colonialism, comparative literature introduces a way of comprehending, researching, and realizing post-colonialism, then for all European scholars, it represents a kind of reflection, a kind of self-criticism and learning, what we might see as a way to extricate ourselves from our colonialist mindset... It amounts to an educating experience of the self and the other. It is "askesis" of some sort.
>
> (Gnisci, 1996)

Without hard introspection as such, the vision of the harmonious coexistence of multiple cultures remains distant.

This overall tendency of gaining self-awareness and introspection in Western academia offers an important epistemological prerequisite for a diverse coexistence of global cultures.

9.3　China's Need for Sincere Cultural Consciousness

In its heyday, Chinese culture showed utter contempt for other cultures, while it surrendered or resorted to Ah Q's "spiritual victory" mentality in times of weakness. In reflecting on this national characteristic, Fei Xiaotong proposes that cultural consciousness can only be obtained with sufficient knowledge of the self, as the ultimate goal of obtaining cultural consciousness is to "help strengthen self-reliance in the transformation of the culture to better fit the new environment of growth in the new era, with more autonomy". He also argues that a culture could only sustain its survival upon full recognition and thorough understanding of its historical "root" or cultural "seed". In the case of China, such legacies can be found in an emphasis on establishing inter-generation connections, showing respect to ancestors, and the education and upbringing of offspring. There is a deeply rooted cultural belief that "the ultimate harmony enables all things to grow and develop; yet if all things are identical, the development shall be hindered", as there is also the belief that different things can come together to form "diversity in unity". In practice, the Chinese culture follows its valued code of conduct, which prioritizes building solidarity with others and winning people over by virtuous deeds rather than by imposing force. Rather than some rhetorical flourishes in a noble discourse, these moral beliefs and practices characterize the realities of Chinese people's daily life, which undergird the country's cultural edifice. Fei (2005) further explains:

> People who live in a certain culture would acquire some awareness of that culture, its origin, history, characteristics, and future. It has nothing to do with "cultural nostalgia" or the intent to "go back to the good old days"; nor does it advocate "thorough Westernization" or "complete subduing to the influence of the other". The process of becoming culturally conscious, however, is demanding. One should first come to know one's own culture, as well as the various other cultures one has been exposed to. This serves as the precondition for locating one's position in the emerging multicultural world. It is through self-adaption, borrowing, and learning from each other to improve on its weaknesses that one culture shall grow along with other cultures. This would create a commonly adaptable order for all cultures to coexist in peace, capitalize on strength, and forge ahead together.
>
> (p. 526)

Having the cultural "seed" alone is not enough; it needs to grow, mature and bear fruit. A life-living role in the growth of the seed is played by creativity, without which a tradition would be moribund. What creativity means in this context is making continuous efforts to "examine the conditions and demands of the past and the present from a development perspective to open up new opportunities for the future growth of the culture" (Fei, 2005, p. 310). Gaining cultural consciousness entails taking into account the past, present, and future; exploiting the resources of tradition and creativity. Hence, rather than clinging to the past, one with such consciousness would stand on reality and look into the future, and would also be aware of the external environment at present, features of which have never been found in any past era. Certain rules and standards are to be commonly observed as we proceed towards globalization. Only by relating to multiple others with sympathy can one culture find its place in the emerging multicultural world, reflect on its current situation, and discover the ethnocultural "self". In the case of Chinese culture and many others, this means coming to know its place amid the multiplicity of world cultures and the role it is to play in future development. In his nineties, Fei looks back on his life and concludes his thoughts as follows: Intellectuals should feel obliged to become culturally aware of oneself as it is their mission of the era, the very last barrier they need to overcome to lead the coming generation of intellectuals to embrace the topic of cultural consciousness. The greatest challenge to Chinese intellectuals, it seems, is the long-existing uninformed nationalistic sentiments. To overcome this, we

90 *Chinese Culture and the Reconstruction of World Culture*

should commit ourselves to exploring and measuring the country's rich cultural resources against the current needs in the development of world cultures. We should pay attention to the unique contributions Chinese culture can make towards resolving cultural conflicts and re-examining and re-recognizing itself in its dialogue with the "other". This is certainly an arduous journey, which is full of conflicts and complex interactions, yet choosing to take the journey in the first place is a decision not to regret.

9.4 Traditional Chinese Culture as a Possible Cure for Cultural Conflicts

The unprecedented development of human society and the accumulation of experiences over the last century have unsettled our perceptions of time and space, leading to startlingly new changes in our physical and spiritual world. Against this background, the intercultural awareness arising in the West and the East has prepared us for a new era of cultural diversity and coexistence; a process that involves constant interaction and adaptation, where Chinese culture may contribute a unique part. The following four aspects showcase how traditional Chinese culture can offer insights into resolving some of the most intense cultural conflicts today.

9.4.1 The Core Idea of "Harmony without Homogeneity"

No cultural conflict can be resolved by conquest or subjugation. Any attempt to uproot the culture from its people can at best cause a temporary and futile disruption, giving rise to hatred and revenge. With regard to relating to other cultures, the Chinese belief has never been to "rescue", subdue, or conquer the other, but to coexist amid multiple cultures towards a healthy and sustaining ecology. A promising cure for solving the cultural conflicts in this regard is offered in the core idea of "harmony without homogeneity" which has been practiced for centuries in Chinese culture. Chinese people believe that different things can be brought together to form a "diversity in unity" and that "the ultimate harmony enables all things to grow and develop; yet if all things are identical, the development shall be hindered". The "harmony" in the quote refers to the coordination among different people and things, which can form and develop as a heterogeneous system rather than a homogeneous whole. The *Book of Shang: The Canon of Yao* teaches "coexistence of all states in harmony; friendly relationships among people". When applied to intercultural relationships, the "coexistence of all in harmony" suggests that various cultures shall coexist in harmony with distinctive characteristics preserved, instead of merging into "one", with the latter indicating "uniformity" rather than "harmony". The character "*he*" (harmony) in ancient Chinese can also be read as "following its course": pursing the mean without going to extremes. Examples of this can be found in Guangyun, "harmony is neither too unyielding nor too soft" and in *Xinshu: The Art of the Dao*, "harmony dwells in a right place between being unyielding and soft; too much of either would defy its place". Both illustrate the sense of appropriateness in harmony. The original meaning of *"he"*, as can be inferred from the quotes, targets the coexistence of different things, to explore how a variety of things coexist in different relationship networks. The coexistence of different things does not happen in static isolation, but with continuous dialogues and interactions, going from contradictions and conflicts to mutual understanding and learning, building connections between universality and uniqueness, hence resulting in a dynamic coexistence in interaction.

Despite some shared meaning, the notion of *"tong"* (homogeneity) differs conceptionally from *"he"* (harmony). The earliest attempt to differentiate the two was recorded at the end of the Western Zhou period when Bo Yangfu (Shibo) discussed the political situation with Zheng Huangong. In distinguishing the two concepts, Bo proposed that "ultimate harmony enables all things to grow and develop; yet if all things are identical, the development shall be hindered". He then further explained, "Different things are put together to achieve harmony, and therefore enrich and nourish other things. Total identity of things ultimately means perishing." The phrase "以他平他" emphasizes differences and correlations. That is, "harmony" is not produced by being different yet unrelated; nor is it produced by being related yet static. In the phrase " things are born to be uneven", "uneven" does not mean being static, but in a constant development towards "evenness", a process which also produces new unevenness. This dynamic process is captured in "以他平他" (subduing differences with differences) and "和" (harmony), from which one may deduce the meaning of "harmony" as competition and upward development. Then one may wonder why would "identity" lead to "perishing"? The term "identity" describes the superposition of the same things which, instead of producing new qualities, stifle the existing ones. Hence, what a "harmonious without homogeneity" system leads to is not convergence or integration, but new qualities generated from within the system, as well as new differences. This is not to deny, however, a natural convergence in values and standards among people over a long period of social practice. Though held as common values and standards, they are perceived and practiced differently across regions and ethnic groups. In China, Confucianism builds itself on the relationships between human beings, while Taoism is founded upon the relationship between man and nature. However, both share the goal of realizing "self-renewal" via "subduing differences with differences". All living things are nurtured without harming one another; all roads run parallel without interfering with one another". While the nurturing of all living things and the parallel running of all roads are states of "being different", the absence of mutual harm or interference indicates the ideal state of "harmony". The highest ideal to attain, as Zhuangzi puts it, is "all things in perfect harmony", a world where harmony is expressed without reserves. Less explicit expressions of harmony can be found in the core ethical values that developed in the Confucian worldview: A father should display love and kindness toward his son, while the son must display obedience and reverence toward his father; an elder brother should be gentle with his younger brother,

92 Chinese Culture and the Reconstruction of World Culture

while the younger brother must display humility and respect toward his elder brother; a ruler should display righteousness in his dealing with others, while his subjects must remain loyal to their ruler. The ideal is to seek balanced reciprocity in these relationships, as encapsulated in the quote, "Extending the high and brilliant, pursuing the way of the mean". Confucius's proposition that "Of the things brought about by the rites, harmony is the most valuable" speaks of harmony, which, together with moderation, provides the premise for developing social norms. Efforts that promote new development towards harmony in the Chinese context can be constantly drawn upon as references for solving cultural conflicts and creating multicultural symbiosis.

9.4.2 Indeterminacy and the Conception of a World Created Out of Chaos

Chinese Taoist philosophy holds that the meaning of things is neither static nor pre-set, but is defined in ever-changing interactions and boundless possibilities, out of which reality is generated by succumbing to a set of chances, as in Laozi's term, "something formless yet complete". It is believed that all things are generated from an invisible "chaos", suggesting that "existence is born out of nonexistence". Ultimately, "existence" will return to "nonexistence", which is the formless semblance. Yet such "nonexistence" is not real because "as a thing, the Way is shadowy and indistinct. Indistinct and shadowy, yet within it, there is form; shadowy and indistinct, yet within it there is substance". The "form" and "substance" here belong to the "nonexistence", yet either is an unsubstantial existence endowed with a vague, undetermined possibility to realize its existence, hence a "non-existent existence", as explained in the quote "Everything in the world is born out of existence, and existence is born out of nonexistence".

The Chinese view of the universe focuses on the assumed "determined" which are actually in constant change. As such, there is a need to assess the possibilities that are current, immediate, problem-solving, and situated in reality. The metaphor of "wading across the river by feeling for the stones" is a case in point. By "feeling for the stones" one can advance towards the "unknown" and forge a new path rather than sticking to the old one where all things are fixed. Since the meaning of all things is neither static nor predefined but is defined in ever-changing interactions and boundless possibilities, some of the taken-for-granted practices, generational revenge for example, which are based on unchanged positions and opinions, may no longer seem reasonable or legitimate. Therefore, the Chinese belief of harmony as a virtue endorses peaceful resolution of conflicts rather than grievance and revenge.

Moreover, the subject perceives the objective world differently based on the changing perspective and frame of reference. Even the subject's understanding of the self is subject to refreshing in its interaction with the "other". Since the late 1970s, China has freed itself from the restricting "regularity" and "universality" promoted by the "Two Whatevers" policy and instead has subscribed to the principle of "treating practice as the sole criterion for testing truth". This shift is meant to remove the excessive emphasis on fixed notions of regularity and universality borrowed from Western thought patterns and to promote subjective initiative as an epistemological legacy of traditional Chinese wisdom. As Zhu Xi notes, "Heaven is Man, and Man is Heaven; the birth of Man was of Heaven; Heaven gave birth to Man and Heaven is within Man". Hence, "Heaven" needs to find its manifestation in "man". It is through the creative endeavors of the individual "man" who acts autonomously and accordingly to changes yet maintains his connection with "Heaven" that the lively ambience of "Heaven" comes into full display.

One could associate the worldviews of "shadowy and indistinct way" and "non-existent existence" stated in *Classic of the Way and the Virtue* with the ongoing scientific discussions on primal chaos. Such a link was suggested by Briggs and Peat (2001), in stating:

> *The Book of Changes* is especially inspirational to us. Chaos theory originates in the complicated and systematic physical research on meteorology, electrical circuits, turbulence, and more. It was obvious that the authors and annotators of *The Book of Changes* reflected over a long period on the relationship between order and disorder in the activities of humankind and finally termed this relationship the "Supreme Ultimate".
>
> (p. 2)

They also explain:

> The societies of Europe, America, and China are in an era of great change. Just like the authors and annotators of *The Book of Changes* in the past, at this very moment, people are engaged in attempting to clarify the relationship between the individual and the collective, seeking stability in unceasing change. Our era is one with huge capacities that have been forged from a vast array of thought and perception… Social conditions in the world today resemble the physical state of disequilibrium. New eras of relative stability and unanticipated architectures may at times be suddenly created. Perhaps when in the future society develops in a direction that we had not even hoped it would, chaos science will be able to assist us in understanding how everything happened.
>
> (Briggs & Peat, 2001, p. 3)

With realizations as such, we may expect to seek an epistemological basis for resolving cultural conflicts.

9.4.3 Thought Patterns that Encourage Diversity

The Western culture has long been subject to thought patterns heavily influenced by the metaphysical objective–subjective dichotomy. As Bertrand Russell notes, Descartes' system identifies the spiritual and the material as two parallel and mutually independent worlds and conveys that that either can be approached without reference to the other. This highlights the

94　*Chinese Culture and the Reconstruction of World Culture*

subject's agency to recognize an object via dissection and classification. The "laws" derived by abstracting from the objective are held as universally applicable and valid generalizations, which go far beyond the peculiarities and realities of the object under observation. In this view, the existing centralized power structures can only administer the world by a generalizing and homogenizing means that dissect the world into mutually exclusive isolations. Overlooking the complexity of the wide-ranging relationships between objects, this administrative pattern is detrimental to the free and creative development of individuals, and, when taken to the extreme, immutable regularity and generality form the ideological basis for cultural hegemony.

The Chinese thought pattern, however, distinguishes itself from this epistemological dichotomy with its tripartite system and the *Zhongyong* (the Mean) thought that arises therefrom. The idea has a long history in Chinese culture as shown in the Eight Trigrams, each of which is made up of three signs with specific meaning and the combination of these signs gives rise to indefinite meaning potentials. Thus, it is said that "the original breath of the Supreme Ultimate comprises three in one" (Ban, 1962, p. 963). It is also noted in *Records of the Grand Historian: The Book of Law*, "Numbers start from one, end with ten, and are complete at three" (Sima, 1959, p. 1251). The reason for this is that when two different things with no hitherto established relationship to one another encounter in a "field", they create a third object which differs from the original two. As Laozi famously notes, "The *Dao* produced One; One produced Two; Two produced Three; Three produced All things." The idea of *Dao* is specified in the *Book of Changes: Commentary on the Appended Phrases*, which states, "The *Book of Changes* is a book that covers a wide range of knowledge, including the *Dao* of heaven, the *Dao* of the earth, and the *Dao* of humans" (Wang & Kong, 1999, p. 318). Therefore, it is explained, in the *Book of Rites: the Doctrine of the Mean*, that "When it can praise the nurturing power of heaven and earth, it can be called a world" (Zheng & Kong, 1999, p. 1448). The heaven and the earth alone cannot make a world, the formation of which requires a third element – "man" to "praise the nurturing power of the heaven and earth", hence a triad of the heaven, earth, and man. The underlying belief of the *Doctrine of the Mean* is also to discover the "middle way" between the "excessive" and the "inadequate", or the so-called "discarding the two ends and use the middle". The "middle" does not result from compromising the two, but is rather a "third" created in the field formed between the "two ends". The *Book of Han: Biography of He Wu* records: "He Wu hated cliques. He asked scholars about officials and asked officials about scholars so that their comments could be compared and tested" (Ban, 1962, p. 3485). Here the scholars and the officials are posited as two extremes and the Mean is a new opinion that neither belongs to an official nor a Confucian scholar. Thus, to understand an object, one shall grasp its "two ends" before seeking its "middle", which constitutes the highest ideal of the Confucian understanding of the Mean. This philosophy has the potential to enlighten cultures beyond the Chinese context.

Then there are the five symbolic elements that are believed to make up the universe, each giving rise to the next and triumphing over each other. The

Chinese Culture and the Reconstruction of World Culture   95

system of five elements was first documented in the *Book of Shang: Hong Fan* and was further discussed in the *Zuo Zhuan* and the *Guo Yu*. It defines all things in the world as composed of five symbolic elements: wood, fire, earth, metal, and water, which are represented by the colors blue, red, yellow, white, and black, as well as the human body parts, namely, liver, heart, spleen, lungs, and kidneys. It finds representations also in the directions of east, south, center, west, and north, as well as the seasons of spring, summer, late summer, autumn, and winter. The five elements engender each other (wood produces fire; fire produces earth; earth produces metal; metal produces water; water produces wood) and triumph over each other (water overpowers fire; fire overpowers metal; metal overpowers wood; wood overpowers earth; earth overpowers water) in a continuous cycle.

If one starts with the broad connections of mutual engendering and mutual subjugation, then it would be natural to attach due emphasis to the diversity of things, their differences and interrelations, the result of which is inevitably the celebration of diversity and respect for nature.

Another idea to draw from is received from "turning back is the motion of the *Dao*". For centuries, the pervasive influence of the evolution theory has been acting on scholastic beliefs in the humanities and social sciences, in both the Western academia and its influenced Eastern counterpart. The urge to exploit natural resources and to enjoy life to the fullest has been strong and relentless, and there is a general desire to accelerate into the future. Yet few have ever considered what the future is. Is the "new" necessarily better than the "old"? And what is this destination that everything is rushing off to? Apart from the grave, which is the ultimate destination for all individuals, there seems to be no real definitive answer that can be offered. A completely different belief is held in Chinese ancient teachings. Starting with Laozi's *Classic of the Way and the Virtue*, which emphasizes "turning back is the motion of the *Dao*", as the emergence of the *Dao* invariably begins with regressions. The movement of all things shares a tendency to return, with an urge to return to their starting points and to set out anew towards a farther horizon based on gained understandings and experiences. This is what the Warring States bamboo annals documented as "restoration", a fundamental condition for the development of all things. Instead of prioritizing linear development along the timeline, Chinese philosophy places a premium on returning to the beginning, i.e., "returning to one's roots and starting anew". Since all things are continually returning to their origin and then sallying forth again, rather than heading blindly towards one direction, there is no need for haste. While emphasizing "let everything take its course", "all things are at peace with themselves", "non-action", and collaborative development, Chinese culture also averts stagnation, as the *Book of Changes*, the ancient source of Chinese culture, essentially teaches development and change. This serves as philosophical underpinnings for the notion of "sustainable development", putting a check on the blind pursuit of the society's aims. Each turning point in history seems to have been marked by efforts of returning to one's cultural roots and seeking a new pathway ahead. There has been an

96 *Chinese Culture and the Reconstruction of World Culture*

emerging tendency in the West to return to and seek inspiration from ancient Greek and Hebrew origins. Some of the tension in cultural conflicts might be significantly relieved if we change our mindset from rushing ahead and taking over to looking back and reflecting further.

There is yet another thought pattern of "non-existence". As Laozi puts it,

> thirty spokes form a wheel, which is hollow inside; blending clay to make a vessel, which is hollow inside; carving out windows and doors to build a room, which is empty inside; only in this way can they carry out their particular functions.
>
> (Wang & Lou, 2008, p. 26)

That means, the functional parts of the wheel, the vessel, and the room are not made up of substantial existence, but the absence thereof. Likewise, the technique in traditional Chinese painting graphically termed as "painting clouds to highlight the moon" suggests that in painting the moon, the painter should paint the clouds that surround it rather than the moon itself. The space left unpainted in the middle would then be the moon. These all serve evidence for the valued practice to give people space, with an emphasis on tolerance and generosity, as expressed in the idiomatic phrase "An open mind achieves greatness."

9.4.4 *The Relationship between Man and Society*

With the insistence on individual rights and free will going to extremes in some Western societies, it is pertinent to acknowledge that as a social being, one can only survive in relation to others. Individual rights can only be obtained with the precondition that these rights are ensured by others to be obtainable. Therefore, in claiming individual rights, one shall take on the responsibility of ensuring others' obtaining theirs, as noted by Dai Zhen (1962): "A benevolent person fulfils oneself and helps others fulfil themselves as well" (p. 8). Instead of subscribing to the liberalistic view of society as a means of achieving individuals' purposes or the collectivist view of individuals as a means of attaining social ideals, the Confucian belief holds that people in social communities serve the foundation of all states. "People are the foundation of the state. Only when people live and work in peace and contentment can the state be peaceful and stable" (Kong & Kong, 1999, p. 177). "The voice of the people is the voice of Heaven" (ibid., p. 277). An advocate for simple government and an active supporter of the establishment of autonomous social communities, Confucius explains his belief of governance, "He who rules by moral force is like the pole star, which remains in its place while all the lesser stars do homage to it" (Yang, 1982, p. 11). He also notes, "Among many others, I aim to make litigation happen no longer" (Zheng & Kong, 1999, p. 1448). Confucius's ideal of society features a stable government and a peaceful population. Confucian teachings as such may offer alternative insights into addressing some of the issues undermining

Western democracy and resolving the cultural conflicts caused by forcing one ideology onto others.

To sum up, the construction of a balanced and multicultural world today calls for deeper cultural consciousness, a better understanding of cultural diversity, and a re-examination of self from the standpoint of others, hence the values of appreciation, coexistence, and interaction in the globalization era. Only with an adequate understanding of the self, a creative interpretation with updated visions, and better tolerance of others can we facilitate the coexistence of diverse cultures, improve intercultural communication, and build a new globalized world of cultural diversity, and hence a reconstructed civilization.

References

Ban, G. (1962). *Book of Han*. Beijing: Zhonghua Book Company.

Briggs, J., & Peat, F. D. (2001). *Seven life lessons of chaos: Spiritual wisdom from the science of change*. (Z. Chen, et al. Trans.). Shanghai: Shanghai Science and Technology Education Press.

Dai, Z. (1962). *Interpretations of Mencius*. Beijing: Zhonghua Book Company.

Fei, X. T. (2005). *Fei Xiaotong's theory on culture and cultural self-consciousness*. Beijing: Qunyan Press.

Gnisci, A. (1996). Comparative literature as a discipline of decolonialization. *Chinese Comparative Literature Bulletin*, *1996*(04), 113–120.

Jullien, F. (2000). Why we Westerners cannot avoid China in our study of philosophy. *Dialogue Transculturel*, *5*, 146–156.

Jullien, F. (2002). *Grounding morals: Mencius' dialogue with an enlightenment philosopher* (G. Song, Trans). Beijing: Peking University Press.

Kong, A. G., & Kong, Y. D. (1999). *Interpretations of the book of documents*. Beijing: Peking University Press.

Morin, E. (2002). Au-delà de la globalisation et du développement, société–monde ou empire–monde? [Beyond globalization and development: World society or world empire?] *Revue du MAUSS*, *20*(2), 43–53.

Pageaux, D. H. (2001). Culture or interculturality: From image to media. In D. Y. Yue & H. Meng (Eds.), (2009), *Esthétique du Divers*. Beijing: Peking University Press.

Sima, Q. (1959). *Records of the grand historian*. Beijing: Zhonghua Book Company.

Wang, B., & Kong, Y. D. (1999). *Interpretations of the book of changes*. Beijing: Peking University Press.

Wang, B., & Lou, Y. L. (2008). *Interpretations to and revisions of the classic of the way and the virtue*. Beijing: Zhonghua Book Company.

Wong, S. K. (Ed.). (2012). *Confucianism, Chinese history and society*. Singapore: World Scientific Publishing Company.

Yang, B. J. (1982). *Translation and interpretation of the Analects of Confucius*. Beijing: Zhonghua Book Company.

Zheng, X., & Kong, Y. D. (1999). *Interpretations of the book of rites*. Beijing: Peking University Press.

10 The Interpenetration of Sinology and *Guoxue*

There seemed to be a distinct demarcation between sinology and *guoxue*, which literally means national learning, or, to be more specific, studies of Chinese Classics and culture. The former refers to Chinese studies by non-Chinese scholars and the latter to studies by Chinese scholars. Some claim that they are unrelated and even mutually exclusive. Many *guoxue* scholars believe that non-Chinese scholars are limited by their own cultural pedigree and are unable to achieve a proper understanding of Chinese culture. Moreover, sinologists of old, often having the purpose of infringing upon other nation's interests or of looting others' cultural treasures, hardly conducted research in an equal and unbiased manner, and therefore could not draw reliable conclusions. In addition, some sinologists rarely recognized the stand-alone value of Chinese scholars' research results; they tended to take advantage of those scholars' achievements to develop their own theoretical systems while denying the existence of China's academic system in itself and for itself. Nevertheless, this situation has been changing ever since the world entered into a stage of greater globalization.

10.1 The Three Phases of Sinology

Sinology has so far undergone three phases of development. The first phase was dominated by European missionaries and some specialized scholars, who did research primarily for their own benefit and at the same time contributed to China's cultural development. The Swedish sinologist Bernhard Karlgren, known for his study of Chinese linguistics, is a case in point. American scholars, including John K. Fairbank and Benjamin I. Schwartz, representatives of Chinese studies overseas, led sinology to the second phase. Fairbank conducted an extensive investigation into the realities of China in terms of politics, economy and society, based on a significant amount of survey data using his "impact and response framework". Subsequently, Paul Cohen, Fairbank's student, analyzed and revised Fairbank's study under the banner of "discovering history in China" and from the perspective of the internal forces driving China's development. Benjamin Schwartz, another student of Fairbank, was particularly interested in the historical roots of China's various fundamental realities. His *The World of Thought in Ancient*

DOI: 10.4324/9781003356240-10

China highlights the diversity of and tension within Chinese culture *per se*, which, to some extent, diverted sinology in the United States from its basic pragmatism of realpolitik. Currently, sinology is going through the third phase, which is elaborated upon below.

The major feature of this third stage, as I see it, is the interpenetration and intersection of sinology and *guoxue*, which is not something entirely new, but is something developing rapidly in today's context. Since the twentieth century, the desire to eliminate cultural hegemony and to build global multiculturality have become the common pursuit of humankind; not only on the part of those previously oppressed nations but also by their former oppressors, the developed nations. Many scholars have become aware of the cultural crisis in their own nation and hope to seek a new path from other cultures. Those who have been studying Chinese culture, in particular, have discovered and stressed the significance of its universal value. As Léon Vandermeersch (2009), a renowned French sinologist, put it:

> With postmodernism posing its challenges,… Western humanism [having offered the world the perfect idea of human rights] is facing challenges in modern society and is not yet able to provide a solution. Therefore, why not give Confucian thinking some consideration, as it might offer ways forward for the world, with its rich legacy of ideas such as respect for nature as proposed in "the unity of heaven and man", a non-religious philosophy embodied in the proposition of "staying close to humanity while keeping a distance from divinity" and the philanthropy in "all men are brothers".
>
> (p. 12)

Prefacing the Chinese version of *Thinking Through Confucius*, Roger Ames and David Hall (2005) stated that what they were dealing with is more than just traditional Chinese culture and that their efforts should go into making it a cultural resource for use in the course of enriching and reconstructing their own world (p. v). They managed to draw attention to the questions: Is it possible to remedy and solidify Western liberalism by way of defining "human" from a sociological perspective as Confucianism proposes? In a society based on "ritual action" (as Roger Ames and David Hall term the Chinese concept "*li*", or rites), is it possible to resort to any existing resources to foster a better understanding of the Western idea of human rights, which is not deeply rooted in philosophy but is of great pragmatic significance? Professor Xavier Walter at Sorbonne University believed that the teachings of Confucius, imbued with faith, hope and charity, are of universal significance and that these teachings can be a cultural guide in both moral and cognitive terms in the twenty-first century (Li, 2009, p. 1).

In brief, in the contemporary academia of sinology, some scholars, though not many, have been trying to seek universal values from other national cultures, especially Chinese culture, as a solution to issues faced by all societies. With this purpose in mind, many have discarded old racial discriminations.

100 *The Interpenetration of Sinology and* Guoxue

For example, the French sinologist Francois Jullien states that Chinese culture presents the most exteriority to Europe, and that both its identity as among the earliest cultures and its path of development can help Europeans cast aside their ethnocentrism.[1]

10.2 The Intersection between Sinology and *Guoxue*

The aforementioned perspective changes stem not only from the needs of multicultural globalization, but also from the transition in Western thought from deconstructive postmodernism to constructive postmodernism. At the turn of the twenty-first century, renowned ecological philosopher John B. Cobb (2002), with Whitehead's "process philosophy" as his groundwork, proposed the philosophy of constructive postmodernism. Whitehead believes that man should not be seen as the center of all things but rather that man and nature should coexist in an interconnected "community of living things" (p. 6). He criticizes the Western dualistic thinking in modern times and advocates instead a holistic approach. On that basis, Cobb incorporated ecologism as a dimension into post-modernity, emphasizing that all beings exist as substances subject to continuous change and that there is no such thing as a never-changing entity; rather, there are only relationships that are constantly evolving.[2] According to Cobb, this organic, holistic philosophy, which "concerns harmony, integrity and the interrelationship of all things", is profoundly commensurable with traditional Chinese thought. Cobb states that postmodernity is where humans live in harmony with each other, and, at the same time, with nature; this era will retain some positive features of modernity but transcend its dualism, anthropocentrism, and patriarchy to build a postmodern world in which the collective well-being of all living things is valued and cared for (Wang, 2002, p. 6). Therefore, Cobb is convinced that when the Chinese embrace and take advantage of his process philosophy, it will flourish in China to a larger extent than in the West, because traditional Chinese culture has always been enriched by its organic holism. He then concludes that such a philosophy will depend greatly on the complementarity and blending of Western and Eastern cultures.

Guoxue is experiencing a new phase of "returning to the origin and ushering in the new". To "return to the origin" is to rediscover the Chinese cultural entity, while to "usher in the new" requires researchers to assimilate the wisdom beyond its cultural context and from the contemporary world, especially to learn from the thriving international sinology and couple it with the latest research results in *guoxue*. In fact, this has long been part of classical Chinese studies. Wang Guowei and Tschen Yin-koh both attached importance to applying the two counterparts in each of the pairs that follow as a mutual measure for each other, namely, things that exist and those that are merely documented, ideas that are imported and those that are indigenous, ancient literatures that belong within and those from beyond the border. Their view actually calls for a combination of sinology and *guoxue*. Recently, I have been reading a book written by Tschen Yin-koh's daughters, in which they

The Interpenetration of Sinology and Guoxue   101

mention that when Chen resumed his teaching at Tsinghua University, he had three assistants (Chen, et al., 2010, pp. 213–215): Mr. Wang Yongxing, who was mainly responsible for teaching; Mr. Wang Jian, who focused on research; and Mr. Chen Qinghua, who dealt with foreign languages. They went on writing:

> Father was still keen to keep up with the latest dynamics of the academic world; he had Mr. Chen Qinghua reading Western journals for him, and Professor Zhou Yiliang would also come for a chat and translate or read Japanese journals and papers.
>
> (Ibid., p. 215)

It is thus evident that Chen's *guoxue* effort has never occurred independent of an international academic context, especially the context of international sinology.

As a matter of fact, sinology and *guoxue* can have diverse intersections with each other. In the context of international sinology, *guoxue* can also adopt a positivistic approach (as Tschen Yin-koh did). The recent conflict between China and the West sets the stage for the exploration of universal values embedded in the two parties (as in studies by Vandermeersch, Roger Ames, Tang Yijie, etc.). A culture can be re-examined through cultural differences so that such studies can initiate a new phase of development without deviating from its own cultural roots (as in studies by Francois Jullien, and other authors). In addition to the systematic and exploratory efforts by researchers specializing in Chinese studies, some other scholars have also investigated the wisdom of the two cultures and even ignited sparks of inspiration. Such researchers include John Cobb, as mentioned above, and Voltaire, Leibniz and numerous Chinese scholars, who have made important contributions to the blending and development of foreign cultures within a mainstream culture. Such diverse intersections, along with tourism and material exchanges, have made it possible for cultures to develop beyond their own borders as exemplified historically by the introduction of Buddhism into China and Aegean culture into Western Europe.

In short, the aforementioned perspectives for, or insights into, sinology are rooted in the vigorous development of *guoxue*, the fall of imperial governance and colonization, China's transition from autocracy to democracy, the crisis of Western values, the relative absence of religious beliefs in China, global power shifts, and so forth. All these realities combined have led to a new stage of intertwining or interplay between sinology and *guoxue*, contributing greatly to driving the globe toward a multicultural symbiotic society. This has become an irreversible historical trend.

Notes

1 See: speech scripts of "The Significance of Francois Jullien's Thoughts on the History of Western Ideas". 2008, Peking University.

102 *The Interpenetration of Sinology and* Guoxue

2 See: (1) Cobb, J. C. (2008, Issue 5). Ecological civilization calls for an organic way of thinking. (Q. Wang, & G. L. Z. Yang, Trans.). *Culture Communication*, p. 1. (2) Cobb, J. C. (2009, Issue 1). On freedom: A new process perspective. (B. Pan, Trans.). *Culture Communication*, p. 2. (3) Wang, Z. H. (2007, January & February). Postmodernism calls for a second Enlightenment. *Culture Communication*, p. 1.

References

Ames, R., & Hall, D. (2005). *Thinking through confucius* (J. L. He, Trans.). Beijing: Peking University Press.

Chen, L. Q., Chen, X. P., & Chen, M. Y. (2010). *With joy and worry: Reminiscent of father Tschen Yin-koh and mother Tang Yun.* Shanghai: SDX Joint Publishing Company.

Cobb, J. C. (2002, August 15). Whitehead's response to the East in harmony. *Social Sciences Weekly*, p. 6.

Li, N. (2009, September 18). Chinese and French scholars discussing Confucius thoughts in Shanghai. *Wenhui Reader's Weekly*, p. 1.

Vandermeersch, L. (2009, August 31). The world significance of *Ruzang* (*Confucian canon*). *Guangming Daily*, p. 12.

Wang, X. H. (2002, June 13). For the common welfare: An interview with John B. Cobb. (Interviewed by Wang, Xiaohua). *Social Sciences Weekly*, p. 6.

11 The Three Phases of the Development of Comparative Literature

11.1 The First Phase

Comparative literature, as an independent discipline, did not appear until between the 1870s and 1880s in Europe. A concatenation of significant literary events marked its establishment. In 1877, the world's first international journal of comparative literature, *Acta Comparationis Litterarum Universarum* (ACLU) (*Journal of Comparative Literature*), was founded in Budapest, with Hungarian comparatist Hugo Meltzl as one of its initiators. Prior to the journal, in 1866, H. M. Posnett, professor of English Literature at the University of Auckland, New Zealand, published the first monograph with the title of *Comparative Literature*. Comparative literature took a further step forward when the first specialized seminar commenced at the University of Lyon in 1897. The French scholar Joseph Texte founded this seminar, which was titled "L'influence des littératures germaniques sur la littérature française depuis la Renaissance" (The Influence of German Literatures on French Literature after the Renaissance). Abel-François Villemain (1790–1870) preceded all the above-mentioned scholars, however; as early as 1829 he gave lectures at the Sorbonne under the course title "Examen de l'influence exercée par les écrivains français du XIII siècle sur les littératures étrangères et l'esprit européen" (Examination of the influence exerted by French 18th-century writers on foreign literature and on the European mind).

In his literary studies, Ferdinand Brunetière (1849–1906), known as the earliest and most accomplished comparatist in France, adopted the Darwinian evolutionary theory in order to interpret international literary relations. His opinions had direct influence on his students, Texte and Betz, who, as we have seen, later became eminent scholars in the early stages of French comparative literature.

Joseph Texte (1865–1900) was the first professor of comparative literature in history and his major contribution was to establish comparative literature as an academic discipline at university. In delivering the first seminar on comparative literature at the University of Lyon, Texte emphasized that comparative literature differs from national literature studies in that the former should preserve the national character of certain literature and meanwhile go beyond national borders to study the mutual influence and relationship

DOI: 10.4324/9781003356240-11

104   *The Three Phases of the Development of Comparative Literature*

between literatures of various countries. His doctoral thesis, *Jean-Jacques Rousseau et les origines du cosmopolitisme littéraire* (*Jean-Jacques Rousseau and the Origins of Literary Cosmopolitanism*) (1895), stands as the first comparative literature monograph. Louis-P Betz (1861–1904) made an indelible contribution to comparative literature with his *La littérature comparée: Essai bibliographique* (*Studies in Comparative Literature*), the earliest reference book in this field, which initially included some two thousand items and later expanded its collection to a total of around three thousand. His achievements also include monographs such as *Heine in Frankreich*.

Fernand Baldensperger (1871–1958) was the first recognized founder of the French School of Comparative Literature and also the first to systematically adopt rigorous positivistic methods to analyze the impact of foreign literatures upon French literature. Amid the huge effort Baldensperger devoted to investigating French publications between 1770 and 1880. He paid keen attention to the evidence within subtle signs and public opinion trends, resulting in works that include *Goethe en France* (1904), *Études d'Histoire Littéraire* (1907, 1910, 1939), *Le Mouvement des Idées dans l'Emigration Française: 1789–1815* (1925), and *Orientations Etrangères chez Honoré de Balzac* (1927). These writings invariably adopt a positivistic methodology and resort to facts in studying the relationship between literatures of different countries, which is seen as a prototype of the French School. In 1921, he founded *Revue de Littérature Comparée* (*Review of Comparative Literature*), a journal that served as an important front for French comparative literature. In collaboration with Van Tieghem, Baldensperger also established an institute of modern comparative literature at the Sorbonne, making the university a center of international comparative literature over the next few decades.

Paul Van Tieghem (1871–1948) took the lead in systematically elaborating on and summarizing the viewpoints of the French School. His 1931 book *La Littérature Comparée* (*Comparative Literature*)[1] offers a comprehensive overview of the history, methodology and achievements of comparative literature. Tieghem argues that comparative literature in itself is a branch of literary history and that, like all historical sciences, it should gather all possible facts of different origins, which are to be expounded and then used as positivistic evidence in studies of connections between literary works of different European countries. He then proposes to "subordinate" national literatures to the general history of European literature. The purpose of comparative literature, as Tieghem puts it, is to demonstrate the correlations between the literary works of various countries by studying what external influences the writers are subject to on the basis of "factual connections" between literatures, thus the positivistic methodology. Another pioneering contribution of Tieghem is his classification of literary studies into national literature, comparative literature and general literature. He explains that national literature studies constitute the foundation and starting point of studies of all literatures, which is then complemented and bridged by comparative literature, while general literature deals with literary connections between a larger number of nations. This 1931 book has become an

The Three Phases of the Development of Comparative Literature   105

important work in the development of comparative literature as it, on the one hand, provides a systematic overview of French comparative literature in both theoretical and methodological terms, and, on the other, lays the foundation for comparative literature to start to develop as an academic discipline in the world.

Tieghem's successors, Jean-Marié Carré and Marius-François Guyard, followed his theoretical path and further developed it, establishing the theoretical framework of the French School. Carré (1887–1958), a student of Baldensperger, inherited his predecessors' viewpoints, setting the goal of comparative literature as studying factual connections between global literatures, and he also attached much weight to studying spiritual connections between writers from different nations. Carré (2009), in his preface to Guyard's *La Littérature Comparée* (*Comparative Literature*), noted that comparative literature is "the study of international intellectual relations, of the actual connections that existed between Byron and Pushkin, Goethe and Carlyle, Walter Scott and Vigny – between the works, the inspirations, or even the lives of writers belonging to various literatures" (p. 159). Guyard (1921–2011) was a student of Carré and his 1951 book *La Littérature Comparée* followed Tieghem closely while developing and improving the French School's theory, and therefore is hailed as an influential handbook in the international academia of comparative literature. Compared with Tieghem's work (also titled *La Littérature Comparée*), Guyard pays more attention to studies on the interrelationship between literatures de facto connected, thus stressing what he terms "rapports de fait" (factual connections). Guyard (1969) defines comparative literature as follows:

> Comparative Literature is the history of international literary relations. The comparatist stands at the frontiers, linguistic or national, and surveys the exchanges of themes, ideas, books, or feelings between two or several literatures.
>
> (p. 5)

The French School was the pioneer of world comparative literature. With a rich harvest of academic results, it proved the value of comparative literature as a science, making it possible and laying the foundation for comparative literature to be recognized as an independent discipline. Yet this school also has its historical limitations. Its defects lie in its defining comparative literature as historical studies of literary relations and its scope being confined to the European academia. In addition, its overreliance on positivism and emphasis on factual connections between writers and literary works belonging to different nations led to the neglect of certain aspects of the literatures, namely, the law of their own evolution and their unique aesthetic properties. Lurking behind these defects, especially the one in which Eurocentrism is taken as the theoretical core of comparative literature, is the developmental crisis of the school. As Loliée (1906) puts it in *Histoire des Littératures Comparées* (*A Short History of Comparative Literature*):

106   *The Three Phases of the Development of Comparative Literature*

Nevertheless, Western humanism has pursued its intellectual, moral, and industrial conquest of the universe. With the exception of certain isolated regions among the mountains Eastern Asia is open to the world. Our customs perforce penetrate into countries even most obstinately attached to their immemorial traditions and their ancient formula... the union of Eastern Asia and the European world is, as we have just asserted, final.

That the nearer acquaintance and consequent mutual influence of the various nations shall have, as an inevitable result, an undermining of their individuality, is not to be doubted.

(pp. 372–373)

11.2 The Second Phase

Comparative literature studies in the United States at around the same time as they did in France. As early as 1871, Chauncey Shackford delivered a lecture course at Cornell University on "general literature" and comparative literature (over two decades prior to Texte's lectures in 1897), spearheading the study of comparative literature in the country. From 1887 to 1889, Charles M. Gayley ran a seminar on comparative literary criticism at the University of Michigan, marking the emergence of comparative literature in the United States. In 1899, the first ever Department of Comparative Literature in the country was established at Columbia University and in 1903, George E. Woodberry, then dean of the Department of Comparative Literature, inaugurated the *Journal of Comparative Literature*,[2] the first of its kind in the country. In 1908, Harvard University also set up its Department of Comparative Literature and, two years later, the journal, *Harvard Studies in Comparative Literature*, was launched by Professor W. H. Schofield.

During the early formative years of comparative literature in the United States, Woodberry and Frank W. Chandler offered some crucial viewpoints. Chandler once proposed that comparative literature should be anchored into literary movements, studying the themes, genres, contexts, sources, influences and communication, exploring aesthetics in literature and seeking commonalities in the development of national literatures. These views have undoubtedly had a vital influence on the development of comparative literature in the country.

The 1940s saw new developments in the field of comparative literature in the United States. In 1942, Columbia University established a Comparative Literature Committee under the initiative and efforts of Arthur Christy, who founded *Comparative Literature Newsletter* in the same year. World War II led to a fundamental change in the global situation and people's mindset. Following the end of the war, American comparative literature achieved rapid growth. Yale University and Indiana University took the lead in commencing comparative literature studies and then others successively established their departments or major of comparative literature. In 1950, the

University of North Carolina published the *Bibliography of Comparative Literature*[3] and, two years later, the *Yearbook of Comparative Literature and General Literature* came out. In 1960, the American Comparative Literature Association was officially founded. All these results are a demonstration of the momentum of the discipline's vigorous development in the United States during this period.

By the 1950s, Yale University and Indiana University had become the cradle of the American School of comparative literature. The school's prominent representatives, including Wellek, Levin, Remak and Weisstein, were all graduates from these two universities. The American School in the true sense was born when their self-contained theories were formed and especially characterized by the theories of parallel studies and interdisciplinary research advanced by these scholars.

In September 1958, the second congress of the International Comparative Literature Association was held at the University of North Carolina (Chapel Hill campus). René Wellek (1903–1995), a professor at Yale University, delivered his speech titled "The Crisis of Comparative Literature"[4], which challenged and sharply criticized the French School. This speech caused a stir in the international community of comparative literature and provoked a dispute between the American and the French Schools. The paper came to be regarded as the manifesto of the American School.

Wellek criticized the French School for its perceived unbalanced focus on the investigation into the correlation between two national literatures and their origins, which narrowed comparative literature to a "foreign trade" in the context of literatures. This practice will not lead to an all-round study of artwork, and, as Wellek (1963) argues, "Works of art, however, are not simply sums of sources and influences" (p. 164), but rather they are complete wholes. Wellek also embraces views of New Criticism. He is quoted as saying: "I have called the study of the work of art 'intrinsic' and that of its relations to the mind of the author, to society, etc., 'extrinsic'" (Wellek, 1963, p. 170). The "intrinsic" studies he points to are studies on "literariness", which he identifies as "the central issue of aesthetics, the nature of art and literature" (ibid., p. 169). Furthermore, Wellek accuses the French School of shunning the collaboration of literary history, criticism and theories and confining comparative literature to the study of literary history, laying a rigid demarcation between general literature and comparative literature. He points out that French scholars tend to accentuate the influence of their own literature on their foreign counterparts and that even when they touch upon the impact in the other direction, they are trying to prove that their own country is more capable of understanding and accepting others as they are. In this way, their studies inevitably run counter to the tenet of comparative literature, which is against nationalism, and their study becomes an instrument for spreading narrow nationalism. He suggests eliminating the contrived delimitation between comparative literature and general literature and maintains that comparative literature shall place literary works *per se* at the center of its cross-cultural studies.

108 *The Three Phases of the Development of Comparative Literature*

Wellek's speech undermined the dominance of the French School and triggered a decade-long dispute between American and French scholars. This disagreement encouraged people's rethinking of the orientation, object of study and research methods of comparative literature, providing considerable impetus for its development as a discipline.

Other figures who have made significant contributions to theory building for the American School include both Henry Remak and A. Owen Aldridge. Remak (1916–2009) was a professor at Indiana University. His essay "Comparative Literature: Its Definition and Function" is a fine representation of the views of the American School. The essay not only analyzes the limitations of the French School's study of influences, but also proposes an entirely new definition for comparative literature:

> Comparative literature is the study of literature beyond the confines of one particular country, and the study of the relationships between literature on the one hand and other areas of knowledge and belief, such as the arts (e.g., painting, sculpture, architecture, music), philosophy, history, the social sciences (e.g., politics, economics, sociology), the sciences, religion, etc., on the other. In brief, it is the comparison of one literature with another or others, and the comparison of literature with other spheres of human expression.
>
> (Remak, 1961, p. 3)

This definition shows Remak's emphasis on the orientation of comparative literature to be the comparison of one literature with one or more other literatures belonging to other countries, which refutes the division between comparative literature and general literature and affirms the applicability of comparative literature in studying literary phenomena across two or more countries. He also acknowledges the interdisciplinarity of comparative literature and its scope reaching out of the literary world, proposing a new idea of studying relationships between literature and other spheres of knowledge and belief.

At the very beginning of his *Comparative Literature: Matter and Method*, a crucial piece of theoretical work for the American School, Aldridge (1969) writes:

> Briefly defined, comparative literature can be considered the study of any literary phenomenon from the perspective of more than one national literature or in conjunction with another intellectual discipline or even several.
>
> (p. 1)

Aldridge shares the same views as Remak and presents a further discussion on the affinity and contrast between literatures. As Aldridge et al. (1963) puts it, "affinity consists of resemblances in style, structure, mood or idea between two works which have no other necessary connection" whereas comparison

The Three Phases of the Development of Comparative Literature   109

lies in terms of identifying both likenesses and differences. He regards comparative literature, as not being based solely on direct, factual connections as pure research, from which the significance of parallel studies is elicited.

Viewed from the above opinions, American scholars give prominence to the cross-nationality and interdisciplinarity of comparative literature. Moreover, while a consensus is reached over the verifiable quality of cross-nationality, the French School confines its scope to two nations and the American School expands it to two or more nations; the former highlights the study of factual connections between nations and the latter is more oriented to the comparison of artistic characteristics and aesthetics in the literatures, hence American comparatists' preference to parallel studies that transcend such factual connections. As for comparative literature in the sense of being an interdisciplinary research field, such is the original idea of the American School.

The American School recommends the use of parallel studies, which value the comparison of intrinsic connections, common rules and national characteristics in literatures from different countries, and emphasizes exploring the aesthetic value in literary works, thereby orienting comparative literature back towards literary studies; refraining from the undue inclination towards history studies. It also advocates interdisciplinary studies; such an approach being conducive to a better and more comprehensive understanding of the traits and essence of literature in itself. It is worth noting that, during that period, American comparatists began to concern themselves with Eastern literature and were particularly attracted by Chinese literature. They valued the exchange between Western and Eastern literatures, which had been bred in diverse cultures. The insights of American comparatists broke the barrier for comparative literature caused by the European division of cultural regions and took another step in bringing about an international discipline.

Around the beginning of the 1970s, the two Schools began to gradually dispel their opposition and divergence and thence progressed toward a fusion where they tended to recognize and make impartial comments of each other. In 1963, Étiemble René, a renowned French comparatist, published his monograph *Comparaison n'est pas Raison: La Crise de la Literature Comparée* (*Comparison Is not Reason: The Crisis in Comparative Literature*). This work reviews the previous contention between the two schools, advocating that the study on literatures not directly related should be included in the domain of comparative literature and arguing that the historical perspective and aesthetic contemplation do not oppose; rather, they complement each other and therefore should be combined in research. In 1970, Wellek provided an overview in his essay "The Name and Nature of Comparative Literature". The essay includes a summary of the common views among international comparatists at that time in five aspects. Firstly, comparative literature is the study of literature without linguistic, ethnic and political boundaries. Secondly, for this discipline, it is of the same significance to consider languages and genres with no prior connections and to trace mutual influences from each author's own reading and from aesthetic parallels. Thirdly, comparative literature

110　*The Three Phases of the Development of Comparative Literature*

shall not be exclusive to the study of literary history; it is also an approach to literary criticism, which can be applied to contemporary literature. Neither national literature nor comparative literature studies can ever evade the discussion of literature as a complete whole of the three domains, namely, literary history, theory and criticism. Fourthly, the subject investigates all literature from an international perspective and acknowledges the unity of all creation of literary works and experience of literary reading, and thus hints at the distant ideal of constructing a global literary history and literary scholarship. Fifthly, the nature and the object of study determine that comparative literature "cannot be confined to a single method: description, characterization, interpretation, narration, explanation, evaluation, are used in its discourse just as much as comparison" (Wellek, 1970, p. 19). The above propositions are typical of the trend of international comparative literature from the 1960s to the early 1980s.

11.3　The Third Phase

Comparative literature has had over a century-long history since the French School's founding, with decades of studies on communication and mutual influence of literature and, after World War II, the American School's parallel and interdisciplinary studies on unrelated literatures. With regard to comparative literature in China, it is by no means a branch of that history. Although comparative literature in China emerged during the same period as its two counterparts and was greatly influenced by world comparative literature, it was generated and developed in its own unique way.

The twentieth century witnessed the transformation of China's academic culture from its traditional mode to modernity, steering its path to maturity and prosperity amidst twists and turns in the cultural engagement and accommodation between Chinese and Western scholarship. In that century, Chinese comparative literature was primarily a concept and methodology of scholarly research, and was then deemed as a relatively independent academic discipline, leaving its own indelible and unique imprint on China's history of scholarship. Comparative literature appeared, developed and prospered in China in the previous century essentially on the grounds of the intrinsic need for a conceptual reform of China's literary research and renovation of its methodology. The fundamental features of China's studies in this field during the twentieth century are determined by such a need. Chinese scholars' historical research of Chinese scholarship indicates that China's comparative literature is not something that has existed since ancient times, nor was it imported; rather, it is founded on the internal demands for the evolution of local literature, and arose in the context of global exchanges as a brand-new civilizational phenomenon with Chinese characteristics.

At the start of the twentieth century, the Qing government began to suppress the prevailing radical propositions and tyrannical behaviors of reformists, and proposed a model calling for the use of traditional [Chinese] ways of learning as a foundation and new [Western] ways for practical application. In

The Three Phases of the Development of Comparative Literature 111

1901, the Qing government issued an edict abolishing the eight-legged essay.[5] In 1905, the imperial examination system came to an end and five senior ministers were appointed to investigate overseas. In the following year, more actions were declared, including working out a preparatory constitution and the reform of governmental bureaucracy. Given such circumstances, all Chinese intellectuals, whether they liked it or not, had to deliberate the problems of how to handle Western culture and how to continue the long-lasting traditional Chinese culture and bring it to a greater height of development. It is in such a situation that the spread of Western learning to the East became an irresistible trend in that era. Therefore, under the impact of Western learning, it was difficult for traditional literati to get on in the world if they confined themselves to Chinese literature; consequently, studying abroad and learning foreign languages became new options. Consider the case of Lin Shu (1852–1924), a renowned man of letters, who had a conservative inclination. Despite his ignorance of any foreign language, he eventually managed to collaborate in the translation of more than three hundred foreign fictions. He lamented in his later years that the greatest regret in his life was that he had failed to master any foreign language. This social reality proposed new social needs, and it was an essential factor that triggered the inception of comparative literature in China.

This unique beginning and subsequent evolution determined the diverse differences between comparative literature in China and the West. Considering the origin of comparative literature in France and Europe as a branch of literary historical research, it first appeared in the classroom as a purely scholarly "phenomenon in the academy." On the contrary, at the beginning of the twentieth century, comparative literature in China was not purely academic, nor was it a product of schooling. Rather, it was intimately connected to the Chinese society and the transition of Chinese literature from its traditional model to modernity; it was first of all a notion, a vision and a perspective. Its birth marks the end of a self-enclosed state of Chinese literature and a conscious entry of Chinese literature into the realm of world literature, and the start of an equal dialogue with its foreign counterparts. Without an awareness of this fact, it would hardly be possible to recognize the significance and value of the subject's rise in China.

The above represents the first facet of difference that sets Chinese and European comparative literature apart, and it also underpins the second difference. Comparative literature in France and other parts of Europe resorts to a positivistic approach to factual connections and communication between diverse literatures in Europe, while comparative literature in China has, from the very beginning, been characterized by a strong consciousness of contrast or cross-referencing between Chinese and foreign, especially Western, literature. Comparative literature in Europe stresses the connection and affinity between various national literatures within Europe while comparative literature in China emphasizes otherness and contrast more than affinity. In this regard, in the earliest stages, Europe focused comparative literature mainly on the ways in which cultures identify and communicate with each other

112 *The Three Phases of the Development of Comparative Literature*

instead of comparing differences; comparative literature in China in the early years occurred exactly the other way around, centering on the comparison of differences, and being aimed at a better understanding of itself by looking for variance and learning from others while distinguishing itself.

With regards to the third difference, having been placed under broad temporal and spatial contexts, China's comparative literature has never entirely deviated from the foundation of traditional Chinese culture. Wang Guowei (2011), one of the founders of Chinese comparative literature, states that there is no such distinction as "new" and "old" learning or "Chinese" and "Western" learning (pp. 110–111). Why is it that any learning is not "new" nor "old"? Wang explains that, when looking at things or pursuing knowledge, one should always seek truth. As he puts it, not all of what sages say is trustworthy, or all that they do flawless, and therefore we should refrain from worshiping everything in the past; all things have arisen from some earlier causes while their ripple effects appear in the future, and therefore we should refrain from despising everything in the past. And why is it that any learning is not "Chinese" or "Western"? Wang (1997b) remarks, "Intelligence, everyone is endowed with, and unsolved problems about the universe and life, everyone encounters." (p. 115) If one can provide a solution to some of the problems, be they our compatriots or not, they shall not be treated differently, for either satisfies our thirst for knowledge and lessens the pain of having doubts. He goes on to say, "All learning falls in one category among the three: science, history and literature. What is being studied in China also has a place in the West, and vice versa; the difference lies in the scope and complexity of study" (Wang, 2011, pp. 110–111). Wang's comments above suggest that China should be concerned about a void of learning rather than an imbalance between Chinese and Western learning.

Wang's approach to learning accords with his above-mentioned propositions. For instance, in making comparison with the West, Wang (1997c) proposes that the philosophies and arts that are intended to satisfy the pursuit of pure knowledge, subtle sentiment and to relieve life doubts and pains are the most honorable and sacred of the kind and therefore are what China has been lacking in (p. 192). Chinese poetry has been dominated by reminiscing and meditating on China's history, expressing nostalgia and sentiments, and by gift poems; less is produced to raise questions in the spiritual dimension, and much less to depict mental sufferings beyond worldly interests. Chinese drama and fiction tend to be expostulatory or exhortatory and, with such a purpose that disqualifies them as pure art, they are undervalued. Non-pure artworks have always been ill-treated with no one doing them justice such that fictionists, dramatists, painters, musicians and the like all belittle themselves as insignificant people and the world treats them in the same way (Wang, 1997a, pp. 120–121).

Comparative literature in China gained new momentum in the early twentieth century and has been developing as a discipline since that time. Despite a latent period of studies in the Chinese mainland between the 1960s and 1970s due to issues arising from the times and politics, comparative literature

The Three Phases of the Development of Comparative Literature   113

prospered first in Taiwan and Hong Kong during this period, pioneering the research field in the country. In 1979, after the start of China's reform and opening-up, the academia of the Chinese mainland, which had been suppressed for years, experienced a spurt of academic enthusiasm and creativity. Comparative literature, one of the most inclusive and avant-garde literary disciplines, then revived and grew by leaps and bounds. Such development is of considerable historical significance. Around the 1980s, the world entered into an era of globalization in a deeper and more comprehensive manner. The requirements imposed by multi-culturalism sharply counterposed imperial cultural hegemony and cultural fundamentalism. There was an urgent need for mutual understanding, communication and exchange between people from different cultures. The primary mission of literary scholarship in general is the study of people and comparative literature, a subject of cross-cultural literary studies, which plays an unequalled role in promoting inter-cultural awareness and understanding.

As a matter of fact, in the information age, human beings are still dealing with the same issues they have encountered repeatedly in history: love and desire, life and death: issues of mind–body harmony; power and identity and of interpersonal harmony; relationships between people and the environment, in other words, humanity–nature harmony. These harmonies have been a common pursuit of all cultures throughout history and also common aspirations of literatures of all cultures. An in-depth knowledge of the exploration of these common perplexities by literatures in various cultures and a persistent effort to advance literary exchange and interaction are likely to be a remedy for the current ideology of globalism, which is unidirectional, meager and biased, and may give rise to a new mode of globalization based on multi-culturalism. Thus, the third phase of modern comparative literature principally features mutual understanding, complementarity, and interaction between diverse cultures, or, in other words, heterogeneous cultures.

Comparative literature in China has become an exemplary embodiment of world comparative literature in its third phase, which can be attributed to factors as follows. First of all, as a developing country, China is unlikely to impose unilateral imperial hegemony on others; instead, it is steadfast in committing itself in the course of promoting multiculturalism. Secondly, China, blessed with a long-standing continuous culture and a strong inherited cultural consciousness, offers an almost inexhaustible source for inter-cultural literary research. In addition, China has long been in a state of profound cultural exchange with countries such as India, Japan and Persia, and over the past century, Chinese people have been keen on the learning of foreign cultures and languages (for instance, by means of sending students and visiting scholars overseas), thereby gaining a far better knowledge of foreign countries (including becoming more cultivated in their languages) than the other way around (especially when compared to Europe and the United States). It thus opens up the possibility that China's comparative literature stands at the frontier of constructing a new mechanism for the subject's scholarship by way of its pioneering inter-cultural literary research.

114 *The Three Phases of the Development of Comparative Literature*

Furthermore, comparative literature in China represents the essence of modern comparative literature with its value of "unity in diversity" and its all-embracing recognition of schools and achievements from other countries. In the early 1930s, Van Tieghem's *La Littérature Comparée* (*Comparative Literature*) and Frédéric Loliée's *Histoire des Littératures Comparées* (*A Short History of Comparative Literature*) were translated into Chinese shortly after their publication. By the end of the twentieth century, tens of foreign (including Russian, Japanese, Indian, South Korean and Brazilian) publications on comparative literature, including monographs and essay collections, had been translated or compiled in China and also hundreds of review papers on comparative literature had been published. Most comparative literature textbooks in China have chapters especially set aside for the introduction of, and comment on, foreign comparative literature. One could assume that no other country attached such importance to, or had been so enthusiastic about, approaching and learning from foreign comparative literature as Chinese researchers. Finally, it is also worth mentioning that traditional Chinese culture makes no demarcation between literature, history and philosophy, and that it does not treat arts, such as musical instruments, Chinese chess, calligraphy, dance and opera, as completely independent items. As such, a Chinese perspective on cultural context offers all-round possibilities for interdisciplinary literary studies.

All in all, not only did comparative literature in China during the twentieth century have profound historical roots; it also demonstrated a distinct worldview and always played a leading role. It embraced the positivistic approach centered on communication and influence, which had been developed by the French School, and was also inspired by parallel and disciplinary studies, as advocated by the American School. In this uniquely Chinese way, the subject is based on past experience and it overcomes its French and American counterparts' parochiality of being either Europe-centric or Western-centric; hence, it is truly committed to an equal exchange between Eastern and Western literature and scholarship, and from different perspectives and covering multiple areas, it guides comparative literature to a brand new third phase of development.

The French School, a symbol of the first phase of world comparative literature, initiated communication and influenced research, which was oriented towards positivism. However, in this regard, China has followed its own unique research path, which was not simply an issue about approach selection, but is also a path necessitated by research demands. For instance, the unceasing translation of Indian Buddhist scriptures and literature lasted for over one thousand years in China, leaving abundant academic resources for comparative literature in China. Bound by religious beliefs and living amid the blending of religion and literature, it was historically difficult for scholars to interpret this lengthy and complicated history. After the 1920s, Hu Shi, Liang Qichao, Xu Dishan, Tschen Yin-koh and Ji Xianlin introduced the positivistic approach into the study of literary relations between China and India, inaugurating studies on the history of literary relations between China

The Three Phases of the Development of Comparative Literature   115

and other countries, demonstrating the exceptional advantages of positivism in China's comparative literature, and yielding the earliest academic achievements in this field. Chinese modern literature's embracing of foreign literature throughout the twentieth century covers such a broad scope and exerts such an influence that it has no equal in the world. In addition, Chinese literature's long-standing spread and influence in North Korea, Japan, and Vietnam, among other East Asian countries, showed the wide prospects of positivistic research of literary relations between China and other countries and also between East Asian countries. In this manner, twentieth-century comparative literature in China did not cast aside positivistic research on the history of literary communication and literary relations; instead, this area was the most fruitful one during that period. Chinese scholars combined the Chinese academic tradition of maintaining reason-based and root-seeking in research and the inter-cultural vision and methods of comparative literature, thereby vitalizing their research. Academic achievements produced in this field are characterized by a sense of solidity of research and rigor and propriety in arguments, and thus has indelible academic value and continuing vitality.

Since the 1950s, comparative literature in the United States, which represents the second phase of world comparative literature, has broken through the disciplinary fence of the French School, and oriented comparative literature towards the study of literary relations. It yielded abundant achievements through its advocacy of parallel studies (of literatures not factually connected) and interdisciplinary studies (between literature and other subjects). Comparative literature in China has also reaped special results in this respect. Trailblazers for parallel studies in China include "Comments on *A Dream of Red Mansions*" by Wang Guowei in 1904, "Russia and China in Literature" by Zhou Zuoren in 1920, studies on mythologies in China and North Europe by Mao Dun in the twentieth century, Zhong Jingwen's "Similarities of Chinese and Indo-European Folktales", and Yaozi's "Reading *Romance of the West Chamber* and *Romeo and Juliet*" in 1935. Later, Qian Zhongshu's "Chinese Poetry and Chinese Painting", "On Reading *Laocoön*", "Synaesthesia" and "Poetry can Give Vent to Grievances" and Yang Zhouhan's "The Function of Prophetic Dreams in *The Aeneid* and *A Dream of Red Mansions*" and "Chinese and Western Mourning Poems" are all exemplary works of inter-cultural and interdisciplinary studies. In the 1970s, seminal parallel studies, represented by Qian Zhongshu's *Limited Views: Essays on Ideas and Letters*, broke new ground and afforded an example to the research field. Naturally, the development has been characterized by twists and turns and also rebounds. In conducting parallel studies, for example, researchers have been consciously seeking new knowledge and an understanding of Chinese literature and culture and have been trying to identify the nature and orientation of Chinese literature in a more complete manner. Yet, for quite some time, senior researchers such as Tschen Yin-koh have questioned the levels of comparability in parallel studies; therefore, the emergence of parallel studies was accompanied by some strained comparisons,

116 *The Three Phases of the Development of Comparative Literature*

such as the intertextual references of "X and Y", which were criticized by scholars such as Ji Xianlin, with Chinese parallel studies achieving better development after such correction. "Interdisciplinary literary research" was once a subject under question; for instance, some raised the question: "Is it the study of the relations between literature and other disciplines or is it using other disciplines as reference while maintaining the methodology and perspective of literary studies?" It is apparent, in fact, that the two suppositions are interrelated and can be self-reinforcing. There are quite a few more opinions; for instance, some argue that comparative literature can only be seen as such when it is both "interdisciplinary" and "cross-cultural". Nevertheless, along this tortuous evolutionary course, interdisciplinary literary research in China still makes progress, as is evidenced in *Transdisciplinary Comparative Literature Studies* published by China Social Sciences Press in 1989. The book is a preliminary representation of what Chinese comparatists have achieved in interdisciplinary literary studies. Professor Yang Zhouhan (1989) states pointedly in the book's foreword that "We need an 'interdisciplinary' research vision: one that transcends both national and linguistic boundaries and disciplinary limits and that examines literature from a broader cultural context" (p. 2).

Furthermore, it is worth noting that, in the early twentieth century, Wang Guowei went off the beaten path and approached comparative literature from another perspective. Wang cast light on Chinese literature by way of imported thinking modes, borrowing Western terminology to interpret Chinese literary works such as *A Dream of Red Mansions*, Chinese poetry, represented by productions of Qu Yuan, and the opera of the Song and Yuan dynasties. He was committed to matching foreign ideas to literary works which inherently originated in China. Although he failed to make further direct comparison, Wang's exploration into comparative literature reflects a cross-cultural perspective of world literature, compared to direct comparison at a superficial level. His investigation embodies the introspective comparative concept of seeking self-improvement by observing others, and thus manages to take a deep look at comparative literature in itself, thereby initiating elucidation research in comparative literature in China. Bidirectional elucidation – to elucidate literary works in Culture B with literary theories from Culture A, and vice versa – occupies such an important place in inter-cultural literary studies in China that some scholars deem elucidation research as embodying the characteristics of the "Chinese School" of comparative literature.

In short, comparative literature in China does not merely have passive access to philosophies from the outside world for developing the discipline; rather, it has consciously departed from its own history and has been making efforts to form its own judgement through its unique research approach. Comparative literature in China, representing the third phase of world comparative literature, is by no means a branch of any foreign school; instead, it has created its own voice, expressed its unique thinking, exhibited its intrinsic features and contributed to world comparative literature in an exceptional manner.

The Three Phases of the Development of Comparative Literature 117

In recent years, while continuing along the above developmental path, comparative literature in China has also opened up some new domains, which can be elaborated upon as follows.

1   A new theoretical exploration of the discipline. Chinese comparatists, on the basis of the practice of comparative literature in China, have been exploring novel ideas and theories of comparative literature, so as to incorporate cultural studies across the East and the West in the era of globalization, thereby advancing the evolution of the concept of comparative literature. For example, they advocate the notion of multicultural coexistence and complementarity denoted by the term "unity in diversity"; highlight differences, mutual recognition, harmony between complementarity and coexistence, and strive to promote multicultural coexistence throughout the world; are devoted to a fundamental theory on literary communication between heterogeneous cultures, and seek out a mechanism and method for the dialogue between the East and the West.

2   The establishment of a new discipline known as literary anthropology. Literary anthropology is a fruit borne out of the intersection of literary studies and anthropology, an extension of comparative studies on Chinese and Western mythologies, and the most active new domain generated by nearly two decades of interdisciplinary research of comparative literature in China. Since 1991, a successive group of publications has come out under the collective title of *An Anthropological Interpretation of Chinese Culture*. The series, encompassing over eight million words, provides a modern anthropological interpretation of a good many ancient Chinese classics, including *The Book of Poetry*, *Verses of Chu*, *Tao Te Ching*, *Zhuangzi*, *Records of the Grand Historian*, *Shuowen Jiezi*, *Doctrine of the Mean* and *Classic of Mountains and Seas*. These intricate classics are subjected to original literary and anthropologic interpretation under a global cultural context.

3   The emergence of translation as an independent discipline. China is a country where translation undertakings prosper. China has a translation history of over two thousand years with a considerable number of scholars involved and works translated, leading the world in this field, by volume at least. Statistics show that in the first decade of the twentieth century, translated literary works accounted for four-fifths of literary publications in China, and currently, translated works of all types make up nearly a half of publications nationwide. Literary translation is not merely the conversion of linguistic symbols (words) but also the transmission and re-forging of cultural concepts. Re-creation in literary translation is unavoidable and the translators' responsibility is to produce a functionally equivalent, creative representation of the original text and to bridge gaps where two languages have no intersection and to create opportunities for exchange where the two languages fail to conform, thus both introducing a foreign language and developing the local one. In this sense, works translated into Chinese form an essential part of Chinese

118 *The Three Phases of the Development of Comparative Literature*

literature and, by the same token, the history of translated literature should be a crucial branch of Chinese literary history, as has become the consensus for conceptualizing comparative literature in China.

4 Encounters between overseas Chinese literature and diasporic literature. Studies on overseas Chinese literature have been dealing with literature by overseas Chinese and their offspring, written not only in Chinese but also in other languages. Such studies focus on observing and analyzing literary imagination of cultural encounters, conflict and blending, and are intended to be used to promote cross-national cultural dialogue and mutual interpretation between cultures. In recent years, such research made its way into the discussion of diasporic literature – literature written by authors who live outside of their native countries – within the current global context. Scholars of diasporic literature are devoted to both introducing the Western theory of diasporic writing and summarizing China's theory making and practice in this field in a bid to enter into a direct, rewarding dialogue with international academia. Chinese emigrants have long been venturing worldwide in significant numbers and the country already has a long history of emigration; therefore, literary studies targeted at those foreign countries' immigrant authors will certainly make significant contributions to rewriting world literary history.

5 The disentanglement of literary relations. Qian Zhongshu pointed out long ago that to unravel the interrelationship between native and foreign literatures and the interplay between native and foreign writers has always been among the priority work in the developmental path of comparative literature in all countries (Zhang, 1981). In more recent years, the greatest progress of the study on literary relations between China and other countries is the discussion of twentieth-century Chinese and world literature as a whole, where comprehensive research is conducted on the interaction between the traditional Chinese culture inherited and reflected by Chinese writers and those writers' influence from Western literature. One evidence that markedly argues for this approach is the publication of the 15-volume series of inter-cultural study cases collectively titled *Modern Chinese Writers in Cultural Time-Space Coordinates*. Studies on Chinese literature's development outside China have also made robust advances. The 12-volume series of *Foreign Writers and Chinese Culture* is without doubt a major academic accomplishment in the twentieth century. According to Prof. Ji Xianlin, unlike the West, China, India, Persia, Japan, North Korea and other Arabian countries have established their enormous and profound independent systems of literary theory thanks to a rich accumulation formed along their long-standing histories. Yet it is such a great pity that most researchers studying literary theories are inclined to pay keen attention to the West while ignoring the East. Lately, comparative literature in the East has welcomed gratifying progress with considerable accomplishments made in areas such as comparative poetics, inter-cultural ecological literary studies, imagology and comparative studies of Chinese minorities literature.

The rise of comparative literature in China has triggered multiple far-reaching changes in Chinese academic culture, manifested by its enlarged research vision, the discovery of new objects of study and the renewal of literary conceptions and approaches. This is all the more the case in literary studies concerning literary theory, criticism and history, as evidenced by works such as *Readings in Chinese Literature from the Perspective of Modern Academics* (by Tong Qingbing et al.), *A History of the Reception of Modern Chinese Literature* (by Ma Yixin), *A History of the Reception of Ancient Chinese Literature* (by Shang Xuefeng et al.), essays produced on the topic of "Literatures, Literary Theories, Literary Histories", *A History of Translated Literature in China* (by Meng Zhaoyi et al.), and, in particular, the 6-volume *China's Symbolic Culture* (by Ju Yueshi et al.) and the 8-volume *Western Images of China* (by Zhou Ning).

To summarize, the essence of comparative literature in China, which exemplifies the third phase of world comparative literature, is to promote mutual understanding and equal dialogue between the literatures of various nations. Comparative literature in China, which opposes both cultural hegemony and cultural fundamentalism, has always upheld humanism and makes corresponding efforts towards a world of balanced multipolarity by facilitating inter-cultural and interdisciplinary communication and standing up for multiculturalism. Looking into the future, there are high expectations for comparative literature in China and the world. Our effort to review and take down the history of comparative literature in the twentieth century is meant to activate China's inherent academic traditions by means of sorting, examining and commenting on academic legacies relevant to this field. Meanwhile, we intend to help comparative literature in the new century to fully benefit and learn from its history of the past one hundred years so as to maintain sound development.

Needless to say, the human species is currently going through an unprecedented and unpredictable period. In the shadows of globalization, the only hope for human civilization may lie in promoting multiculturality, enhancing people-to-people understanding and inclusiveness, and blazing new trails and widening paths for all kinds of exchange. Comparative literature in China, with Chinese cultural traditions as its cornerstone and as a third phase of inter-cultural and interdisciplinary literary studies in the world, is bound to play a crucial role in eliminating imperial cultural hegemony and amending the diaspora, and the isolated and insulated situation caused by post-modernism.

Notes

1 The book was translated into Chinese by Dai Wangshu in 1937 and the Chinese version was published and issued by the Commercial Press (Shanghai).
2 French comparatist Fernand Baldensperger and Italian comparatist Benedetto Croce were both editors.
3 The book was co-authored by Fernand Baldensperger and Swiss scholar Friederich, W. P.

120　*The Three Phases of the Development of Comparative Literature*

4 See: Wellek, R. (1963). The crisis of comparative literature. In D. Damrosch, N. Melas & M. Buthelezi (Eds.), *The Princeton sourcebook in comparative literature*. Princeton & Oxford: Princeton University Press. pp. 161–172.

5 The eight-legged essay (八股文) was a kind of stereotyped writing in imperial examinations during the Ming and Qing dynasties in China, which required test takers to conform to certain sets of rules and was later criticized for narrowing people's innovative thinking and minds and having a constraining effect on both the people and the nation.

References

Aldridge, A. O. (1969). *Comparative literature: Matter and method*. Urbana: University of Illinois Press.

Aldridge, A. O., Balakian, A., Guillén, C. & Fleischmann, W. B. (1963). The concept of influence in comparative literature: A symposium. *Comparative Literature Studies, Special Advance Number 1963*, 143–152.

Carré, J. M. (2009). Preface to *La littérature comparée*. In D. Damrosch, N. Melas & M. Buthelezi (Eds.), *The Princeton sourcebook in comparative literature*. Princeton & Oxford: Princeton University Press.

Guyard, M. F. (1969). *La littérature comparée*. In R. J. Clements. (1978). *Comparative literature as academic discipline: A statement of principles, praxis, standards*. New York: The Modern Language Association of America.

Loliée, F. (1906). *A short history of comparative literature: From the earliest times to the present day*. (M. D. Power, Trans.). London: Hodder and Stoughton.

Remak, H. (1961). Comparative literature, its definition and function. In N. P. Stallknecht & H. Frenz (Eds.), *Comparative literature: Method and perspective*. Carbondale: Southern Illinois University Press.

Wang, G. W. (1997a). On the bounden duties of philosophers and artists. In G. W. Wang. *Jing'an collection*. Shenyang: Liaoning Education Press.

Wang, G. W. (1997b). On recent years' scholarly circle. In G. W. Wang (Ed.), *Jing'an collection*. Shenyang: Liaoning Education Press.

Wang, G. W. (1997c). Remarks on literature. In H. X. Xu (Ed.), *Pursuing goodness, pursuing beauty, pursuing truth: Selected works of Wang Guowei*. Shanghai: Shanghai Far East Publishers.

Wang, G. W. (2011). Preface to *National studies serial*. In H. X. Xu (Ed.), *Selected works of Wang Guowei*. Shanghai: Shanghai Far East Publishers.

Wellek, R. (1963). The crisis of comparative literature. In D. Damrosch, N. Melas & M. Buthelezi (Eds.), *The Princeton sourcebook in comparative literature*. Princeton & Oxford: Princeton University Press.

Wellek, R. (1970). *Discriminations: Further concepts of criticism*. New Haven: Yale University Press.

Yang, Z. H. (1989). Foreword. In D. Y. Yue & N. Wang (Eds.), *Transdisciplinary comparative literature studies*. Beijing: China Social Sciences Press.

Zhang, L. X. (1981). Qian Zhongshu on comparative literature and literary comparison. *Dushu, 1981*(10), 134–140.

12 "The Death of Comparative Literature" and Its Regeneration

12.1 "The Death of Comparative Literature" and the New Turn

In the late twentieth century, there appeared clamorous claims about the perceived death of comparative literature as a discipline, and yet recent years have seen some reversal in such claims. The previously announced death was mainly grounded on the observation that "[c]ross-cultural work in women's studies, in post-colonial theory, and in cultural studies has changed the face of literary studies generally" (Bassnett, 1993, p. 161), which denied the existence of comparative literature as it had been previously thought of. Moreover, overemphasis on the "prescriptiveness" of comparative literature, in other words, a methodology excessively delimiting the object of study, virtually extinguished its prospects. Markedly, Spivak, among other scholars, deemed globalization as the "imposition of the same values and system of exchange everywhere" and pointed out that the "earlier model, promoted by the colonial powers, of univocality" (Bassnett, 2006) had already ended up in failure.

In recent times, a number of comparatists have changed their views. Susan Bassnett (2006), perhaps the first to announce the death of comparative literature, concedes that the assertion "was as much about trying to raise the profile of translation studies as it was about declaring comparative literature to be defunct. Today, looking back at that proposition, it appears fundamentally flawed." Gayatri C. Spivak, author of *Death of a Discipline*, stresses that polyphony is at the core of post-colonialism and that if comparative literature were to "move beyond its Eurocentric origins" and "outside the global exchange flows determined by international business" (Bassnett, 2006), it would have to assume new development and form a new discipline.

To steer the regeneration and progress of comparative literature, a good many scholars have offered their constructive suggestions. Spivak (2003), for instance, argues that new comparative literature will need to "undermine and undo" the inclination of dominant cultures to "appropriate" those having just emerged as an independent culture (p. 100). This implies, as Bassnett (2006) summarizes it, that the regeneration requires it to "move beyond the parameters of Western literatures and societies and reposition itself within a planetary context." Haun Saussy (2006) points out that the future of

DOI: 10.4324/9781003356240-12

122 *"The Death of Comparative Literature" and Its Regeneration*

comparative literature calls for efforts to "reexamine the idea of 'literariness' and to reclaim literary studies that present new perspectives and the possibility of new insights" (p. 231). As is indicated by Oswald de Andrade, among other Brazilian writers and theorists, "the denial of univocality means assertion of the Brazilian polyphonic and pluricultural space and, ultimately, liberation from mental colonialism" (Bassnett, 2006). Then, we have Bassnett (2006), who writes:

> The future of comparative literature lies in jettisoning attempts to define the object of study in any prescriptive way and in focusing instead on the idea of literature, understood in the broadest possible sense, and in recognizing the inevitable interconnectedness that comes from literary transfer.

12.2 The Regeneration of the Discipline: A Chinese Idea for the Third Phase

The new turn in Western comparative literature substantially matches the reflections of Chinese comparatists regarding the third phase of the development of comparative literature. Years ago, the idea of such a third phase[1] was put forward, pointing out that China's comparative literature emerged in close relation to the transition the country was making toward modernity in both its society and literature. It sets off in a heterogeneous context, spanning Eastern and Western cultures, transcends regional boundaries and features a broader view of world literature. Cross-cultural and interdisciplinary literary research have long since been regarded as the fundamental nature and scope of comparative literature as a discipline, stressing a historical method and advocating in-depth literary research in spatial and temporal dimensions, or even beyond the boundaries of time and space. In fact, it is not possible that China, a developing country, could become a unilateral hegemonic power; rather, the country is determined to continue its efforts of forging multiculturalism and promoting the globalization of pluralism. China has been, and is set to continue, injecting new energy into inter-cultural literary research thanks to its lasting, continuous culture and rich cultural heritage. The country has also achieved its fame in its proactive and in-depth cultural exchanges with the outside world, especially with countries such as India, Japan and Persia, and, during the last century, its people have been enthusiastic learners of cultures and languages around the globe so that they learned much more about their foreign counterparts than people from other countries commonly did. As a result, Chinese comparative literature is able to spearhead the third phase of comparative literature through its inter-cultural literary research.

The article "Reflections on Comparative Literature in the Twenty-first Century" advances quite a few contentious issues worthy of reflection and discussion that are highlighted by its author and many others in the contemporary Western community of comparative literature. We can point, for example, to a seeming contradiction between Bassnett and Spivak. While

Spivak holds the aforementioned idea of "planetarity", Bassnett believes that traditional Western culture still makes its way right into contemporary writers' minds without exception. Bassnett (2006) opposes the possibility to "undermine and undo" European traditions and instead notes: "A fundamental question that comparative literature now needs to address concerns the role and status of the canonical and foundation texts that appear to be more highly valued outside Europe and North America." She accuses Spivak's proposal of being too "politicized", reminding that crucial issues in contemporary comparative literature are "as much esthetic as political" (Bassnett, 2006). The Chinese comparative literature perspective resists both the appropriation and the "undermining and undoing". Emergent and canonical cultures hold equal importance; the demise of any culture or literature is a great loss to humankind. Therefore, the mission of the scholars is to promote the dialogue between the two, where mutual recognition, complementarity and interaction arise. This communication is not to result in cultural "assimilation", or "fusion", or "merging"; rather, they turn out to be a perfect complement for each other, bringing their respective traits to new heights, thus fueling global multiculturalism. Such is what we anticipate for comparative literature: the third phase of its development.

Indeed, Spivak is not that confident of her proposition of comparative literature situating itself in a planetary context. As she puts it, the dying discipline is "a definitive future anteriority, a 'to come'-ness, a 'will have happened' quality" (Spivak, 2003, p. 6). In this way, Spivak denies its presence as a discipline. Yet, apparently, that is neither true nor logical, for all "things-becoming" can only be born of "things-become". With no such thing already existing, what could possibly give birth to anything yet to come into being or from what could anything regenerate? Divorced from the over two centuries' development of comparative literature, the possibility of a new comparative literature emerging is foreclosed: not appearing out of the void. Even Bassnett (2006), who made the first announcement of its kind that "comparative literature as a discipline has had its day", ends up admitting that comparative literature is flourishing beyond its birthplace, whereas the subject is in decline. Moreover, as is mentioned above, European classics and foundational works, in which Bassnett is especially interested, are much more highly appreciated outside Europe and North America than in countries with a history of colonialism and imperialism. Eventually, Bassnett (2006) comes to recognize comparative literature is attributed with "the existence of a solid field of study"; and any denial of this very existence is undoubtedly unwise.

In "Reflections on Comparative Literature in the Twenty-first Century", Bassnett provides quite a few pioneering ideas, which are worth referencing and are thought-provoking for comparatists in China. First of all, she again draws attention to Croce's call for "a complete explanation of the literary work, encompassed in all its relationships, disposed within the composite whole of universal literary history" and "seen in those connections and preparations that are its raison d'être" (Croce, 1973, p. 222). Bassnett (2006) goes on to explicate what comparative literature is supposed to study, such

124 *"The Death of Comparative Literature" and Its Regeneration*

being not only "the history of the moment of actual textual production", but also "the history of the reception of texts across time." Next, she points to, with special emphasis, the significance of readers to comparative literature, arguing that the opportunity of comparative literature making sense as a discipline and of advancing a genuinely innovative methodology for literary studies lies in highlighting the role of the reader. That is when "the act of comparing happens during the reading process itself, rather than being set up a priori by the delimitation of the selection of specific texts" (Bassnett, 2006) and thence when essential changes are caused to people's reading and the whole concept of comparison. Therefore, comparative literature lies in different scholars studying the same topic, and, more importantly, it exists in the reading process. Comparison in its true sense is to juxtapose multiple works, examining readers' reactions to the juxtaposed pieces and analyzing the texts in certain historical contexts. Bassnett goes on to repeat and highlight that the core issue of comparative literature is simultaneously both political and esthetic, and she attaches special significance to the return of comparative literature to the study of "literariness". Finally, she states that comparative literature researchers can benefit from the global discourse, where worldwide circulation networks are formed. Comparison can happen during the exchange and transformation within literary and philosophical movements and that, in the global information flow, the theory of cultural capital and its transmission is a valuable approach to comparison; and the list goes on.

To sum up, it has been a tradition of comparative literature in China, since the very beginning of its establishment about a century ago, to learn about and to learn from the instructive and original thoughts of communities from all over the world, which constitutes the fundamental reason underlying its robust development. During these one hundred years or so, comparative literature in China has embraced a positivistic approach, centered on dissemination and influence, which had been developed by the French School of comparative literature, and was also inspired by parallel and interdisciplinary studies upheld by the American School. In this way, the subject's development in China is based on former experience and overcomes its French and American counterparts' parochiality of being Eurocentric; hence, by sticking to an inter-cultural and interdisciplinary approach, it is truly committed to the exchange between Eastern and Western literature and scholarship and joins comparative literature worldwide in constructing the third phase of the discipline.

Note

1 The third phase refers to a new stage after the French and American Schools and in the era of globalization. See: Yue, D. Y. (2005). On the third phase of the development of comparative literature. *Journal of Social Sciences, 2009*(9), 170–175.

References

Bassnett, S. (1993). *Comparative literature: A critical introduction*. Oxford: Blackwell Publishers.

Bassnett, S. (2006). Reflections on comparative literature in the twenty-first century. *Comparative Critical Studies*, *3*(1–2), 3–11.

Croce, B. (1973). Comparative literature. In H. J. Schultz & P. H. Rhein (Eds.), *Comparative literature: The early years*. Chapel Hill: University of North Carolina Press.

Saussy, H. (Ed.). (2006). *Comparative literature in an age of globalization*. Baltimore, MD: Johns Hopkins University Press.

Spivak, G. C. (2003). *Death of a discipline*. New York: Columbia University Press.

13 The Beginning and Early Development of Comparative Literature in China from 1900 to 1910

Comparative literature in China is neither a branch of European or American comparative literature nor a subject born in college classrooms as in the case in Europe and the United States. In June 1987, Yang Zhouhan, professor of English at Peking University and the first president of the Chinese Comparative Literature Association (CCLA), delivered a fascinating lecture on "The Past and Present of Chinese Comparative Literature" at the annual conference of the Japanese Comparative Literature Association (JCLA) in Kyoto. This was a significant debut in the international community of the emerging Chinese comparative literature. Yang (1990) highlighted two characteristics of the origin of comparative literature in China, stating:

> I examined Chinese and Western comparative literature as to the differences in their origin. Western comparative literature came into being in schools, whereas in China it has been closely connected with political and social reform movements as an integral part of those activities.
>
> (p. 5)

Yang also identified another starting point of comparative literature in China as the intention to interpret Chinese literature and culture by way of imported theories from the West. According to Yang, a stronger historical awareness and the desire to find the underlying cause of everything are salient features of the Chinese culture and the minds of Chinese scholars. "This inherited cultural influence determines that where any impact of foreign literature on Chinese literature is seen, or vice versa, people are prone to probe into the root causes" (Yang, 1990, p. 7).

Overall, from Yang's perspective, comparative literature in China, an indigenous product of the country, rose from the nation's demands for its understanding and the growth of its own literary development. Chinese comparative literature is a result of the contact between Chinese and Western cultures and China's economic, political, social and cultural development. The subject's birth in China is inseparable from the aspiration to rejuvenate the nation and the ambition to renew and develop its literature. It started from introducing foreign literature and strived for a rediscovery of the self in such a context, seeking a new path for development. Meanwhile, it is worthy

DOI: 10.4324/9781003356240-13

to note that comparative literature in China is fundamentally rooted in Chinese society and time-honored Chinese literary traditions.

13.1 Emerging from the Study and Translation of Novels

At the start of the twentieth century, Chinese intellectuals were deeply aware of the necessity of expanding their vision, maintaining a world-oriented view and learning from the cultures of other nations. While there was the practical need of arousing the masses, literature, fiction in particular, drew unprecedented attention. Pioneering intellectuals at that time reached a consensus that "to renew the people of a nation, one must first renew its fiction." Yan Fu (1901) pointedly remarked after the failure of the Wuxu Reform (1898) that as long as the people were not enlightened, neither the conservative nor the reformist approach would work and that a significant step towards the people's enlightenment was to make them acquire a knowledge of both China and the West, such that "the number of people with a thorough and unbiased understanding of China and the West went up every day" (pp. 524–526). Hence he took translation as his sole undertaking, neglecting other intellectual pursuits. In 1897, when Yan established the *National News* in Tianjin, he co-authored an important essay with Xia Zengyou titled "Announcement of Our Intention in Publishing Fiction Supplements for *National News*", in which they stated that European countries, the United States and Japan all became civilized by drawing on the lessons learned from fiction. At that point, Kang Youwei (1958) made an investigation into publications in Shanghai and wrote a poem:

> Touring Shanghai I shuttle in and out of bookshops.
> And among all genres, which is the most popular?
> Eclipsed are classics and history by eight-legged essays,
> And eight-legged essays by fiction.
> Folk music goes on all day and night, while
> Classical melodies are nowhere to be heard.
> Man's natural preferences are never swayed by the sovereign.
>
> (pp. 226–227)

Kang composed the poem upon hearing of the intention of his friend Qiu Shuyuan (Singaporean journalist and poet) to write a novel on political reforms, thus encouraging Qui in this practice. Viewed from this perspective, it is apparent that Kang also attached importance to using fiction in enlightening the people. Liang Qichao had expounded such a view in a keen manner. In 1898, Liang explained, in "Preface to the Publication of Political Novels in Translation", first published in the periodical *Qingyi Bao* (*Upright Discussion Newspaper*), that people were naturally afraid of solemnity and fond of pleasantry and therefore not at ease while trying to sit properly when listening to classical music but obsessed with folk music; such was indeed common, even for the sages (Liang, 1989, p. 34). He quoted Kang Youwei as saying:

128   *Comparative Literature in China from 1900 to 1910*

> Those who can read may not read classics but would invariably read fiction. Therefore, where classics fail, fiction can be used to instruct the people; where official histories fail, fiction can help them reach the people; where wise sayings fail, fiction can spread wisdom; where laws fail, fiction can encourage compliance.
>
> (Ibid., p. 34)

Liang (1996) concluded that if "one intends to renovate the people of a nation, one must first renovate its fiction" and he asserted that the same went for the renovation of a nation's morality, religion, politics, social customs, learning and art, and even the people's minds and national character (p. 74). He attributed this to the incredible power of fiction to rein the human mind. From this point of view, Liang (1989) paid special attention to the translation of fiction and noted:

> As reform came together in European countries, men of letters, the erudite and aspirants always conveyed their personal experiences, their ambitions and their political arguments in fiction... Upon each publication, the public opinion nationwide would change. Political fiction has been a crucial contributing factor to the political development in countries including the United States, Britain, Germany, France, Austria, Italy and Japan.
>
> (p. 34)

Liang then made an allusion to a British scholar (whose name was not mentioned) and affirmed his view of regarding fiction as the soul of a people. To fulfill this solemn task, traditional fiction was certainly not enough, which resulted in an indispensable need to introduce new fiction from the West, especially political fiction. Thus, it is easily seen that fiction translation sprang up in close relation to the historical demands of rejuvenating the nation, enlightening the people, and promoting a more cultivated nation.

In 1903, Xia Zengyou (1863–1924) published a 5,000-word article titled "The Principle of Fiction" in the third issue of the periodical *Illustrated Fiction* [*Xiu Xiang Xiao Shuo*], pointing out that fiction has a far broader scenario than painting, is flexible with the passage of time, and is more enticing than history books. In this sense, he stated, the pleasure of reading fiction can compare with the two basic human needs: food and sex. Xia then concluded that the reception of Western culture should give priority to Western fiction and that fiction is the one and only channel for cultural import.

Liang Qichao believed that Chinese literature had a glorious history wherein Mencius, known as the second sage and ranked only after Confucius, cited instances of the noble pursuing desires of the flesh; Qu Yuan composed odes praising beauties, wherein people voiced their opinion in a jocular way and expressed affection and loyalty in a worldly manner; these were all regarded as being more influential than solemn and outright remarks. Nevertheless, fiction failed to attain smooth development in China. Liang

(1989) further explained that although fiction had long been among the main businesses in ancient China, masterpieces were rare since the outstanding Yuchu novels[1] and that when referring to heroic stories, people invariably thought of *The Water Margin* and, with regard to romance, *A Dream of Red Mansions* (p. 34). He pointed out that Chinese fiction had been fettered by stereotypical practice and was unable to bear the same task as Western fiction. Thus, the development of Chinese literature in itself entailed a big leap and Western literature constituted a vital stimulus and reference for this change.

In another contribution, Wang Zhongqi (1880–1913), whose pseudonym was Tian Lusheng, emphasized the shortcomings of fiction at that point in both its creation and appreciation, which is reflected in his articles including "On Relationship between Fiction and Social Reform", "On the History of Chinese Fiction in All Dynasties", and "On Three Chinese Novels". In all of these works, Wang proposed to vitalize the country's fiction as a remedy for the people. In appealing for people's attention to Western fiction, Wang did not hold that fiction should be merely transplanted from the West to China; instead, they proposed that the traditions in Chinese fiction shall be examined and reviewed first of all. He pointed out that Chinese fiction had had a focus on lamenting political depression, chaotic society and no freedom of marriage and that typical Chinese fiction writers included Cao Xueqin (author of *A Dream of Red Mansions*), Shi Nai'an (author of *Outlaws of the Marsh*) and Wang Shizhen (thought to be the author of *The Golden Lotus*). Wang (1907) explicitly stated that this situation was in line with the trend of Western literature.

It was under such an abovementioned situation that the translation and introduction of foreign fiction proliferated in China. According to the *Hanfenlou Library Catalogue of New Books*, more than 600 translated fictions appeared in China between the Hundred Days' Reform (1898) and 1911 (Guan & Zhong, 1991). In 1908, Xu Nianci published "Tables of Fiction Works Published in 1907" in the literary periodical, *Forest of Fiction*, and reported that 80 translated fictions came out during that single year, among which 32 were translated from British books, 22 American, 9 French, 8 Japanese, 2 Russian, and 7 from other countries. During that decade, five major fiction magazines were launched successively: Liang Qichao's *New Fiction* (1902), Li Boyuan's *Illustrated Fiction* (1903), Chen Jinghan's (under his pen name of "Leng Xue") *New Fiction* (1904), Wu Jianren and Zhou Guisheng's *The All-Story Monthly* (1906), and Huang Moxi's (Huang Ren) *Forest of Fiction* (1907), all of which produced large quantities of translated works of fiction. At the same time, many notable translators emerged, with Lin Shu the most distinguished of them. Other translators included Su Manshu, who translated *Les Misérables* (1903–1904) and *Selected Poems by Byron*; Ma Junwu, who translated *The Sorrows of Young Werther*, *The Song of the Shirt* (by Thomas Hood), and the drama *William Tell* (by Friedrich Schiller); Shen Zufen, who translated *Robinson Crusoe*; and Wu Guangjian, who was the first to translate *The Three Musketeers* into vernacular Chinese. Each of these works attracted a wide readership.

130   *Comparative Literature in China from 1900 to 1910*

By its very nature, fiction translation is a cross-cultural activity making it an integral part of comparative literature. The translation of fiction and relevant studies during this period all started from the commonalities between Chinese and Western literature because, at that time, when there was nothing in common, there would be no point of translation, nor would there be any chance of convergence or cross-referencing between different cultures. People then believed that the most salient common grounds of Western and Chinese literature were that literature should serve to vitalize the nation, enlighten the people and foster a more cultivated population. In 1902, Liang Qichao (1996) pointed out that "this is true of human beings of all nationalities and not just the Chinese alone" (p. 78). In addition, Jin Songcen, a regular contributor to *New Fiction*, further proposed that literature was a common channel for Chinese and Western culture. He stated that human beings are born with emotions, which is the same for people all around the world, and people around the world all tend to express their emotions in literature so that while there had been enmity and objection between the East and West, men of letters had the responsibility to bridge their common emotions through fiction (Jin, 1997, pp. 170–172). Xia Zengyou and others also examined specifically the commonality of human beings. Xia co-authored with Yan Fu in writing "Announcement of Our Intention in Publishing Fiction Supplements for *National News*", which regards China as a part of the world and sets up discussions from a global perspective. For instance, they observed:

> No matter in Asia, Europe, America or Africa during the Stone, Bronze or Iron Age, from China, Mongolia or the Cimmerian group, tracing their roots, we can always find commonality. The commonality is bestowed by nature and comes in the form of sarvathā-jñāna (the wisdom of all entities). On such a foundation. all religions and philosophical schools, including Confucianism, Mohism, Buddhism, Christianity and Islamism, have arisen, and monarchy, democracy and monarchical-democratic mixed governance are all established. Thus, both politics and philosophies are born out of commonality, not the other way around. So, what is held in common by all peoples? One commonality should be heroic spirits and another, desires of the flesh.
>
> (Yan & Xia, 1981, p. 188)

This "commonality" is embodied in common themes and genres of literature.

Huang Ren (1869–1913, original given name Zhenyuan and alias Moxi), the author of *History of Chinese Literature*, also pointed out that all people share the same heart and reason.[2] He believed that despite the diverse customs of the East and West, there must be some points where the two converge; for instance, while Greek mythology and tales in *The Arabian Nights* may appear absurd to the Chinese, they were conceived in a similar manner to Chinese fantasy novels (Huang, 1908). He then reached his conclusion that since all human beings are at the same stage of evolution, they are not

Comparative Literature in China from 1900 to 1910   131

alien to each other in nature. As Huang put it, at that "same stage of evolution", people from different cultures create literary works that always have something in common with those belonging to a different culture: such a point was of great significance at the time when Huang lived. In sum, there are many remarks in the literary publications mentioned above that highlight the commonality of literatures of different cultures; these included, for example, "human feelings and sentiments are universal", "all lands exist in the same world", "all words in different languages convey the same meanings" and "fiction has no national boundaries".

In addition to plentiful discussion on the commonality in the contents of Chinese and Western literature, "unification of speech and writing", which makes sense for both Chinese and Western literature, became a core topic, for in translating Western literature, the first and foremost issue translators encountered was to tackle the language. In 1887, Huang Zunxian wrote, in *National Records of Japan*, that English and French literature assumed great development when their writers began to create works in their own vernaculars instead of the previously used Latin language and China should also reach such a unification of language used in both writing and speaking. Huang's view was manifested in his poem "Miscellaneous Feelings", which read: "Writing my views with my own hand, why should I be constrained by old-fashioned formats?" Liang Qichao also proposed that the key to the evolution of literature lay in the transformation of literature from being written in classical language to being written in vernacular language and that all countries inevitably followed such a developmental path for their literature. Such an insight is also an attempt to seek common patterns in different literatures.

In the discussion of fiction translation, most effort was devoted to examining the features or weaknesses in the development of Chinese literature by reference to Western fiction so that Chinese literature could make greater progress. One example of this is Zhou Guisheng, translation editor of *The All-Story Monthly*, who made plenty of such attempts in translating foreign works. In the translator's notes to the Chinese translation[3] of *Margot la Balafrée* (by Du Boisgobey), Zhou argued that Chinese fiction had a custom of starting with an introduction to the main characters before narration; or, some works had prologues, introductions, prefaces or forewords at the very beginning. It seemed that without such an opening the authors had no idea where to set about their writing. He further explained that French fiction needed no such props and compared it to steep peaks that rise abruptly and to firecrackers exploding from which sparks fly, which may seem like disorderly clusters, but, if observed closely, are actually rather organized. Lin Shu often committed to comparing Chinese and Western fiction in the forewords to his translations, reflecting on Chinese literature by reference to the originality of Western literature and thereby pointing out the shortcomings of Chinese literature. Liu compared Dickens' *The Old Curiosity Shop* with *A Dream of Red Mansions* in terms of their contents, and another Dickens' novel *David Copperfield* with *Outlaws of the Marsh* in terms of their

132 *Comparative Literature in China from 1900 to 1910*

structures. He observed the defects of Chinese literature based on the Western works he translated for the purpose of promoting the improvement of Chinese literature. From 1904, such comments were often seen in the "Miscellaneous Notes on Fiction" [Xiaoshuo conghua] column of the magazine *New Fiction*. For instance, Su Manshu remarked that Western fictions did not always have many characters and the narration was constantly focused on one or two people and, to the contrary, Chinese fictions invariably consisted of a multitude of characters and were devoted to presenting a social history (*Miscellaneous notes on fiction*, 1997, p. 88). He further noted that Chinese fiction tended to recount the past while Western fiction was more concerned with the present. An analysis of fiction was published under the pen name of Xia Ren, which explored Chinese fiction's "one shortcoming and three things well-done" and Western fiction's "three shortcomings and one advantage" (ibid., p. 92). Others argued for the superiority of Western fiction over Chinese fiction; for example, some compared reading Chinese fiction to visiting Western gardens, where upon entry, the whole scenery unfolded right before one's eyes; and reading Western fiction to visiting Chinese gardens, where, without touring the whole place, it was unlikely to fully appreciate its flavor (ibid., p. 101). Afterwards, Lv Simian (courtesy name Chengzhi) made a notable analysis of the difference between narrative modes of Chinese and Western fiction, stating:

> The narrative of fiction falls mainly into two categories: subjective and objective narration. Subjective narration is when the story is told through the lens of the main character and the author personally is that character... Western fiction mostly belongs to this category (fictional works translated during recent years mostly come under this type). Objective narration is when the narrator remains external to the story... Chinese fiction mainly fits into this category.
>
> (Ibid., p. 418)

Such divisive discussion on literature, though often half-baked and unavoidably biased, represents the practice of reflecting on the "self" by reference to "others", thereby recognizing the characteristics of the former that were unlikely to be seen merely through the "self" isolated from the outside world. This marked the beginning of comparative literature becoming one aspect of elucidatory research and the "self" and "other" cultures entering into "mutual recognition".

Translation stands at the frontier of cultural communication and mesology in traditional comparative literature has translation studies as its core. Translation studies in China have delivered rich theoretical results and practical experience; even within the context of translation surging throughout the world, China stands out among its counterparts. As early as 1894, Ma Jianzhong, who was well versed in several languages including English and French, proposed to establish a "translation academy" to train professional translators. His article "Proposal on Establishing a Translation Academy" highlighted the importance that translators shall develop a keen interest in the two languages and deliberate over every single word and sentence in those languages so as to make sense of their similarities and divergences by revealing the ideational origins of the languages. He also suggested examining different languages in terms of phonetics, language complexity, literary forms and causes of subtle differences in meanings embedded in the two languages, and trying to grasp their sentiments and tones. Ma (1960) put forward the requirement for "good translation" that the translated text shall be equivalent to the original text without deviating from the original meaning (p. 90). At the turn of the twentieth century, Yan Fu advanced "faithfulness, expressiveness, and elegance", later widely exalted as the three criteria of translation. It is worth noting that these three principles were not merely concluded from experience but derived from the profound traditional Chinese culture. Yan (1933) wrote: "*The Book of Changes* states that the first requisite of rhetoric is truthfulness; Confucius says that expressiveness is all that matters in language." (p. 51) He adds that "if one's language lacks grace, it won't go far. These three qualities then are the criterion of good writing and, I believe, of good translation too. Hence besides faithfulness and expressiveness I also aim at elegance" (Yan, 1933, p. 51) These three criteria are still chased by Chinese translators today, but remain fairly hard to achieve. During the early twentieth century, the effort of translators such as Yan Fu, Liang Qichao and even Lin Shu took the lead in understanding Western literary creations within the frame of Chinese culture, and was therefore of unique significance in comparing Chinese and Western cultures, tackling problems in the exchanges of the two cultures, and understanding their contradictions.

When discussing the contact between Chinese and Western cultures, the eminent Chinese scholar and translator Gu Hongming (in his time known as Ku Hung-ming) forever comes to mind. Gu's translation *The Discourses and Sayings of Confucius* was published by Kelly & Walsh (Shanghai) in 1898 with a subtitle of "A New Special Translation, Illustrated with Quotations from Goethe and Other Writers". Prof. Wei Maoping's 2004 book *On the History of German Literature Translation in China* has quite a few positive remarks in this regard. Gu's translation can be seen as a dialogue between Confucius and Goethe beyond time and space with Gu as the medium. Gu's attempt opened up a fresh outlook and was a demonstration of mutual affirmation and recognition between Chinese culture represented by Confucius and the German culture represented by Goethe. This was also a predecessor of the approaches Qian Zhongshu adopted in his book *Limited Views: Essays on Ideas and Letters*.

Fiction translation and studies during the first decade of the twentieth century, in other words, at the outset of comparative literature in China, were fruitful and admirable. Zheng Zhenduo published his endorsement of Lin Shu's historical achievements in his *Studies of Chinese Literature*, which was also a review and summary of the development of comparative literature at this stage. Zheng (1957) made three points when concluding Lin's contributions (pp. 1228–1229): Firstly, Chinese people's knowledge of the world had

134 *Comparative Literature in China from 1900 to 1910*

been quite shallow and limited. They had always thought that there was nothing in common between "them" and "us" and that "China" and the "West" had a huge gap between the two parties. It was not until Lin introduced over 150 Euro-American fictions that some intellectuals in China began to realize that "they" and "we" are all "humans" and to learn about "their" (Westerners') families, internal society and national characteristics. These intellectuals came to realize that "China" and the "West" were not absolutely disparate. Secondly, at that time, most intellectuals considered China inferior to other countries in only one aspect: political corruption. With regard to Chinese literature, it was regarded as the superb and most splendid of its kind and no Western works could ever exceed those of Sima Qian, Li Bai or Du Fu. Then, when Lin brought in a bunch of Western literary works and approved of Walter Scott, regarding him comparable with Sima Qian, people started to be aware that the West also had their own literature and their own writers Comparable to Chinese ones. Thirdly, Chinese literati always viewed fiction as the "lesser way" of learning and belittled fiction writers. When composing fictions, Chinese writers invariably used their pseudonyms, unwilling to reveal their real identity to their writers. Lin completely broke that conventional opinion and set about translating European fiction as a classical Chinese writer, claiming that their writers could equal masters in China, which was bold and adventurous. From then on, some Chinese men of letters professed to be fictionists and a trend of translating world literature began in the country. Zheng further stated that many people had been dedicated to fiction writing or translation during those two decades and attributed it to the influence of Lin Shu, as evidenced by Zhou Zuoren's preface to his "Dian Di" collection of translation, where he admitted that he was heavily influenced by Lin Shu in his earlier translation of fiction. As a matter of fact, not only fiction translators represented by Zhou Zuoren but also creators of fiction were under the effect of Lin Shu. Zheng concluded that the greatest merit of Lin Shu was to break through the stereotype of fiction and bring European writers such as Scott, Charles Dickens, Washington Irving, and Alexandre Dumas to the attention of Chinese people. Such was Lin Shu's accomplishments, which marked the initial contact, mutual recognition and interaction between Chinese and Western literature.

13.2 The Positioning of Comparative Literature in Time-Space Coordinates

It is safe to say that Wang Guowei's was at the forefront of bridging cultures and literatures, in the past and with present importance, in China and the West. Wang had been immensely fond of Chinese classics from a young age and he also gained an extensive knowledge of the West in terms of sociology, logic, psychology, philosophical theories and the history of philosophy, so that he became versed in both Chinese and Western learning throughout history. In 1902, Wang translated Japanese philosopher Genyoku Kuwaki's *Tetsugaku-gairon* (*Introduction to Philosophy*), which offered a systematic

Comparative Literature in China from 1900 to 1910   135

introduction to the fundamental theory and contents of Western philosophy. In the same year, his translation of renowned Japanese psychologist Yujiro Motora's *Rinrigaku* (*Ethics*) provided a comprehensive discussion over psychological and ethical issues concerning sentiments, such as "good and evil" and so forth, on the basis of modern psychology. In the following year, Wang translated *Outline of the History of Ethics* by Henry Sidgwick, professor at the University of Cambridge, which enabled him to learn at the beginning of his academic career how to transcend the previous contention over "new" and "old" or "Chinese" and "Western". Therefore, Wang managed to explore life and society in the sense that China and the West, as well as the present and the past, are interlinked and by conducting comparative studies, researched how to analyze the history and status quo of Chinese culture by incorporating new ideas imported from the West. He mentioned at a very early point that learning shall not be segmented as "new" and "old" or "Chinese" and "Western" and provided his reasons for this claim (Wang, 2011, pp. 110–111). As to the time-based classification, Wang explained that a truth-seeking spirit is essential in perceiving and understanding the world and thus undiscriminating ancient worship is not desirable since the great minds may also be faulty in their sayings and conducts; similarly, indiscriminate disdain for anything old would make little sense in that everything has its past causes and future effects. Regarding the national boundaries of learning, Wang (1997d) writes, "Intelligence, everyone is endowed with, and unsolved problems about the universe and life, everyone encounters" (p. 115). Therefore, whoever can solve part of such issues, regardless of nationality, is no different from any other as they each gratify and comfort people by offering fresh insights and dispelling doubts in a like manner. Wang (2011) goes on to propose:

> All learning falls in one category among the three: science, history and literature. What is being studied in China also has a place in the West, and vice versa; the difference lies in the scope and complexity of study.
>
> (p. 110)

Based on the aforementioned perception, Wang revealed that the peril in China was not that there was a bias between Chinese and Western learning but that there was no such thing that can be looked upon as learning. It is thus clear that Wang had been pursuing knowledge in time-space dimensions from the very beginning.

As for the relationship between the present and past or China and the West, Wang (2011) believed:

> Chinese learning and Western learning prosper and decline together. As a trend develops in either of them, it will give a push to the other party so that the two always boost each other. In today's world, talking about today's learning, we have not seen a single case where Western learning fails to grow while Chinese learning thrives alone, and vice versa.
>
> (p. 111)

136 *Comparative Literature in China from 1900 to 1910*

Furthermore, an urgent need at that point, which was around 1911, was to introduce things of the most practical use from Western learning. Wang (1997f) had published an article "Refutation of Doubts About Philosophy" in the journal *The World of Education* in 1903, stating: "Those who will raise Chinese philosophy to greater heights are bound to be those who are knowledgeable about Western philosophy" (p. 5). Since he considered a profound knowledge of Western philosophy as an inevitable course of prospering Chinese philosophy, in 1903, Wang (1903) included in the Humanities Curriculum he drafted, courses such as Comparative Linguistics and Comparative Mythology in addition to Chinese Literature, Foreign Literature, History of Chinese Philosophy, History of Western Philosophy and Sociology and Anthropology (p. 181). On the other hand, Wang also noted that the blending of Chinese and Western literature was not a simple task. He observed:

> It is also natural that Western thoughts cannot be imported into China all at once. Besides, Chinese people have a practical inclination instead of an interest in theoretical exploration; therefore, even though Western ideas are introduced to China now, they cannot persist in the country if they fail to be reconciled with inherent Chinese thoughts. The Tipitaka has been put on the shelf while the teachings advocated about a millennium ago during the Song Dynasty are still welcomed by officials nowadays. Such experience gives a hint of what will happen in the future.
>
> (Wang, 1997d, p. 115)

Thus, we can safely deem that the abovementioned "profound knowledge" shall go beyond mere understanding of the two objects or acceptance of the both, but, most importantly, shall be a blend of Chinese and Western thoughts. At that time, Wang laid special stress on having a comprehensive discussion on the long-standing issues in China by reference to Western theories. For instance, he successively published three influential articles: "Lun *Xing*" ("On Human Nature") in 1903, "Shi *Li*" ("Interpretation of *Li*") in 1904 and "Yuan *Ming*" ("On the Origin of *Ming*") in 1906. The three articles examine, respectively, the Chinese idea of the goodness and evil of human nature with Kantian epistemology, explored the etymological origin and semantic changes of the notion "*li*" in both China and the West (viewed from which Wang asserted that rationality was not conducive to "transforming evil into goodness") and used Arthur Schopenhauer's "freedom of the will" to explain that freedom is hard to achieve due to the various kinds of constraint people are subject to and to propose the concept of responsibility. It can be seen that Wang's contribution to Chinese philosophy and literature was all made on the basis of his managing to bridge China and the West, and the past and present.

It was on such a foundation that, for the first time, Wang explicitly affirmed in China the independent value of philosophy and art (more commonly discussed as aesthetics today). As he put it, in addition to works expressing aspirations or created as a means to a moral end, the philosophy and art intended to satisfy the pursuit of pure knowledge and subtle sentiment and to relieve life doubts and pains are the most honorable and sacred of their kind and are what China has been lacking in, which is much to be regretted (Wang, 1997c, p. 192). Chinese poetry has been dominated by reminiscing and meditating on history, expressing nostalgia and sentiments, and by gift poems; less is produced to raise questions in the spiritual dimension, and much less still to depict mental sufferings beyond worldly interests. Chinese opera and fiction tend to be expostulatory or exhortatory and, with such a purpose that denies defining them as pure art, they are undervalued as well. Non-pure art works had always been ill-treated with no one doing them justice so that fictionists, dramatists, painters, musicians and the like all belittled themselves as being insignificant people and the world treated them in the same way (Wang, 1997e, p. 120).

It was with great courage and wisdom that Wang went against the common consensus that had existed in China for over a thousand years, by exalting pure philosophy and art, things deemed useless in that age, as the most sacred, the most respectable and of the highest value to pursue for a lifetime. Without being fuelled by foreign imports, it is unthinkable that Wang would have been able to make such achievement. His going beyond conventional Chinese utilitarian aesthetics and social aesthetics can clearly be attributed to the blending of China and the West as well as a sense of innovation.

From this point on, Wang blazed the way for Chinese literary criticism grounded on the blending of China and the West, providing an entirely new mode of studying literature. His 1904 "Comments on *A Dream of Red Mansions*", 1906 "The Spirit of Qu Yuan's Literary Works" and 1910 *Renjian Cihua (Notes and Comments on Ci Poetry)* formed a prospectus for this new perspective of literary criticism.

Wang first noticed the shortcomings of Chinese literature during its comparison with Western literature. Upon reading and studying Western philosophy and literature, Wang came to believe that the demerit of Chinese literature lay in its over-emphasis on literature as tools for political cultivation or social reform, which was always dominated by "sublime words with profound meaning", sarcasm or words that are meant to have social functions, so that it ignored the independent nature of literature, which is not defined by any worldly interests but is somewhat like a "play". Wang (1997c) approved of Friedrich Schiller's theory of play, stating that, "Literature is an undertaking of human play. When their energy is surplus to the demands of competition to survive, they find vent in play" (p. 191). Literature should be independent of politics, economy, and the like; yet, it is not purposeless but rather is an end in itself. Literature should be devoted to inquiring into the soul, answering the fundamental question of what life is for, and helping people escape from the sufferings of life. In sum, Wang showed an explicit resonance with Kant's "purposiveness without a purpose", Schopenhauer's insight that wanting and desiring are at the root of life sufferings, and Schiller's theory of play. In the second chapter of his "Comments on *A Dream*

138 *Comparative Literature in China from 1900 to 1910*

of Red Mansions", he cited and translated Bürger's poem, which has the following lines:

> Ye men of lofty wisdom, say
> What happened to me then;
> Search out and tell me where, how, when,
> And why it happened thus.

Some twentieth-century scholars, such as Daniel Bell (1919–2011), observe that primordial questions (existential questions) "confront all men in all times and places" and "derive from the finiteness of the human condition and the tensions generated by the aspiration, constantly, to reach *beyond*" (Bell, 1976, p. 166). Wang believed that this was also the fundamental question that was advanced by traditional Chinese culture. He quoted Lao Tzu and Chuang Tzu respectively as saying: "Mankind's great misfortune is that they have a (physical) body" and "The great clod burdens me with form and labors me with life." Wang (1997b) then went on to state that life had always been accompanied by worry and toil (p. 65). Wang followed his customary approach, setting out his discussion on long-standing problems in China and on the "greater desires"[4] of life and he deemed the primary responsibility of literature to be the addressing of such questions. As Wang saw it, *A Dream of Red Mansions* is a magnificent piece of work inasmuch as it responds to these fundamental questions and accordingly makes inquiries into the soul in search of liberation. Among European literature around his time, Wang applauded Goethe's *Faust* as the best of all, praising the ingenuity and sophistication in depicting Faust's sufferings and his struggles out of such pains. He further compared *A Dream of Red Mansions* to *Faust*, particularly comparing Jia Baoyu to Faust, the former story giving an account of Baoyu caught in entanglements and trying to thread his way out. In Wang's view, Baoyu suffers far more profound pain than Faust in that "Faust suffers what geniuses suffer while Baoyu suffers what everyone suffers. Baoyu's pain reaches exceptionally deep into the root of human nature and represents an especially keen eagerness for seeking salvation" (Wang, 1997b, p. 72).

How, then, can people get liberated? Wang classified the approach into two kinds: liberation for ordinary people and liberation for the extraordinary. Common people suffer from their painful experience and then seek to bring it to an end. For example, in the novel *A Dream of Red Mansions*, a few characters commit suicide, by jumping into a well, hitting a wall, or stabbing themselves. As a matter of fact, when people realize that life and sufferings are inseparable and yearn to let go of their worldly desires, they should realize such ends are not the real liberation that people should be seeking. In the novel, only Jia Baoyu, Jia Xichun (cousin of Jia Baoyu) and Zijuan (maid of Lin Daiyu) obtain true liberation in that only these three characters' suffering are derived from their awareness that desire is at the root of all sufferings. Meanwhile, Xichun and Zijuan are not the same as Baoyu: the suffering of the former two lies within themselves while Baoyu is subject to exceptional

Comparative Literature in China from 1900 to 1910 139

pains. Xichun and Zijuan find their desires becoming more acute because they fail to satisfy their desires and, in turn, it becomes even harder to have them satisfied. Trapped in such a cycle, they are finally so frustrated that they become awakened and then choose to bring their predestined labor to a close (by either suicide or tonsure). In contrast, Baoyu is in practice "the extraordinary"; one who is exceptionally insightful and able to see the essence of life and the universe, realizing that life and suffering always go together and thus intent on casting off his worldly desires in order to seek liberation. Such liberation is artistic, sentimental and splendid ("the beauty", as Goethe defined, "What in life doth only grieve us, that in art we gladly see."). In the light of such a difference, the protagonist of the novel is Baoyu, but not Xichun or Zijuan. Considering liberation, as Wang put it, *A Dream of Red Mansions* differs from *The Peach Blossom Fan* (a grand historical play set in the late Ming dynasty) in terms of its artistic value. According to Wang, among Chinese literature, only the above two works are embodied with the sentiment of world-weariness and pursuit of liberation; yet the "liberation" in the latter is not liberation in any true sense: it is "liberation" imposed by others (while that in the former is "liberation" under people's own aspirations). Moreover, Wang added, the author of *The Peach Blossom Fan* plotted the story of the two main characters to lament the previous dynasty but not to tell life stories, and, therefore, it is a political, national and historical piece of work (while *A Dream of Red Mansions* is philosophical, universal and literary). Thus, *A Dream of Red Mansions* stands as an important work, although it runs counter to what Chinese people commonly hold: the national optimism represented by the two derivative works *Southern Peach Blossom Fan* and *Return A Dream of Red Mansions*. Wang (1997b) then concluded, "Contrary to all comedies, *A Dream of Red Mansions* is a completely tragic piece" (pp. 73–74).

In brief, tragedy occurs when people become aware that pain is inevitable, then seek to be liberated, going through all kinds of hardships and sufferings, but finally fail to find the way out. Wang maintained that only when the writing reached such a dimension could it produce true literature. Wang's vision of literary criticism is something that traditional Chinese literature in itself is not likely to generate. Since *A Dream of Red Mansions* was composed commentaries, odes, indexes, reviews, and textual research on the book have emerged in an endless stream; yet none have matched Wang's insights. Even Wang's avant-garde contemporaries failed to inquire into the soul, pursue disengagement, and touch upon the tragedy of worldly significance. Lin Shu (2015), for example, while recognizing *A Dream of Red Mansions* as Chinese fiction's culmination, only acclaimed its narration of "the changes of fortune and the vicissitudes of life, in a refined, meticulous style, with rich, varied colorings and a carefully worked-out overall plan" (p. 57). In addition, Xia Ren also extolled the work, saying, "As for Chinese novels, nothing could be more splendid than *A Dream of Red Mansions*." Nevertheless, Xia Ren (1997) attributed this novel to a political one, an ethical one, a social one, a philosophical one, and a moral one (p. 89). No one other than Wang Guowei managed to relate *A Dream of Red Mansions* to spiritual inquiry, pursuit of liberation and world tragedy.

140   *Comparative Literature in China from 1900 to 1910*

The reason why Wang could scale such heights was that he managed to treat the past and present, and China and the West as an integrated whole, and chose what to accept or reject according to his knowledge and demands as a Chinese person. Anyone able to settle some of these perplexities contributes to slaking people's appetite for knowledge and easing their sufferings arising from doubts, so, whether they be our fellows or not, they shall be regarded without distinction or partiality. With that perspective in his pursuit of solving problems about the universe and life, Wang constantly found illumination in Western theories. He stated that, from summer 1903 to winter 1904, he was immersed in Schopenhauer's works and he remarked, "What I was particularly gratified with is Schopenhauer's epistemology, which had been largely inspired by Kant's studies. As for his 'philosophy of life', it is also a great pleasure and relief to see Schopenhauer's perceptive observations and incisive critiques" (Wang, 1997a, p. 25). Wang saw *A Dream of Red Mansions* in the sense that it took the same foothold as Schopenhauer's theory. Nonetheless, he remained skeptical and critical about Schopenhauer, and even Kant. In his "Comments on *A Dream of Red Mansions*", Wang sensed that Schopenhauer's ideas were mostly born of his own temperaments and subjective experience but had little to do with objective knowledge. Thus, he raised a major doubt in the fourth chapter of the "Comments on *A Dream of Red Mansions*": Is true deliverance possible; and what about the objective world afterwards? Moreover, "the world has a limit but the life living on it doesn't; hence, among the infinite number of humans on this finite world, it is inevitable that some people cannot manage to accommodate themselves on this land" (Wang, 1997b, p. 80). Therefore, it is not realistic in the wishes of Buddha or Jesus for the nirvana or salvation for human beings at large. Wang was forthright in pointing out Schopenhauer's contradiction, stating:

> Schopenhauer's works are littered with classical allusions, but they are not theoretically grounded. After Buddha passed into Parinirvana and Jesus was crucified, what happened to the will to live of all flesh? And how about their sufferings? As I see it, there was no difference than before. Then, was Schopenhauer's contention grounded when he attributed everything to God? Or, was it only an assumption that denied all factual corroboration? If the latter is the case, whether Buddha or Jesus themselves had obtained liberation is unknowable.
>
> (Ibid., p. 80)

In Wang's article "Schopenhauer and Nietzsche", he further identified the root of this contradiction as the finiteness of human beings and the infinity of the universe. Wang (1997g) wrote:

> The will is beyond all material reality but the body has a limited physical frame; causality and space-time constraints are external shackles while the endless motivations and national morals constitute internal pressure on the will. The talents [Schopenhauer and Nietzsche] have exceptional

insights and will, are conscious of what others fail to be aware of, aspire for what common people do not dare to shoot for, but are also subject to the same shackles and pressure as others.

(pp. 92–93)

As such, Wang anchored himself to traditional Chinese culture, with an insight into both its weaknesses and strengths, and extensively absorbed from Western culture while having a profound knowledge of the contradictions between the two cultures. His great foresight and breadth of mind has made it possible for him to transcend time and space, thus contributing to the great turn in Chinese culture throughout the course of cultural development anchored both in the present and the past, and the East and the West. His approach is neither traditionally Chinese nor traditionally Western; especially in pursuing the "trueness" and the fundamental principles of literary criticism, leading to his achieving an unprecedented literary vision.

13.3 Know Thyself and Others, and Absorb the Best of the Present and the Past[5]

Lu Xun (1881–1936) lived at a time slightly later than Lin Shu and Wang Guowei. While he was involved in extensive social engagement, contradictions within the Chinese society were becoming sharper and more complex, and Western ideas of all kinds were flooding into China on a large scale and in a disorderly manner, the influence of which was both profound and complicated. While Wang Guowei was fully immersed in soulful pursuit of pure reflection and pure literature, it was impossible for Lu Xun, living in such a context, not to consider the future of the nation and especially the people. Lenin (1975) pointed out: "The Chinese Narodnik combines the ideology of militant democracy, firstly, with socialist dreams, then with hopes of China avoiding the capitalist path and of preventing capitalism" (p. 165). Also, Lu inevitably gave more regard to the fact that Western philosophy and aesthetics had a dimension that was negative and not fit for China's status quo, and, therefore, he laid greater stress on criticism and making condemnatory choices.

During his study in Japan, Lu was among the Chinese student group that possessed the fiercest revolutionary thoughts. He once recalled that period, commenting: "at the end of the Qing dynasty, revolutionary thoughts were vigorous in the minds of some young Chinese. Anyone who screamed for revenge and resistance would easily find echoes" (Lu, 2005c, pp. 233–234). The foothold of Lu's remarks on the past and present as well as China and the West was that China already had its intrinsic flaws and, during that time, was confronted with new drawbacks brought about by external exchanges, the two of which crisscrossed, expediting the country's fall (Lu, 2005d, p. 58). Out of his intense aspiration to change that situation, in his early years, Lu delved into Western culture and reflected on life and future. Having examined and compared several different cultures, Lu put forward the fundamental principle of "self-examination, knowing others, sound comparison, and self-consciousness".

142 *Comparative Literature in China from 1900 to 1910*

Lu's focuses were firstly on indigenous Africans and aboriginal Australians, the status quos of countries such as Spain and Portugal, and the Jews. He commented on the reigning doctrine of the time as being one of pursuing material wealth and constitutional democracy, stating (as cited in Yue, 2016, p. 18):

> If wealth is to be taken as the criterion for determining civilization, then what of the descendants of the Jews who have amassed so much wealth that none of the great merchants of Europe can compare with them: what has been the lot of their people? Are railroads and mines the mark of civilization? In the last fifty years, Africa and Australia have certainly witnessed an expansion in these industries, yet how have the indigenous cultures of these two continents fared? Is majority rule tantamount to civilization? Did not Spain and Portugal establish constitutions long ago? And what of the state of these nations at present? If you say material is the sole basis of culture, then will a display of advanced war machines and vast stores of grain suffice to give a nation sway over the rest of the world? If the inclinations of the majority are to be taken as the sole criterion for judging what one ought to and ought not to do, then if a man were to find himself living near a group of apes, would he be obliged to swing from trees and eat bananas?

Lu then came to ask: What kind of civilization did his time need most? As he saw it, all of the above contentions were merely "grasping at branches and picking up leaves" and were based on practices which were subject to constant alteration and thus deflection and which had become obsolete outside China. Lu reminded people of the danger they might involve themselves in if these thoughts were to be assimilated and overly exalted in China.

Lu identified the "superficial and imbalanced" elements in Western culture during the nineteenth century as materialism and majority rule, and he further explained the two notions and illustrated their consequences. According to Lu, materialism is the inclination that "in their rush to adopt the objective standards of the material world, people are ready to discard the subjective inner spiritual realm with no further thought whatsoever". He stated that its outcome would be:

> Spiritual values were corroded with each passing day and the popular mood verged on new depths of mediocrity and philistinism. In their rush to adopt the "objective" standards of the material world, people were ready to discard the subjective inner spiritual realm with no further thought whatsoever. This emphasizing on the exterior while abandoning the inner, grasping at material while discarding its spirit, the teeming masses' desire for material things that obscures all else, bled society white halted progress.

(Ibid., pp. 18–19)

Majority rule is when only what is practiced by the majority is regarded as correct while those who do not conform are without question wrong, and individual originality and personality are defied. Under such a circumstance, the majority turns to tyranny and rules minorities. Wang raised the important point that, while ancient empires were governed by one lone autocrat, the society at that time was experiencing an abrupt transfer of power to millions of shameless rascals, rendering the people into living in misery. He then queried the role majority rule can play in national prosperity. As Lu put it, Western civilization has reached the current stage of development not by conscious choice but through forces that lay outside voluntary control. China today, on the other hand, enjoys full freedom of choice to cater to its own demands. Wang Guowei remarked:

> It is material[ism] and majority [rule], and that theirs is an imbalanced path for development. Certain phenomena manifested themselves in the West as a result of historical conditions and were inevitable there, but to arbitrarily take these things and implement them in China is wrong.
>
> (Ibid., p. 19)

So, what can China extract from Western civilization? To answer this question, Lu, in his "On Imbalanced Cultural Development", gave a retrospect of the several centuries of the history of Western civilization, especially the history of ideas during the second half of the nineteenth century. He compared ideologists from different cultures, including Stirner, Schopenhauer and Nietzsche from Germany, Kierkegaard from Denmark and Ibsen from Norway. On this basis and with China's circumstances in view, Lu (1908) proposed: "We should repudiate the material and stress the development of the native intelligence of the human mind, relying on the individual and dismissing sheer numbers." He argued:

> These men would of necessity possess unwavering faith in their own principles and would never be swayed by the praise or the condemnation of society. If the world lauds them, they must not be taken in by its flattery; if it reviles them, they should not feel disheartened; if people wish to follow them, they should be allowed to do so, but if instead laughter and mockery are hurled at them in order to isolate them from others, they must not fear that either. The possibility of bringing light into our gloom and darkness, and striking the spark that can illuminate the inner-souls of our compatriots all hang on this. When each person realizes his or her own identity and no longer merely drifts with the tide, this will enable China to stand on her own feet. As the situation exists today, the citizens of old and vanquished states that were formerly ignored or held in contempt by our men of ambition have all entered a state of self-awareness. They can speak from the depth of their hearts in clear and sonorous tones with their spirits running high and will, in time, no longer be subjugated through the powers of force and deception.
>
> (Lu, 2011)

144 *Comparative Literature in China from 1900 to 1910*

It is manifested that, although Lu was comparing the philosophical positions of ideologists from various cultures, he reached his own conclusion. Lu was committed to self-examination, knowing others, and making comparison with the sole aim to awaken the self-awareness of the populace and arouse their innate creativity that was still latent, thereby enabling China to stand on its own feet in the family of nations.

Lu not only weighed Western cultures based on comparison, but also made critical choices according to China's practicalities, and even brought about alterations to them. During his stay in Japan, Lu was most significantly influenced by the theory of evolution and absorbed Nietzsche's views most of all; however, he adopted a rigorous critical attitude towards both.

The theory of evolution once offered Lu a relatively thorough concept of development, which convinced him that everything is under constant change, which, though extremely complex, is always tending to be upward and progressive. Applying this evolutionary point of view to the analysis of social history, Lu could agree with neither those who had a bigoted belief in the ancients nor those who despised everything ancient. He stated:

> It is not without precedent for the past to triumph over the present in terms of creative imagination, while knowledge acquired and generalized, which is doomed to be tested, must progress with the times. Thus, what our predecessors failed to perceive is no shame to future generations, nor is it something to shun.
>
> (Lu, 2005a, p. 26)

This means that everything develops in several historical stages, evolving form a lower to a more advanced level. Things set to arise but not yet existing are constantly coming up; old and decayed things are constantly declining. To think that everything "has already existed in the past" is wrong, and so is to deny history. When being evaluated, everything must be examined in the context of a particular historical stage. Lu mostly accepted the positive aspect of the theory of evolution, which played a role in the development of his thoughts later on, while he remained critical of its negative aspect because the social environment and status he was in determined that he could never identify with Social Darwinism. Supposing that Social Darwinism upholds "the law of the jungle" to suppress the "inferior" or to devour the "weak", Lu took an entirely contrary position, aiming to use the same principle to motivate the "inferior" to catch up with the "superior" and to turn the "weak" to the "strong". He believed that weak states should strengthen themselves. Lu (2011) stated:

> If our own foundation is stable, and we have surplus strength, let us then act as the Polish general Bem did in supporting Hungary, or as the English poet Byron in aiding Greece, that is, to promote the vital cause of freedom and to topple oppression, so that the world will finally be rid of tyranny. We should offer aid and support to all nations in peril or

distress, starting with those which have been our friends and extending our aid throughout the world.

Lu Xun had always had deep sympathy for weak nations, sparing no effort to introduce the literature of Poland, Hungary, the Czech Republic, and other countries, as well as people's lives there. Meanwhile, he expressed intense hatred for the invasion of "weak" nations by the "strong" under the guise of the theory of evolution. He regarded the imperialists as "bestial patriots", unmasking them, and saying:

> Jingoists must ordinarily hail from large, strong nations—countries awesome and powerful enough to ride roughshod over the rest of the world. For this reason, jingoists show respect for their own countries alone and look disdainfully upon others. Seizing upon the doctrine of the "survival of the fittest," they attack the weak and small in order to realize their own desires. They will know no satisfaction until they have taken over the entire globe and made all other races their subjects.
>
> (Lu, 2011)

Therefore, while Lu accepted the theory of evolution, he refuted it as a guise and shield for imperialist invasion. This contention was very much in line with his patriotic anti-imperialist position at that time.

Lu took a similar attitude towards Nietzsche. When Lu was studying in Japan, Nietzsche's thoughts and the philosophy of will were prevailing the Japanese academic circle (Guo, 1959, p. 535). Among the abovementioned great philosophers Lu had investigated, Nietzsche's criticism of capitalist civilization and persistent pursuit of "innovation" soon attracted Lu's attention, and the insightful philosopher Nietzsche, who spotted the superficial and imbalanced side of modern civilization, was the one to whom Lu Xun devoted most of his discussion. In "On Imbalanced Cultural Development", Lu (2005d) mentioned Nietzsche and his *Thus Spoke Zarathustra*, conveying Zarathustra's idea regarding the present world:

> When I travelled back to see the present, in front of me is the "land of education", a society full of colors. What I saw was a community lacking in solid, established beliefs, a place where the mass did not have a pioneering attitude towards knowledge. How can I possibly stay in such a land?[6]
>
> (p. 50)

"Lacking in solid, established beliefs" suggests mere emphasis on material possessions with no spiritual conviction, while that "the mass did not have a pioneering attitude" infers people simply go with the flow and have no originality. Lu Xun took these sentences as his basis for concluding the shortcomings of nineteen-century civilization as being "materialism" and "majority rule". Notably, upon receiving Nietzsche's thoughts, Lu took them as a weapon to save his own nation from decline. The conundrum he was confronted with was primarily about the liberation of the Chinese nation that he himself belonged to from the shadow of imperialism and feudalism. Nietzsche, on the other hand, born in a powerful capitalist nation during its transition toward monopolistic imperialism, was first and foremost concerned about how to curb the rising tide of the mass revolutionary movement. Hence, while Lu echoed Nietzsche, with the same appeals and some of the same forms of thoughts, his purpose and thus the actions he proposed differed from Nietzsche. For instance, Lu aimed at the grand awakening of the collectivity in his advocacy of "respecting individuality" (*zun gexing*), intending to break the commotion where all the mindless people were active in making themselves heard yet without their own judgment and to see to it that everyone would have an individual identity: being able to think for themselves and retaining originality. In addition, he advocated "engendering spirit" (*zhang jingshen*), which embodied his expectation that the superior descendants of the ancient land, with their unyielding willpower, would manage to open up for themselves a way out against the headwinds. Lu believed that, such an undertaking accomplished, the whole nation would be able to smash through the darkness and silence like first flowers blooming at the advent of spring and like the day dawning with the end of night.

All the above clearly indicates that Lu's pursuit was fundamentally for the dawning of the nation; in other words, the "grand awakening of the collectivity". He deemed that only in this way could this loosely bound country develop into a coherent whole united by its people, which Lu termed a "country of people". He was convinced that once such a "country of people" was established, it would be an unprecedentedly mighty power standing out in the world (Lu, 2005e, pp. 25, 57). This was the youthful Lu's highest ideal. It can be seen that Lu accepted Nietzsche's Superman doctrine and shared the same belief as Nietzsche's: "Only with the appearance of a Superman can the world be governed ideally. If this is not possible, then we should entrust governance to the most outstanding of our luminaries", and "rather than force the enlightened and wise to trail after the common and mediocre, would it not be better to disregard the masses and place our hopes instead upon the enlightened and wise?" (as cited in Yue, 2016, p. 162). However, as Lu sees it, the Superman and the enlightened and wise were those who bore the mission to awaken mass consciousness. This is an idea fundamentally different from Nietzsche's ideal of striving to cement the control by the tiny minority over the vast majority of the population. Long before Lu had accused Nietzsche's theory of being full of contradictions, Lu picked out its merits and by absorbing and reconstructing them, he enriched and elaborated his own ideas, for example, in his early years, Lu took Nietzsche's new idealism and voluntarism as his ideal, yet, in contrast to Nietzsche, he had intended to exclude China from the defects of capitalism, aiming instead at rebuilding the national character and, through self-empowerment, saving the nation from subjugation.

From the above it can be concluded that whether it from the theory of evolution or Nietzsche's ideology, Lu fully embodied the precious spirit of both criticizing and reforming Western thought in light of China's actual situation and needs. His ultimate ideal was "to neither lag behind the outside world in the trend of thoughts nor discard our inherent national qualities: extracting from the present and restoring the ancient, so as to establish new principles" (Lu, 2005d, p. 56). Such was Lu's pursuit in his cultural and literary comparison.

Unlike Wang Guowei, who focused more on spiritual inquiry, Lu Xun concentrated on the more immediate matter of awakening the populace, therefore, they had different attitudes toward literature in many ways. In this regard, Lu provided his answer to the question, "what is art":

> All human beings are capable of two things: to receive and to create. For the former, anyone who is not intellectually disabled will appreciate and be moved by such scenes as the sun rising over the sea or a blade of green grass teeming with life. With those scenes firstly received and emotions provoked, they may then be represented in certain art forms by certain observers; such is the creation part. Therefore, underlying art are perceptions, without which art would not be possible. Yet, natural objects unfolding before people's eyes are not necessarily perfect, as flowers may have withered and forests be barren, and thus they are always subject to deliberate alteration in artistic representation; such is the beautification process.
>
> (Lu, 2005b, p. 50)

Lu pointed out that, on the one hand, art was the reproduction of objective things and, on the other, only human emotional perception and creativity could render the reproduction possible. Therefore, Lu claimed that "there are three elements in art, namely things by nature, thought and beautification" and that "the artist could compose and beautify natural objects". In this way, he put "things by nature" in the primary position and thoughts that serve to beautify the former in the secondary position. Like his perception of art that reflected natural phenomena, Lu held the same opinion in the social field. Lu (2005d) stated:

> In poetry and novels, most of the protagonists are untamed. This is not a coincidence, where the writers are merely using their imagination, but rather a precursor to the emergence of new social trends, which are reflected in literature and art.
>
> (p. 51)

Such is Lu's view on the relationship between literature and society.

Based on this principle, Lu wrote "On the Power of Mara Poetry" and "On Imbalanced Cultural Development" in 1907, comparing and analyzing the unique characteristics of the development of a range of national literatures. He first noted that Indian, Hebrew, Iranian and Egyptian civilizations, among others, were all ancient cultural pillars "famous at the brink of history, and

148 *Comparative Literature in China from 1900 to 1910*

who fashioned the dawn of culture" but as they "lost [their] vigor and [their] culture shriveled, grand voices gradually ceased to issue from the minds of the nation" and political decline was brought about literary stagnation (Lu, 1996, p. 97). Lu also made a comparison between these ancient civilizations and Russia, which was once a great nation that sank into silence. "Russian silence; then stirring sound. Russia was like a child, and not a mute; an underground stream, not an old well" (ibid., p. 98). Consequently, "the early nineteenth century produced Gogol, who inspired his countrymen with imperceptible tear-stained grief" (ibid., p. 98). By comparing a range of cultures, Lu demonstrated the significance of literature, especially poetry, to national culture and spirit. Such a cross-cultural review of the relationship between literature and culture was a trailblazing idea in the course of the development of Chinese literature, marking the emergence of the intercultural and interdisciplinary approach to comparative literature.

The gist of "On the Power of Mara Poetry" was to offer a thorough examination of "those, among all the poets, who were committed to resistance, whose purpose was action but who were little loved by their age" (ibid. p. 99). Lu took Byron as the focal point of this work, laying special emphasis on his passion for freedom, his fight against violence and for independence, liberty and human dignity, and his dedication to the extermination of all false, hypocritical, and vulgar conventions. Meanwhile, Lu (2006) highlighted Byron's distinctive attitudes towards love and hatred, his commiseration with the weak, and his capacity as "a champion of strength who gave his enemies no quarter, yet he displayed sympathy toward them during the deprivations of captivity" (p. 93). As Lu concluded, Byron's poetry was characterized by being full of passion and possessing a lively spirit. Lu cited Byron's words: "I have written from the fullness of my mind, from passion, from impulse, from many motives" (Byron, 1982, p. 190) and commented (as cited in Yue, 2016, p. 21): "It becomes apparent how Byron's every word, every turn of phrase, are manifestations of his life's breath and spirit." Lu Xun argued that Shelley, also a poet of the "Satanic School", was likewise "a man of great imaginative faculties who gave unrelenting pursuit to his every ideal, never shirking or turning from his goals... an extraordinarily moral character, with ideals lofty as the clouds; surging, irrepressible passions" (ibid. p. 21). In his comparison, Lu revealed Shelley's dissimilarity with Byron in that he "ha[d] been familiar from boyhood with mountains and lakes and the sea, and the solitude of forests" (Shelley, 1839, p. 149) so that he "harmonized the rhythm of his heartstrings with the sounds of nature, enabling him to create a body of inimitable lyric compositions" (as cited in Yue, 2016, pp. 21–22). Lu also spotlighted Shelley's pursuit of the mystery of life and death. With Byron as the pivot, Lu also discussed other poets who dwelt on the topic of rebellion, and analyzed their respective differences. He offered insightful remarks on Pushkin and Mikhail Lermontov, the three Polish poets Mickiewicz, Slowacki and Krasińsk, and Hungary's Petőfi. This comparative analysis of grouping works with similar themes and similar spirits is one of the methods still used in comparative literature's thematology.

Comparative Literature in China from 1900 to 1910   149

In researching the "Mara School" represented by Byron and Shelley, Lu paid special attention to its dissemination and influence. He noted that Byron and Shelley

> took up the fight. With the power of a tidal wave, they smashed into the pillars of the ancien régime. The swell radiated to Russia, giving rise to Pushkin, a poet of the nation; to Poland, creating Mickiewicz, a poet of revenge; to Hungary, waking Petőfi, a poet of patriotism; their followers are too many to name.
>
> (Lu, 1996, p. 108)

Looking through a multitude of cultures, Lu discussed the spread and influence of the "Mara School" led by Byron and Shelley in a way whereby all cultures, from England to Russia, Poland and Hungary, were studied in the same breath, thus analyzing its origin and diffusion. Although, technically speaking, Lu's attempts cannot be termed empirical influence research, at least he adopted the methodology of influence research and delivered unprecedented achievements.

In sum, Lu firmly believed that "to praise the true greatness of your native land takes introspection and knowing others as awareness comes from careful comparison. Once awareness finds its voice, each sound strikes the soul, clear and articulate, unlike ordinary sounds" (ibid., p. 99). An ultimate approach to this belief is "to neither lag behind the outside world in trend of thoughts nor discard our inherent national qualities, extracting from the present and restoring the ancient, so as to establish new principles" (Lu, 2005d, p. 56). Be it his effort in interdisciplinary cultural and literary research, or cross-cultural comparative research, or research into reception and influence, Lu Xun's contribution in his early life was always unique, and he is rightly praised as a forerunner of China's comparative literature.

All the above early twentieth-century fiction translation and research, especially Wang Guowei, the pioneer of coalescing Chinese and Western culture and literature, and the young Lu Xun, fostered by the mutual cultural cross-influencing between Chinese and Western literature, is sufficient to demonstrate that China's comparative literature is not entirely innately pre-existing, nor is it imported from abroad, but, rather, it is a response to the demands of the development of Chinese literature itself.

Notes

1 Yu Chu (虞初) was the name of a man in the West Han Dynasty, known as the earliest ancestor of novelists in China. Later, "Yuchu novels" became a term generalizing classical Chinese novels written in such a style. The maturity of Yuchu novels was marked by the appearance of *Yu Chu Xin Zhi* (*A New Collection of Yuchu Novels*) compiled by Zhang Chao of the Qing Dynasty.
2 A similar notion was put forward by the English poet Matthew Arnold: "The same heart beats in every human breast."
3 The translation was published on *New Fiction*, 1903(8).

150 *Comparative Literature in China from 1900 to 1910*

4 As Mencius put it, desires conform to a ranking. In brief, the desires for bodily pleasure are lesser desires (小欲) and greater desires (大欲) concern mental aspirations.
5 See: Lu, X. (2005). On the power of Mara Poetry. In *Collected works of Lu Xun* (Vol. 1). Beijing: People's Literature Publishing House. p. 67; Lu, X. (2005). On imbalanced cultural development. In *Collected works of Lu Xun* (Vol. 1). Beijing: People's Literature Publishing House, p. 57.
6 See: Nietzsche, F. (2006). On the land of education. In K. Ameriks & D. M. Clarke (Eds.), *Thus spoke Zarathustra* (A. Del Caro, Trans.). New York: Cambridge University Press, pp. 93–95.

References

Bell, D. (1976). *The cultural contradictions of capitalism.* New York: Basic Books, Inc., Publishers.

Byron G. G. (1982). Byron to Murray, 6 April 1819. In L. A. Marchand (Ed.), *Lord Byron: Selected letters and journals.* Cambridge, MA: The Belknap Press of Harvard University Press.

Guan, L., & Zhong, X. P. (Eds.). (1991). *History of modern Chinese literature.* Beijing: The Publishing House of the China Literary Federation.

Guo, M. R. (1959). *Collected works of Guo Moruo* (Vol. 12). Beijing: People's Literature Publishing House.

Huang, R. (1908). Brief remarks on fiction. *Forest of Fiction, 1908*(9), 1–1.

Jin, S. C. (1997). On the relationship between love novels and new society. In P. Y. Chen & X. H. Xia (Eds.). *Materials on twentieth-century Chinese fiction* (Vol. 1). Beijing: Peking University Press.

Kang, Y. W. (1958). Hearing that Shuyuan plans to write a novel about the coup d'état, I'm writing this poem to spur him on. In W. Shu, et al. (Eds.), *Kang Youwei's poems and essays.* Beijing: People's Literature Publishing House.

Lenin, V. I. (1975). Democracy and Narodism in China. In *Lenin collected works* (Vol. 18). (S. Apresyan, Trans.). Moscow: Progress Publishers.

Liang, Q. C. (1989). Preface to the publication of political novels in translation. In *Collected works of Liang Qichao* (Vol. 3). Beijing: Zhonghua Book Company.

Liang, Q. C. (1996). On the relationship between fiction and the government of the people. In A. D. Kirk (Ed.), *Chinese literary thought: Writings on literature, 1893–1945.* Stanford: Stanford University Press.

Lin, S. (2015). Preface to the Chinese translation of *The old curiosity shop.* In Wang, Z. L. *Degrees of affinity studies in comparative literature and translation by Zuoliang Wang.* Heidelberg, New York, Dordrecht, London: Springer.

Lu, X. (1908). On imbalanced cultural development. In J. E. von Kowallis, (2013). Lu Xun's early essays and present-day China. *Studia Orientalia Slovaca II, 12*(1), 1301–1313.

Lu, X. (1996). On the power of Mara Poetry. In A. D. Kirk (Ed.), *Chinese Literary Thought: Writings on Literature, 1893–1945.* Stanford: Stanford University Press.

Lu, X. (2005a). Lessons from the history of science. In *Collected works of Lu Xun* (Vol. 1). Beijing: People's Literature Publishing House.

Lu, X. (2005b). Letter on the promulgation of the fine arts. In *Collected works of Lu Xun* (Vol. 8). Beijing: People's Literature Publishing House.

Lu, X. (2005c). Miscellaneous memories. In *Collected works of Lu Xun* (Vol. 1). Beijing: People's Literature Publishing House.

Lu, X. (2005d). On imbalanced cultural development. In *Collected works of Lu Xun* (Vol. 1). Beijing: People's Literature Publishing House.

Lu, X. (2005e). Toward a refutation of malevolent voices. In *Collected works of Lu Xun* (Vol. 1 & 8). Beijing: People's Literature Publishing House.

Lu, X. (2006). On the power of Mara Poetry. In P. G. Zarrow (Ed.), *Creating Chinese modernity: Knowledge and everyday life, 1900–1940*. New York: Peter Lang.

Lu, X. (2011). Toward a refutation of malevolent voices. (J. E. von Kowallis, Trans.). *Boundary 2, 38*(2), 27–65.

Ma, J. Z. (1960). *Words from the Shike Studio* (Vol. 4). Beijing: Zhonghua Book Company.

Miscellaneous notes on fiction. (1997). In P. Y. Chen & X. H. Xia (Eds.), *Materials on twentieth-century Chinese fiction* (Vol. 1). Beijing: Peking University Press.

Shelley, P. B. (1839). The revolt of Islam. In M. W. Shelley (Ed.), *The poetical works of Percy Bysshe Shelley*. London: Edward Moxon.

Wang, G. W. (1903). Some remarks on the "Imperial regulations for the faculties of classical learning and literature in the university". In G. W. Wang (Ed.), *Jing'an collection*. Shenyang: Liaoning Education Press.

Wang, G. W. (1997a). Author's preface. In G. W. Wang (Ed.), *Jing'an collection*. Shenyang: Liaoning Education Press.

Wang, G. W. (1997b). Comments on *A dream of red mansions*. In G. W. Wang. *Jing'an collection*. Shenyang: Liaoning Education Press.

Wang, G. W. (1997c). Incidental remarks on literature. In G. W. Wang. *Jing'an collection*. Shenyang: Liaoning Education Press.

Wang, G. W. (1997d). On recent years' scholarly circle. In G. W. Wang. *Jing'an collection*. Shenyang: Liaoning Education Press.

Wang, G. W. (1997e). On the bounden duty of philosophers and artists. In G. W. Wang. *Jing'an collection*. Shenyang: Liaoning Education Press.

Wang, G. W. (1997f). Refutation of doubts about philosophy. In G. M. Yao & Y. Wang (Eds.), *Collected works of Wang Guowei* (Vol. 3). Beijing: Chinese Literature and History Press.

Wang, G. W. (1997g). Schopenhauer and Nietzsche. In G. W. Wang. *Jing'an collection*. Shenyang: Liaoning Education Press.

Wang, G. W. (2011). Preface to *National studies serial*. In H. X. Xu (Ed.), *Selected works of Wang Guowei*. Shanghai: Shanghai Far East Publishers.

Wang, Z. L. (1907). On the history of Chinese fiction through dynasties. *The All-Story Monthly, 1907*(11), 12–19.

Xia, R. (1997). Miscellaneous notes on fiction. In P. Y. Chen & X. H. Xia (Eds.), *Materials on twentieth-century Chinese fiction* (Vol. 1). Beijing: Peking University Press.

Yan, F. (1901). To Zhang Yuanji. In S. Wang (Ed.), *Collected works of Yan Fu* (Vol. 3). Beijing: Zhonghua Book Company.

Yan, F. (1933). Foreword (to *Tian Yan Lun*, Chinese translation of *Evolution and Ethics*). In Wang, Z. L. (2015). *Degrees of affinity studies in comparative literature and translation by Zuoliang Wang*. Heidelberg, New York, Dordrecht, London: Springer.

Yan, F., & Xia, Z. Y. (1981). Announcement of our intention in publishing fiction supplements for *National news*. In *Selected works of modern Chinese literature* (Vol. 1). Beijing: People's Literature Publishing House.

Yang, Z. H. (1990). *The mirror and the jigsaw puzzle*. Beijing: China Social Sciences Press.

152 *Comparative Literature in China from 1900 to 1910*

Yue, D. Y. (2016). *China and the West at the crossroads* (S. Geng, & D. Dorrington, Trans.). Beijing: Foreign Language Teaching and Research Publishing Company, Limited & Singapore: Springer.

Zheng, Z. D. (1957). Mr. Lin Qinnan. In *Studies of Chinese literature* (Vol. III). Beijing: The Writers Publishing House.

14 Where to, Where from, and When
The Quest of Wang Guowei

14.1 Going Beyond Disputes Over the Old vs. the New and China vs. the West

Rooted and versed in classical Chinese studies and Western learning from the very beginning of his academic research, Wang Guowei (1877–1927) managed to identify social and existential issues from a perspective beyond the boundaries between the East and West, as well as between the past and present, especially in his attempts, in his comparative studies, to analyze the history and current status of China at that time through the lens of new thoughts emerging in the West. Wang summarized the mainstream discussion on learning to be dichotomizing the whole matter, the new versus the old, China versus the West, and the useful versus the useless, and went on to elucidate that there was in fact no such distinction as "new" and "old", "Chinese" and "Western", or "useful" and "useless" learning. He pointed out that scholars who held a biased viewpoint were mediocrities failing to touch the core of learning (Wang, 2011b, p. 109). Why is it that any learning is not "new" nor "old"? Wang explains that from a practical point of view, when looking at things or pursuing knowledge, one should always seek the truth and that not all of what the great minds say is trustworthy, nor is all what they do flawless, so we should refrain from worshiping everything in the past and from a historical point of view, all things have arisen from some earlier causes while their ripple effects appear in the future; thus, we should also refrain from despising everything in the past. And why is it that any learning is neither "Chinese" nor "Western"? Wang (1997e) remarks, "Intelligence, everyone is endowed with, and unsolved problems about the universe and life everyone encounters" (p. 115). If one can provide a solution to some of the problems, be they our compatriots or not, they shall not be treated differently, for either satisfies our thirst for knowledge and lessens the pain of having doubts in the same way. He goes on to say,

> All learning falls in one category among the three: science, history and literature. What is being studied in China also has a place in the West, and vice versa; the difference lies in the scope and complexity of study.
> (Wang, 2011b, p. 110)

DOI: 10.4324/9781003356240-14

154   *Where to, Where from, and When*

Viewed from the above, Wang comments that China should be concerned about a void of learning rather than an imbalance between Chinese and Western learning.

As for the relationship between the present and past or China and the West, Wang Guowei believed: Chinese learning and Western learning prosper and decline together. As a trend develops in either of them, it will give a push to the other party so that the two always boost each other. In today's world, talking about today's learning, we have not seen a single case where Western learning fails to grow while Chinese learning thrives alone, and vice versa (ibid., p. 111).

Furthermore, an urgent need at that time was to introduce those things of the most practical use from Western learning. Wang (1997g) published an article "Refutation of Doubts about Philosophy" in the journal *The World of Education* in 1903, stating: "Those who will raise Chinese philosophy to greater heights are bound to be those who are knowledgeable about Western philosophy" (p. 5). Since he considered a profound knowledge of Western philosophy as an inevitable prerequisite for prospering of prospering Chinese philosophy, in 1903, Wang Guowei (1903) included in the humanities curriculum he drafted courses such as Comparative Linguistics and Comparative Mythology in addition to Chinese Literature, Foreign Literature, History of Chinese Philosophy, History of Western Philosophy and Sociology and Anthropology (p. 181). On the other hand, Wang Guowei (1997e) also noted that the blending of Chinese and Western literature was not a simple task, and he observed:

> It is also natural that Western thoughts cannot be imported into China all at once. Besides, Chinese people have a practical inclination instead of an interest in theoretical exploration; therefore, even though Western ideas are introduced to China now, they cannot persist in the country if they fail to be reconciled with inherent Chinese thoughts. The Tipitaka has been put on the shelf while the teachings advocated about a millennium ago during the Song Dynasty are still welcomed by officials nowadays. Such experience gives a hint of what will happen in the future.
>
> (p. 115)

Thus, we can safely deem that the above-mentioned "profound knowledge" shall go beyond mere understanding of the two objects or acceptance of the both, but, most importantly, shall be a blend of Chinese and Western thoughts. At that time, Wang laid special stress on having a comprehensive discussion on the long-standing issues in China by reference to Western theories. For instance, he successively published three influential articles: "Lun *Xing*" ("On Human Nature") in 1903, "Shi *Li*" ("Interpretation of *Li*") in 1904 and "Yuan *Ming*" ("On the Origin of *Ming*") in 1906. These three articles examine, respectively, the Chinese idea of the goodness and evil of human nature with Kantian epistemology, explored the etymological origin and semantic changes of the notion "*li*" in both China and the West (viewed from which Wang asserted that rationality was not conducive to

Where to, Where from, and When 155

"transforming evil into goodness") and used Arthur Schopenhauer's "freedom of the will" to explain that freedom is hard to achieve due to the various kinds of constraint to which people are subject and to propose the concept of responsibility. It can be seen that Wang's contribution to Chinese philosophy and literature was all made based on his managing to bridge China and the West, and the past and present.

14.2 Chinese Literature in an Integrated, Inclusive Cultural Context

It can be said that Wang Guowei's greatest contribution is that he navigated a major turning point in Chinese literature through his studies, which were conducted within an integrated and inclusive context, this being a move away from the utilitarian and towards anti-utilitarianism. He first proposes that in Western cultures philosophy and art are believed to have the aim of pursuing truth. Philosophers unveil the truth and artists bring it out with representations of such truth. Since what they are after is immortal, their endeavors might not conform with, and may even be incompatible with, the interests of a certain period or within a certain nation, which manifests their sacredness exactly. China, conversely, lacks such a tradition of pursuing truth for no utilitarian purposes. Wang points out that moral and political philosophies are the most established in China. Even the emergence of metaphysics during the Zhou, Qin and Song dynasties was merely aimed to cement moral and political philosophies. Thus, almost all Chinese philosophers desire to have a say in politics, and the same goes for men of letters. Chinese poetry has been dominated by reminiscing and meditating on China's history, expressing nostalgia and sentiments and by gift poems; less is produced to raise questions in the spiritual dimension, and much less to depict mental sufferings beyond worldly interests. Chinese opera and fiction tend to be expostulatory or exhortatory and, with such a purpose that disqualifies them as pure art, they are undervalued. Non-pure artworks have always been ill-treated with no one doing them justice. To illustrate this view, Wang takes a few ancient Chinese intellectuals as examples.

The great poet Du Fu (712–770) expressed his ambitions with his poem:

> I thought that I would stand out as quite exceptional,
> and at once occupy some crucial position.
> I would make my lord greater than Yao or Shun,
> and cause our customs again to be pure.
>
> (Du, 2016, p. 51)

Similarly, Han Yu (786–824) advised intellectuals: Why not submit a memorial to the throne and give your talent full play to make the whole country prosper again?[1] Lu You (1125–1210) lamented: In loneliness and helplessness, I still wished to help with flood control.

Those poets, as Wang (1997f) writes, are acclaimed as immortals, and thus generations of poets have given the highest priority to the same themes such

156 *Where to, Where from, and When*

as loyalty, patriotism, enjoining good and forbidding evil (pp. 119–120). However, Wang believes that no philosophy in its true sense is centered on the interests of society and politics, and neither is literature. He labels literature oriented by politics, society or even morality as "literature for living"; conversely, literature aimed at fame or personal interests, or as a tool in competition, is regarded as "literature for ornament". As Wang puts it, such types are disqualified as true literature, for they are produced out of the will to live rather than for pure knowledge and subtle feelings, or the need to relieve life's doubts and pains. While "in affirming its will to life each living thing also naturally seeks its own well-being" (Schopenhauer, 2010, p. xxxvi), only human beings can share pure knowledge and subtle feelings to release themselves from life's doubts and pains. True litterateurs, therefore, shall be those who live their life for literature but who do not live a literature-bound life. Through Wang Guowei's creative endeavors, for the first time in history, a Chinese scholar reflected on China by way of Western cultures, affirming the independent values of Chinese philosophy and art in addition to his expressing aspirations and preaching his perspectives.

On this basis, Wang, with the cross-connected development of Chinese and Western cultures as his reference, was the first to highlight the pursuit after "the True" (*zhen*) in Chinese philosophy and aesthetics, based on which he proposed a few new concepts, including poetic state (*jingjie*), intuitive cognition and the states of being veiled (*ge*) and non-veiled (*buge*). Classical Chinese philosophy inclines to view the True as a spiritual pursuit rather than an essential entity. For example, as Confucianism puts it, "Sincerity is the way of Heaven. The attainment of sincerity is the way of men" (Confucius, 1971, p. 413). Sincerity, a form of the True, naturally exists but its actualization must be achieved by human beings. Similarly, Zhuangzi (286–369) regarded the True as purity and sincerity in their highest; without the two ideals people cannot be moved (Wang & Liu, 1987, p. 197). Yet, for Zhuangzi, the True is also an ever-present state subject to Heaven and is thus unchangeable. That is to say, the True proposed by both Confucianism and Daoism is objective (the unchangeable law of Heaven) and subjective (the purity and sincerity of humans) at the same time. With such thoughts as the foundation, Wang investigated the essence of the True through the core concepts he proposed within the realm of aesthetics, namely, the poetic state, intuitive cognition and the states of being veiled and non-veiled.

In Wang's definition, the True is the key to identifying the poetic state (*jingjie*) in that the state he refers to only exists when real scenery and objects are depicted and real feelings embodied. Then, the question becomes this: what is "the True"? According to Wang, the True has its meaning in two senses: true subjective emotions and true objective matters. He further summarizes it as the unification of subjectivity and objectivity. Though it originated in nature, the True of objective matters must be experienced and interpreted by poets and then combined with the poets' aesthetic ideals; thus, Wang sees the intuitive cognition in depicting objects and the expression and conveying of sentiments of poets as two unified and complementary sides. In

Wang's mind, having a poetic state epitomizes the True and, in turn, the True is manifested by intuitive cognition and the state of being non-veiled. The intuition therein means "aesthetic intuition" transcending any utilitarian intentions and unrestricted by any concepts, i.e., being non-veiled. Feng Youlan (1895–1990, known in his time as Fung Yu-lan) agreed that the true means being non-veiled and further explained, "What writers derive from their intuition is restricted by no concept or dogma, and when these things are expressed instantly without any deliberation or embellishment, such is the state of being non-veiled" (Feng, 1989, p. 197). In a nutshell, attaining a poetic state means being intuitive and non-veiled, and as such it represents the True.

The terms proposed by Wang, from the poetic state to intuitive cognition and to being non-veiled, all reveal his commitment to integrate the True of Heaven with the True of humans; two matters of great interest in traditional Chinese culture. Clearly, this exploration has been inspired by both Kant and Schopenhauer. Wang's "true scenery and objects" and "true emotions and feelings" fall within the True of ideas. In his article "Schopenhauer's Philosophy and Education Theory", Wang declares that what art displays is neither concepts nor certain objects, but rather ideas which unveil the whole picture consisting of certain objects; that which exists in nature and can be appreciated by human intuition. For instance, architecture, sculpture, painting, music, etc., are all presented in a way that they can be received either by eyes or ears. Poetry (as well as drama and novel alike), although resorting to conceptual manners to evoke readers' intuition, has its value completely in the attainment of intuitive cognition (Wang, 1997h, pp. 62–63). Wang (2011a) writes in his article "Confucius's Aesthetic Educationism":

> Beauty is independent of personal gains or losses. When appreciating beauty, people are unaware of any personal interests. German philosopher Kant said: the appreciation of the beautiful is "disinterested" in pleasure and Schopenhauer proposed the essence in appreciating the beautiful in two senses: (1) the object observed; not the thing *per se* but the form and way it is presented; (2) the consciousness of the spectator; not the "self" *per se* but the pure "self" void of any desire.
>
> (p. 251)

Presumably, Wang's discussion about the True of philosophy and aesthetics is rooted in such thoughts.

14.3 Wang Guowei's New Insights into Chinese Literary Criticism

Intended to oppose utilitarianism and seek truth, Wang Guowei devoted himself to the confluence of China and the West, forging a completely different path for Chinese literary criticism. His "Comments on *A Dream of Red Mansions*" (1904), "The Spirit of Qu Yuan's Literary Works" (1906), and *Renjian Cihua* (*Notes and Comments on Ci Poetry*) (1910) delineated the outline of his novel vision for literary criticism.

158 *Where to, Where from, and When*

Wang first noticed the shortcomings of Chinese literature under comparison with Western literature. He writes:

> How has the spiritual world of the Chinese people been? I wonder if the greatest literati of the Chinese nation are great enough to represent the spirit of the populace, just as Homer, Shakespeare and Goethe were. I cannot provide a definite answer. Why? Is it because China has no such great literati? Or because we fail to name them? It has to be one of the two reasons, and if the first one is true, China fails to equal the West in literature; and if it is the other case, China has given less prominence to literature compared with its Western counterparts. I am not sure about the former, but the latter is attested by factual situations and is the issue scholars concerned should not evade.
>
> (Wang, 1997c, p. 125)

Upon reading and studying Western philosophy and literature, Wang came to believe that the demerit of Chinese literature lay in its over-emphasis on literature as a tool for political cultivation or social reform, and which was always dominated by "sublime words with profound meaning", sarcasm or words that are meant to have social functions, so that it ignored the independent nature of literature which is not defined by any worldly interests but is somewhat like a "play". Wang (1997d) approved of Friedrich Schiller's theory of play, stating, "Literature is an undertaking of human play. When their energy is surplus to the demands for competition for survival, they find vent in play" (p. 191). He further illustrates this point of view. Children well clothed and fed and carefully sheltered by their parents have nothing to worry about for their survival; thus, their energy has nowhere to be devoted but play. Then, when they have to concern themselves with their living, the play is brought to a halt. Only those who are strong in spirit and free from living worries can preserve their nature of play for a lifetime. Yet grown-ups are no longer satisfied with childhood play, and will consequently resort to portraying what they see and expressing what they feel to let out the surplus energy. Therefore, if national culture hasn't yet developed to a certain stage, the emergence of literature is impossible; no one hustling and bustling for survival is qualified as a litterateur. In other words, literature should be independent of political and economic utilities but that is not to say that literature is purposeless, but rather it is an end in itself.

What is that "end" of literature? As Wang sees it, although literature is born out of play, it is not confined as such, but instead has a most solemn purpose; to inquire into the soul, to answer the fundamental question of what life is for, and to help people extricate from the sufferings of life. Wang (1997a) made an account of himself in the preface to his *Jing'an Collection*, describing himself to always have been weak and melancholy and confessing that life issues have always been lingering in his mind (p. 119). Those lingering questions about life can be concluded as "what life is for", along with the spiritual pain due to such questions being unsolved. Wang showed an explicit resonance with

Where to, Where from, and When 159

Kant's "purposiveness without a purpose", Schopenhauer's insight that wanting and desiring are at the root of life sufferings, and Schiller's theory of play. In the second chapter of his "Comments on *A Dream of Red Mansions*", he cited and translated Bürger's poem, which has the following lines:

> Ye men of lofty wisdom, say
> What happened to me then;
> Search out and tell me where, how, when,
> And why it happened thus.

"Where to" and "where from" are exactly the primordial questions proposed by Daniel Bell (1976), who believes that these questions "confront all men in all times and places" and are "derived from the finiteness of the human condition and the tensions generated by the aspiration, constantly, to reach beyond" (p. 166). Wang believes that the fundamental meaning of literature lies in answering such questions.

In Wang's view, *A Dream of Red Mansions* is a magnificent piece of work inasmuch as it responds to these questions and accordingly makes inquiries into the soul in search of liberation. He points out that the novel not only raises the question of "greater desires", but also attempts to provide a solution to it (Wang, 1997b, p. 70). Wang thinks that the question of "desire" is brought up at the beginning of the book. The origin of Jia Baoyu (the main character in the novel) demonstrates that all life sufferings derive from desire, as Baoyu was the only stone left by the goddess in mending the sky because of its deficiency and was then immersed in self-pity and grief. Wang writes:

> What is the essence of life? Nothing more than desire. Desire is the nature of life as being insatiable, and originates from the state of deficiency. Deficiency is painful... However, the desire of life never transcends life itself, while the nature of life is coupled with pain. Thus, desire, life and pain are indeed joined... *A Dream of Red Mansions* in fact reveals that life and pain are the consequences of one's own deeds and that liberation can only be achieved by way of one's own efforts.
>
> (Ibid., pp. 65, 66, 71)

The mission of art is to depict the pain of life and the approach to relief. Therefore, among European literature around his time, Wang applauded Goethe's *Faust* as the best of all, praising the ingenuity and sophistication in the depicting of Faust's sufferings and struggles out of such pains. He further compared *A Dream of Red Mansions* to *Faust*, particularly Jia Baoyu to Faust, since the former gives an account of Baoyu caught in entanglements and trying to thread his way out. In Wang's view, Baoyu suffers far more profound pain than Faust in that "Faust suffers what geniuses suffer while Baoyu suffers what everyone suffers. Baoyu's pain reaches exceptionally deep into the root of human nature and represents especially keen eagerness for seeking salvation" (ibid., p. 72).

160 *Where to, Where from, and When*

Then, how can people get liberated? Wang classified the approach into two kinds: liberation for ordinary people and liberation for the extraordinary. Common people suffer from their painful experience and then seek to bring it to an end. For example, in *A Dream of Red Mansions*, a few characters commit suicide, by jumping into a well, hitting the wall, or self-stabbing. As a matter of fact, such is not real liberation, which should be what people are after when they realize that life and sufferings are inseparable and yearn to let go of their worldly desires. In the novel, only Jia Baoyu, Jia Xichun (cousin of Jia Baoyu) and Zijuan (maid of Lin Daiyu's side) obtain true liberation in that only the sufferings of these three figures are derived from their awareness that desire is at the root of all sufferings. Meanwhile, Xichun and Zijuan are not the same as Baoyu: the suffering of the former two lies in themselves while Baoyu is subject to exceptional pains. Xichun and Zijuan have their desires becoming more acute because they fail to satisfy their desires and, in turn, it becomes even harder to get them satisfied. Trapped in such a cycle, they are finally so frustrated that they become awakened and then choose to bring their predestined labor to a close (by either suicide or tonsure). In contrast, Baoyu is in practice "the extraordinary" one, who is exceptionally insightful and able to see the essence of life and the universe, realizing that life and suffering always go together and thus intending to cast off his worldly desires so as to seek liberation. Such liberation is artistic, sentimental and splendid (the beauty as Goethe defined, "What in life doth only grieve us, that in art we gladly see."). In the light of such a difference, the protagonist of the novel is Baoyu, but not Xichun or Zijuan.

Considering liberation, as Wang put it, *A Dream of Red Mansions* differs from *The Peach Blossom Fan* (a grand historical play set in the late Ming dynasty) in terms of artistic value. According to Wang, among Chinese literature, only the above two works are embodied with the sentiment of world-weariness and pursuit of liberation; yet, the "liberation" in the latter is not liberation in true sense: it is "liberation" imposed by others (while that in the former is "liberation" under people's own aspirations). Moreover, Wang added, the author of *The Peach Blossom Fan* plotted the story of the two main characters to lament for the previous dynasty but not to tell life stories, and, therefore, it is a political, national and historical piece of work (while *A Dream of Red Mansions* is philosophical, universal and literary). Thus, *A Dream of Red Mansions* stands as an important work, although it runs counter to what Chinese people commonly hold: the national optimism represented by the two derivative works *Southern Peach Blossom Fan* and *Return A Dream of Red Mansions*. Wang then concluded, "Contrary to all comedies, *A Dream of Red Mansions* is a complete tragic piece" (ibid., pp. 73–74).

What is tragedy? Schopenhauer (2010) believes that "the true sense of tragedy is the deeper insight that the hero does not atone for his particular sins, but for original sin instead, i.e., the guilt of existence itself" (p. 281). He classifies tragedy into three categories (Schopenhauer. 2010, p. 254): the first type is caused by the "extraordinary wickedness of a character" and when the character touches the "extreme bounds of possibility", the second type takes place due to "blind fate" and the third type happens through "the mere attitude of the persons to one another through their relations". The last type is not triggered by any misadventure or wickedness of the character, but happens between normal characters in their normal positions relative to each other and it is exactly in such positions that the characters have been constantly forcing each other ahead towards tragedy. They force their tragedy knowingly but none have done anything wrong. Schopenhauer regards the third one more desirable than the former two in that it indicates the greatest misfortune is no exception in life but something that might happen naturally in all lives. He further explains:

> And if in both of the other categories of tragedy we catch sight of an appalling fate and horrific evil as powers that are indeed terrible but that threaten us only from a great distance so that we ourselves will probably escape them without being driven to renunciation, then this last genre shows us the sort of powers that destroy life and happiness and that can at any moment make their way towards us as well, where the greatest suffering is brought about by entanglements essentially the same as those assumed by our own fate, and through actions that we too might perhaps be capable of committing, so that we may not complain of injustice: then we shudder as we feel ourselves already in the middle of hell.
>
> (Ibid., p. 282)

Wang brings *A Dream of Red Mansions* under the third kind of tragedy and deems it tragedy in its highest extent (Wang, 1997b, p. 75).

"Comments on *A Dream of Red Mansions*" offers a conclusion:

> Then, is the significance of *A Dream of Red Mansions* devalued in that it takes liberation as the ultimate ideal? When such life sufferings and toils are present, any living person will hope to see salvation, and if not by action, they will seek it by way of art. This book, however, attempts at salvation in both ways. So, if liberation is not obtained by suicide, this grand piece of work merits keen and wide applause.
>
> (Ibid., p. 81)

In brief, tragedy occurs when people become aware that pain is inevitable, then seek to be liberated, going through all kinds of hardships and sufferings, but finally fail to find the way out. Wang maintained that only when the writing reached such a dimension could it produce true literature. Wang's vision of literary criticism is something that traditional Chinese literature in itself is not likely to generate. Since *A Dream of Red Mansions* was published, commentaries, odes, indexes, reviews, and textual research on the book emerged in an endless stream; yet none could match Wang's insights. Even avant-gardes contemporary with Wang failed to inquire into the soul, pursue disengagement, and touch upon tragedy of world significance. Lin Shu (1907), for example, while recognizing *A Dream of Red Mansions* as Chinese

162   *Where to, Where from, and When*

fiction's culmination, only acclaimed its narration of "the changes of fortune and the vicissitudes of life, in a refined, meticulous style, with rich, varied colorings and a carefully worked-out overall plan" (Lin, 1907, p. 57). In addition, Xia Ren also extolled the work, stating, "As for Chinese novels, nothing could be more splendid than *A Dream of Red Mansions*." Nevertheless, Xia Ren attributed this novel's themes to a political one, an ethical one, a social one, a philosophical one, and a moral one (Xia, 1997, p. 89). No one other than Wang managed to relate *A Dream of Red Mansions* to spiritual inquiry, pursuit of liberation and world tragedy.

The reason why Wang could scale such heights was that he managed to treat the past and present, and China and the West as an integrated whole, and chose what to accept or reject according to his knowledge and demands as a Chinese person. As he put it:

> Intelligence, everyone is endowed with, and unsolved problems about the universe and life, everyone encounters. If one can provide a solution to some of the problems, be they our compatriots or not, they shall not be treated differently, for either satisfies our thirst for knowledge and lessens the pain of having doubts in the same way.
>
> (Wang, 1997e, p. 115)

With that pursuit of solving problems about the universe and life, Wang Guowei constantly found illumination in Western theories. He said that, from summer 1903 to winter 1904, he was immersed in Schopenhauer's works and he remarked, "What I was particularly gratified with is Schopenhauer's epistemology, which had been largely inspired by Kant's studies. As for his philosophy of life, it is also a great pleasure and relief to see Schopenhauer's perceptive observations and incisive critiques" (Wang, 1997a, p. 25). Wang saw *A Dream of Red Mansions* in the sense that it took the same foothold as Schopenhauer's theory. Nonetheless, he remained skeptical and critical about Schopenhauer, and even Kant. In his "Comments on *A Dream of Red Mansions*", Wang sensed that Schopenhauer's ideas were mostly born of his own temperaments and subjective experiences but had little to do with objective knowledge. Thus, he raised a major doubt in the fourth chapter of the "Comments on *A Dream of Red Mansions*": Is true deliverance possible and what about the objective world afterwards? Moreover, "the world has a limit but the life living on it doesn't; hence, among the infinite number of humans on this finite world, it is inevitable that some people cannot manage to accommodate themselves on this land" (Wang, 1997b, p. 80). Therefore, it is not realistic in the wishes of Buddha or Jesus for nirvana or salvation for human beings at large. Wang was forthright in pointing out Schopenhauer's contradiction, stating:

> Schopenhauer's works are littered with classical allusions, but they are not theoretically grounded. After the Buddha passed into Parinirvana and Jesus was crucified, what happened to the will to live of all flesh?

Where to, Where from, and When 163

And how about their sufferings? As I see it, there was no difference than before. Then, was his contention grounded when Schopenhauer attributed everything to God? Or, was it only an assumption that denied all factual corroboration? If the latter is the case, whether Buddha or Jesus themselves had obtained liberation is unknowable.

(Ibid., p. 80)

In Wang's article "Schopenhauer and Nietzsche" he further identified the root of this contradiction as the finiteness of human beings and the infinity of the universe. Wang (1997h) wrote:

The will is beyond all material reality but the body has a limited physical frame; causality and space-time constraints are external shackles while the endless motivations and national morals constitute internal pressure on the will. The talents [Schopenhauer and Nietzsche] have exceptional insights and will, are conscious of what others fail to be aware of, aspire for what common people do not dare to shoot for, but are also subject to the same shackles and pressure as others.

(pp. 92–93)

As such, Wang anchored himself to traditional Chinese culture, with an insight into both its weaknesses and strengths, and extensively absorbed from Western culture while having a profound knowledge of the contradictions between the two cultures. His great foresight and breadth of mind has made it possible for him to transcend time and space, thus contributing to the great turn in Chinese culture along the course of cultural development anchored both in the present and past, and the East and the West. His approach is neither traditional Chinese nor traditional Western; especially in pursuing the "trueness" and the fundamental principles of literary criticism, leading to his achieving an unprecedented literary vision.

Note

1 From Han Yu's poem "Presented to Tang Qu".

References

Bell, D. (1976). *The cultural contradictions of capitalism*. New York: Basic Books, Inc., Publishers.

Confucius. (1971). The doctrine of the mean. In *Confucian analects, the great learning and the doctrine of the mean* (J. Legge, Trans.). New York: Dover Publications, Inc.

Du, F. (2016). Respectfully presented to Vice-Director of the Left, the Senior Wei. In S. Owen (Trans. & Ed.), *The poetry of Du Fu* (Vol. 1). Boston/Berlin: Walter de Gruyter Inc.

Feng, Y. L. (1989). *A new history of Chinese philosophy* (Vol. 6). Beijing: People's Literature Publishing House.

164 *Where to, Where from, and When*

Lin, S. (1907). Preface to the Chinese translation of *The old curiosity shop*. In Z. L. Wang (2015). *Degrees of affinity studies in comparative literature and translation by Zuoliang Wang*. Heidelberg, New York, Dordrecht, London: Springer.

Schopenhauer, A. (2010). *Arthur Schopenhauer: The world as will and representation* (Vol. 1). (N. Judith, et al. Trans.). Cambridge: Cambridge University Press.

Wang, G. W. (1903). Some remarks on the "Imperial Regulations for the Faculties of Classical Learning and Literature in the University". In G. W. Wang (Eds.), *Jing'an collection*. Shenyang: Liaoning Education Press.

Wang, G. W. (1997a). Author's preface. In W. Y. Xie & X. L. Fang (Eds.), *Full collection of Wang Guowei*. Hangzhou: Zhejiang Education Publishing House.

Wang, G. W. (1997b). Comments on *A dream of red mansions*. In G. W. Wang (Ed.), *Jing'an collection*. Shenyang: Liaoning Education Press.

Wang G. W. (1997c). Four random thoughts on education. In G. W. Wang (Ed.), *Jing'an collection*. Shenyang: Liaoning Education Press.

Wang, G. W. (1997d). Incidental remarks on literature. In G. W. Wang (Ed.), *Jing'an collection*. Shenyang: Liaoning Education Press.

Wang, G. W. (1997e). On recent years' scholarly circle. In G. W. Wang (Ed.), *Jing'an collection*. Shenyang: Liaoning Education Press.

Wang, G. W. (1997f). On the bounden duties of philosophers and artists. In G. W. Wang (Ed.), *Jing'an collection*. Shenyang: Liaoning Education Press.

Wang, G. W. (1997g). Refutation of doubts about philosophy. In G. M. Yao & Y. Wang (Eds.), *Collected works of Wang Guowei* (Vol. 3). Beijing: Chinese Literature and History Press.

Wang G. W. (1997h). Schopenhauer's philosophy and education theory. In G. W. Wang (Ed.), *Jing'an collection*. Shenyang: Liaoning Education Press.

Wang, G. W. (2011a). Confucius's aesthetic educationism. In H. X. Xu (Ed.), *Selected works of Wang Guowei*. Shanghai: Shanghai Far East Publishers.

Wang, G. W. (2011b). Preface to *National studies serial*. In H. X. Xu (Ed.), *Selected works of Wang Guowei*. Shanghai: Shanghai Far East Publishers.

Wang X. Q., & Liu, W. (Eds.). (1987). *Zhuangzi: The old fisherman*. Beijing: Zhonghua Book Company.

Xia, R. (1997). Miscellaneous notes on fiction. In P. Y. Chen & X. H. Xia (Eds.), *Materials on twentieth-century Chinese fiction* (Vol. 1). Beijing: Peking University Press.

15 The Enquiries of Lu Xun in His Early Years

Born a few years after Lin Shu and Wang Guowei, Lu Xun (1881–1936) had a quite different life experience. At the time when Lu began to be extensively involved in society, China was confronted with domestic social conflicts of increasing complexity and intensity, along with the coincidence of a large-scale influx of various Western thoughts, in a way that was leading to a state of chaos and that has rarely been seen throughout the history of literature worldwide. Therefore, in contrast to Wang, who was completely engrossed in unworldly pure reflection and pure literature, and thereby made spiritual inquiries, Lu could not but primarily be concerned about the prospects of the nation and its people. As Lenin (1975) put it, "The Chinese Narodnik combines this ideology of militant democracy, firstly, with socialist dreams, then with hopes of China avoiding the capitalist path, and of preventing capitalism" (p. 165). In this sense, it was natural that Lu Xun was more critical in examining Western philosophy and aesthetics and remarkably mindful of their negative aspects, especially those that were incompatible with China's actualities.

15.1 Lu Xun as a Youth in Japan

Lu Xun studied in Japan for a much longer time (1902–1909) than Wang Guowei, which enabled him to have a more distant foothold in observing the social reality of China and allowing him more time and opportunity to investigate Western culture and literature thoroughly.

During the decade between the signing of the Boxer Protocol in 1901 and the Xinhai Revolution in 1911, thousands of Chinese students went to Japan for study, among whom a large portion tended to be supporters of the anti-Qing revolution. They wrote books and started newspapers, with more than ten published by or in the name of hometown associations in Japan. These publications mainly focused on reporting political, social, and cultural issues emerging in China's provinces, and were committed to enlightening the people and arousing public awareness in science. Lu arrived in Japan in April 1902; in November of the same year, Xu Shoushang and Tao Chengzhang organized a hometown association of Zhejiang province in Tokyo and it attracted over one hundred members. They also founded the monthly magazine *Zhejiang*

DOI: 10.4324/9781003356240-15

166   *The Enquiries of Lu Xun in His Early Years*

Trend. Lu's "Brief Outline of Chinese Geology", and excerpts of his translated works, including *The Soul of Sparta* and *Traveling to the Underground*, were published in *Zhejiang Trend* in 1903. Most of his important later essays, which were finished in Japan, such as "On Imbalanced Cultural Development" and "On the Power of Mara Poetry", were published in *Henan* magazine (1907). "Toward a Refutation of Malevolent Voices" was published under another pen name of Xun Xing in the eighth issue of *Henan* in 1908.

While studying in Japan, Lu was among the groups of Chinese students exhibiting the most provocative revolutionary trend of thought. He once recalled the situation at that time and commented that "at the end of the Qing dynasty, revolutionary thoughts were vigorous in the minds of some young Chinese. Anyone who screamed for revenge and resistance would easily find echoes" (Lu, 2005g, pp. 233–234). Unlike some scholars at that time, Lu never dreamed of relying on external support (from capitalist countries) for the rejuvenation of the Chinese nation, nor did he ever have the naïve thought that imperialism would not intervene in or had nothing to do with China's revolution. He had always emphasized the dire threats of imperialism to China: "Many an imperialist power flocked around China, casting their covetous eyes, drawing maps, scheming, and plotting. I don't know how we can survive without elaborate schemes in one hand and weapons in the other" (Lu, 2005c, p. 6). He unmasked all the imperialist powers under the banner of "friendship" and "assistance", exposing their true purpose of coming to China:

> We stand as China, a nation of the Chinese… However, they have travelled arduously enormous distances to reach deep into our territory, with the look of predators in their eyes. What are they plotting? The *Book of Songs* says, "You have drums and horns but you will not have them beat or struck. You will perish, and another person will possess them." It doesn't seem so strange, after all, to have the accounts checked first before one arrives, provided that one was to become the new master of a place. The names I am about to mention are all the most notorious. As for spies disguised as travelers, we have no idea what scale they come in.
>
> (Ibid., p. 6)

He then stated in "Toward a Refutation of Malevolent Voices":

> Of course, our own land of China has long chafed under oppression at the hands of stronger nations, and though we are not yet dead, carrion kites already circle overhead. As if our loss of territory were not enough of a blow, it has been accompanied by indemnities. Consequently, the people suffer from all forms of privation, and the countryside is strewn with the corpses of the starving and the frozen.
>
> (Lu, 2011)

Those imperialist powers dispatched ambassadors, businesspeople, politicians, priests, and scientists to the Chinese mainland to conduct detailed

The Enquiries of Lu Xun in His Early Years 167

research and investigations from every aspect. Lu then realized that their sole purpose was to prepare for further looting of China, which would result in Chinese people dying from cold and hunger with corpses exposed in the wild. Therefore, he was very sympathetic to the anti-imperialist movement of the populace. After the failure of the Boxer Rebellion in 1903, Lu (2005c) stated:

> On seeing these pale-faced, green-eyed foreigners engaged in exploiting on a daily basis this land and its resources, how can one not be overwhelmed with shock, fear, and then anger? One cannot help but reach for weapons, dying to root them out once and for all.
>
> (p. 19)

Thus he expressed his wholehearted endorsement for the millions of people's anti-imperialist sentiments and demands.

Lu believed that under such dire threats, to survive without "elaborate schemes in one hand and weapons in the other" was impossible. Introspecting the feudal system dominant in China, he all the more sensed the danger of China's fall, attributing its "decline" to domestic authoritarianism and foreign imperial aggression combined. Lu explained that the domestic deep-rooted maladies and the plague newly brought in by intruders were accelerating the decline of China (Lu, 2005h, p. 58). Lu then gained a profound insight into the several-thousand-year feudalism, which was the main reason for the long-term stagnation of the Chinese society. He criticized the feudalism by arguing:

> In Chinese politics, curtailing "disruption" has always been the ideal… Anyone with the capacity to disrupt others or anyone with a marked susceptibility to such "disruptions" would be suppressed by our emperors. This was done out of fear that disruption might somehow threaten the throne and the emperor's right to secure the line of succession for generations to come as the exclusive domain of his own offspring. So, whenever genius appeared, every possible effort was expended to destroy it.
>
> (Lu, 2013)

Lu noticed that the ruler had to block all the channels of progress and development to preserve his long-term dominance to maintain the status quo of the society. Any able and wise individual, who promoted progress and development, was bound to be strangled in such a society. Obscurantism is the weapon the ruler used for stifling progress. It was against the backdrop of this state of mind that Lu was exposed to Western culture in Japan.

15.2 "Self-examination, Knowing Others, Sound Comparison, and Self-Consciousness"

Lu Xun first attempted to seek a development route of civilization out of the comparison of "self-examination and knowing others". Having compared

168　*The Enquiries of Lu Xun in His Early Years*

several different cultures, he commented on the reigning doctrine of the time (as cited in Yue, 2016, p. 18):

> If wealth is to be taken as the criterion for determining civilization, then what of the descendants of the Jews who have amassed so much wealth that none of the great merchants of Europe can compare with them: what has been the lot of their people? Are railroads and mines the mark of civilization? In the last fifty years, Africa and Australia have certainly witnessed an expansion in these industries, yet how have the indigenous cultures of these two continents fared? Is majority rule tantamount to civilization? Did not Spain and Portugal establish constitutions long ago? And what of the state of these nations at present? If you say material abundance is the sole basis of culture, then will a display of advanced war machines and vast stores of grain suffice to give a nation sway over the rest of the world? If the inclinations of the majority are to be taken as the sole criterion for judging what one ought to and ought not to do, then if a man were to find himself living near a group of apes, would he be obliged to swing from trees and eat bananas?

What civilization was needed at the time? According to Lu, all of the above propositions were merely "grasping at branches and picking up leaves", touching upon only superficial aspects of the issues and lacking solidarity; being in a constant state of flux and having become obsolete in other parts of the world. He then cautioned against the danger of adopting these things in China and excessively upholding and exalting them.

By means of comparing and examining the Jews, indigenous Africans and Australians, in addition to Spain, Portugal, and other countries, Lu came to his conclusion that the "superficial and imbalanced" elements in nineteenth-century Western culture were materialism and majority rule. Materialism refers to the attitude that is oriented by material processions such that the subjective aspect—the inner realm—is overshadowed by the physical world. Lu (2005h) further elaborated upon the result of materialism as a world where everything is materialized, spiritual values are corroded, the taste of the people turns towards mediocrity and vulgarity; with overwhelming emphasis laid on external, physical pleasure and with internal, spiritual aspects put aside, all the people are blinded by material desires, rendering the society diminished and bringing progress to a halt (pp. 57–58). The majority rule represents a principle where those who conform are naturally justified while those who deviate are faulted, whereby the majority reigns and individuality and originality are paled. Lu (2005h) stated that, unlike the former tyranny by one single ruler, the nation then was experiencing an abrupt transfer of power to the hands of a mass of dishonorable people, imposing on the populace burdens that they could hardly live through, and such practice was of no good for reviving the nation (p. 54). According to Lu, Western civilization did not voluntarily choose to come to this phase of development—it was a forced result; as for China, it could decide its own path suited for its own

The Enquiries of Lu Xun in His Early Years   169

needs. Lu (2005h) pointed out, "Materialism and majority rule are what lead to an imbalanced path. The two have arisen as inevitable historical products of western civilization, and it would not be desirable to simply take them and apply to China" (p. 47).

Such being the case, what can China derive from Western civilization? To respond to this question, in his "On Imbalanced Cultural Development", Lu explored through the lens of the history of Western civilization spanning a few centuries, especially its ideological history in the second half of the 1800s. He touched upon a wide range of thoughts, from Stirner's "extreme individualism" and Kierkegaard's "ethical individualism" to Schopenhauer's "will to power" and Ibsen's view of fight as "an integral part of life", Nietzsche's hope for "supermen who overcome human nature", etc. Among these people, Lu paid most attention to Ibsen and Nietzsche. In particular appreciation of Ibsen's reflection on his time, Lu (2005h) wrote:

> He witnessed how society, though often in the name of equality, had become ever more vicious, with mediocrity and superficiality growing, stupidity and ignorance prevailing, and hypocrisy and deceit gaining ground. Those distinguished by their extraordinary bearing and virtues were disparaged as inferior and fell victim to humiliation. The dignity of the individual and the values of humanity were being reduced to nothing. He was often overwhelmed by these emotions, which is evident in his *An Enemy of the People*. The book tells the story of a man who, due to his persistence of the truth and unwillingness to pander to the world, is not compatible with the mass of people; to the contrary, a philistine man is able to lead the ignorant mass, manipulating the majority, bullying the minority, forming cliques driven by personal interests. Consequently, a fight is sparked and thence the whole book concludes.
>
> (p. 47)

As for Nietzsche, Lu (2005h) praised him thus:

> He was an ultimate individualist, who believed that the future of society lay only in geniuses and that the evils of a system oriented by the majority of unenlightened people were like scorpions. In a nutshell, he held that if the world was always ruled by the majority, the spirit of the society would become mediocre, and the impetus for change and evolution would rapidly disappear. A better situation is to sacrifice the interests of the masses and hope for the emergence of one or two geniuses; once they emerged, social progress would begin. This is Nietzsche's "Superman theory", which once shocked the European intellectual community.
>
> (pp. 52–53)

In light of his comparison between thinkers from various cultures, including Stirner, Schopenhauer, Nietzsche, Kierkegaard and Ibsen, and with China's circumstances in view, Lu proposed his optimistic argument of "encouraging

170 *The Enquiries of Lu Xun in His Early Years*

spiritual aspirations and abstaining from the pursuit of material wealth, and valuing individuality rather than popular opinions." He further claimed:

> Thus, what is of primary value and offers us the greatest hope at present is that men of learning might appear with their own convictions and the subtlety and critical distance necessary to insulate themselves from the pompous claims and rash deceptions that presently abound and who thoroughly critique [our] civilization. These men would of necessity possess unwavering faith in their own principles and would never be swayed by the praise or the condemnation of society. If the world lauds them, they must not be taken in by its flattery; if it reviles them, they should not feel disheartened; if people wish to follow them, they should be allowed to do so, but if instead laughter and mockery are hurled at them in order to isolate them from others, they must not fear that either. The possibility of bringing light into our gloom and darkness, and striking the spark that can illuminate the inner-souls of our compatriots all hang on this. When each person realizes his or her own identity and no longer merely drifts with the tide, this will enable China to stand on her own feet. As the situation exists today, the citizens of old and vanquished states that were formerly ignored or held in contempt by our men of ambition have all entered a state of self-awareness. They can speak from the depth of their hearts in clear and sonorous tones with their spirits running high and will, in time, no longer be subjugated through the powers of force and deception.
>
> (Lu, 2011)

These words provide clear insight that while Lu drew his conclusion from the comparison between and reference to the philosophical positions of thinkers belonging to different cultures, his own aim was to awaken the self-awareness of the populace and bring out their latent creativity so that China could take its rightful place in the world. His perception was at odds with the propositions of the above-mentioned Western thinkers. In encouraging self-examination, knowing others and comparison, Lu had one single goal; to raise self-awareness.

15.3 Inclusiveness and the Establishment of a New Tradition

In terms of Western cultures, Lu Xun not only weighed them through comparison, but also received them with choices and even adjustments according to China's actual conditions. He was most significantly influenced by the theory of evolution and drew upon Nietzsche's thinking to the greatest extent when he was studying in Japan, yet he was critical towards both.

When examining the exchange of ideas between Chinese and Western cultures, one can often notice that certain ideas that have been challenged or have become outdated in the West manage to have a new significance and play a different role in China. Lu and his appreciation of the theory of evolution is a typical example. The theory of evolution constituted the starting point for Lu to perceive the world. Lu, an atheist, first and foremost took a

The Enquiries of Lu Xun in His Early Years   171

scientific understanding of the origin of life. His orientation can be seen in his satire of those diehards rejecting the idea that humans evolved from monkeys, and his unremitting advocate of the history of human evolution wherein "the existence of all living things originates from non-living substances". In addition, the theory also offered Lu a sound concept of development, convincing him that everything is in a state of flux. Therefore, for each issue discussed in his early works, he would invariably trace its historical development, which is evident in "Lessons from the History of Science", "The History of Mankind", "On the Power of Mara Poetry", and "On Imbalanced Cultural Development". Lu (2005h) emphasized:

> Everything within the natural world evolves in a continuous sequence with the origins deeply buried, just as flowing water must have originated from the headstream, and flowers and trees must have grown out of their roots. Some of the origins are manifest while some are obscure and beyond all reason. Therefore, if we were to investigate the ins and outs, we would most likely find they are inextricably linked.
>
> (p. 48)

Such is Lu's reasoning to demonstrate that the emergence of things must be historically based and follows a developmental process. He firmly believes that despite the enormous complexity of how everything proceeds, the direction it goes is always upward and progressive (Lu, 2005e, p. 28). It was the influence of the theory of evolution that convinced Lu of progress and a promising future.

Applying this evolutionary point of view to the analysis of social history, Lu could not agree with either those who respected or those who despised everything ancient. He stated:

> When evaluating any ancient work and judging whether it is respectable or not, it is necessary to weigh it against other works by its creator's contemporaries. Only by comparing what those writers living in the same age were capable of can we reach a conclusion as proper as possible. Yet, the exaggeration that all thoughts today are originated from some sort of predecessor, in that they seem to be new but are in fact ancient creations related and passed down, is as bigoted as the indiscriminative contempt of the ancient. It is not without precedent for the past to triumph over the present in terms of creative imagination, while knowledge acquired and generalized, which is bound to be tested, must progress with the times. Thus, what our predecessors failed to perceive is neither shame to future generations nor is it something to shun.
>
> (Ibid., p. 26)

The point is that everything has its historical stages and keeps developing from lower to higher. Constantly emerging are futuristic things and things previously non-existent, while what is old and decayed is withering away. To

172   *The Enquiries of Lu Xun in His Early Years*

deem everything as having had its existence in the past is not right, nor is to deny history. When put under evaluation, everything must be examined in the context of a particular historical stage. With such an insight, Lu (2005i) assailed those longing for regressing to ancient days, remarking that they must be discouraged, unmotivated, and sluggish and that their best hope in life was no other than killing themselves to follow the ancients, or otherwise they would not be able to achieve anything (p. 69). As to those unknowledgeable mediocrities criticizing old things, they were not exemplars to follow. In concordance to what Lu had been pursuing, he wrote: "externally not lagging behind intellectual developments of the world, and internally not deviating from our own cultural root; by taking in the new and restoring the old, we shall establish a new tradition" (Lu, 2005h, p. 57).

Similarly, under the influence of the theory of evolution, Lu believed that things evolve through continuous struggle, but not in a peaceful way. Lu stated: "Peace and harmony is mere non-existence in the human world. What is alleged to be so is only an interlude between wars" (Lu, 2005i, p. 68). He continued as follows:

> Upon the birth of humankind, the species was involved in an ongoing fight for survival... Those who dare to make a departure from the due course will invariably fall into decline... Unfortunately, evolution is like a flying arrow that won't stop unless it falls or lands on top of an object. It makes no sense to hope for such an arrow to turn around and fly back to the string from which it has been shot... Armed with this power, humankind gets to survive, develop, progress, and reach the best they could possibly be.
>
> (Ibid., pp. 69–70)

Stagnation is relative, temporary, and phenomenal; only evolution and development are absolute, permanent, and essential.

As mentioned above, Lu mainly accepted the positive aspect of the theory of evolution, which played a constructive role in the later development of his thought; meanwhile he had always been critical of its negative aspect. Under the social environment and status of his time, Lu could not approve of social Darwinism in the least. While social Darwinism might be said to uphold "the law of the jungle" to suppress the "inferior" or devour the "weak", on the contrary, Lu intended to use the same principle to motivate the "inferior" to catch up with the "superior" and to turn the "weak" into the "strong". He believed that weak nations should strengthen themselves, stating:

> If our own foundation is stable, and we have surplus strength, let us then act as the Polish general Bem did in supporting Hungary, or as did the English poet Byron in aiding Greece, that is, promote the vital cause of freedom and to topple oppression, so that the world will finally be rid of tyranny. We should offer aid and support to all nations in peril or distress, starting with those that have been our friends and extending our aid throughout the world.
>
> (Lu, 2011)

The Enquiries of Lu Xun in His Early Years   173

Lu had always been deeply compassionate for the weaker nations, making considerable efforts to introduce the literature and people's lives of Poland, Hungary, the Czech Republic, and the like. At the same time, he expressed intense hatred for the "strong" who invade "weak" nations under the guise of the theory of evolution. He regarded the imperialists as "bestial patriots", or jingoists; revealing:

> Jingoists must ordinarily hail from large, strong nations; countries awesome and powerful enough to ride roughshod over the rest of the world. For this reason, jingoists only show respect for their own country and look disdainfully upon others. Seizing upon the doctrine of the "survival of the fittest," they attack the weak and small in order to realize their own desires. They will know no satisfaction until they have taken over the entire globe and made all other races their subjects.
>
> (Ibid.)

Lu accepted the theory of evolution, but simultaneously contradicted it, deeming it as a mask and shield for imperialist invasion. This is closely connected with Lu's anti-imperialist patriotic thoughts at that time.

Lu assumes the same attitude towards Nietzsche. During his study in Japan, Nietzsche's thoughts, and even the philosophy of will, were all the rage in Japanese academia. Among the thinkers and philosophers Lu probed into, Nietzsche's criticism of capitalist civilization and persistent pursuit of originality soon attracted his attention. Therefore, he most frequently mentioned Nietzsche in his works, who, as an insightful thinker, witnessed the superficial and imbalanced modern civilization. Tang Tao (1939) argues: "I believe that Lu Xun went from Ji Kang's anger at the world and Nietzsche's Superman, under the impact of the theory of evolution, and finally reached the idea of class struggle." Guo Moruo (1959) points out that "Lu Xun and Wang Guowei were both once fascinated by Nietzsche", and stresses it cannot be ignored "that both of them had been through a time when they had an inclination towards romanticism. Wang Guowei admired the philosophy and art in German romanticism, and Lu Xun favored Nietzsche, who was fundamentally a romantic" (p. 535). They both gained an acute insight from the connection of Lu's ideas with Nietzsche's, which was an important characteristic of a certain stage of Lu's thinking.

Lu (2005h) interpreted Nietzsche's words in *Thus Spoke Zarathustra* in his "On Imbalanced Cultural Development":

> When I travelled back to see the present, in front of me is the "land of education", a society full of colors. What I saw was a community lacking in solid, established beliefs, a place where the mass did not have a pioneering attitude towards knowledge. How can I possibly stay in such a land?[1]
>
> (p. 50)

The void of "solid, established beliefs" infers emphasis only on material things and lack of spiritual conviction, while not having "a pioneering attitude" means going with the flow and lacking originality. These words laid the foundation of Lu's interpretation of the defects of nineteenth-century civilization as "materialism" and "majority rule". It is worth noting that Lu took in Nietzsche's thinking as a weapon to rescue his mortally endangered motherland and the primary problem he faced was how to liberate himself and his compatriots from the oppression of imperialism and feudalism. On the other hand, Nietzsche lived in a robust capitalist nation transitioning towards monopolistic imperialism and the first problem he faced was how to contain the rising tide of revolutionary mass movement. Therefore, while Lu borrowed Nietzsche's slogans and adopted some of Nietzsche's thinking in terms of the form, intention and content, his ideas were utterly different from Nietzsche. For example, Lu's advocacy of "respecting individuality" (*zun gexing*) was meant to smash the turmoil of numerous unlearned people calling in unison in an unadvised manner, since what he aimed at was a community where all were able to think for themselves and had original ideas, that is, each individual stood as their specific selves. According to Lu, when everyone has their own self, the grand awakening of the mass will be nigh. Furthermore, Lu advocated "engendering spirit" (*zhang jingshen*), hoping that the exceptional people of this land of rich history could harbor an indomitable will and then amidst all the havoc, forge a path to survival. Nevertheless, Lu realized that few people were truly capable of respecting individuality and expanding their spirit, and "cherished the hope that one or two scholars would take a stand, setting an example for the rest". "With them in the crowd, it is like the thunder in early spring, because of which the grass sprouts. Now the light in the eastern sky appears and the dark night recedes." Therefore, Lu's fundamental pursuit is for the "light in the eastern sky" to lead to the "grand awakening of the masses", and "to transform this country of loose sand into a nation of human beings". "When the nation of human beings is established, we will become capable of mighty and unprecedented achievements, elevating us to a unique position of dignity and respect in the world" (Lu, 2005l, pp. 25, 57). This is the youthful Lu's highest ideal. It can be seen that Lu accepts Nietzsche's Superman doctrine and shares the same belief as Nietzsche's: "Only with the appearance of a Superman can the world be governed ideally. If this is not possible, then we should entrust governance to the most outstanding of our luminaries", and "rather than force the enlightened and wise to trail after the common and mediocre, would it not be better to disregard the masses and place our hopes instead upon the enlightened and wise?" (Lu, 2005h, pp. 53–54). However, in Lu's mind, the Superman, the enlightened and wise are the small number of visionary individuals whose task is to awaken the masses to consciousness and aspiration. This is clearly fundamentally different from Nietzsche's ideal of striving to consolidate the control of the tiny minority over the vast majority of the population. Lu's philosophy of "respect for individuality and the nurturing of intellect and spirit" indeed hails from the new idealism and voluntarism of the last years of the nineteenth century, especially from Nietzsche; however, regardless of the influence of this ideology, it has a vigorous and progressive influence on

The Enquiries of Lu Xun in His Early Years   175

Lu himself. It enables him to break through the shenanigans of the Westernization Group's "clamor for the acquisition of modern weaponry" and the Reformists' concentration on creating a national body to frame a constitution and realize that the crux of national salvation is in awakening the consciousness of the people.

Lu also adopted a critical attitude towards Nietzsche. If his view in 1907 was "the world will not become peaceful until a Superman emerges", then by 1919, he already felt that Nietzsche's Superman was "too nebulous". Lu had criticized his previous acceptance of Nietzsche's philosophy of "ignoring the masses and placing one's hopes on the sages", believing that the most realistic and promising prospect was if all were able to offer up their own albeit weak power. That said, Lu by no means totally rejected Nietzsche's Superman doctrine, and his focus was clearly on the "belief that noble and near-perfect human beings will appear in the future". Where Lu parted with Nietzsche was that he believed it was not necessary to wait for that "torch", but rather we should "do what we can, say what we can, shine if we have warmth, like summoning a fairy light as it can shine some light into the darkness" (Lu, 2005k, p. 341). At the same time, Lu still believed that Nietzsche's advocacy of "destroying all idols" had a considerable impact on Chinese society. He notices that Chinese traditions are deep-rooted and that even minor reforms would require great sacrifice. If a Chinese said or did something that conflicted with tradition, they would be effectively muted and accused of being eccentric, or even treacherous, so unacceptable that even everyone related to them deserves to be incriminated. Therefore, Lu believed that in China, if one is determined to be a reformer, then, like Nietzsche, one should not be afraid of isolation, "totally ignoring the scolding and compliments of idol protectors". He quoted from Nietzsche's famous "Of the Flies in the Marketplace" in *Thus Spoke Zarathustra*: "They buzz around you even with their praise: their way of praising is pushiness. They want the proximity of your skin and blood" (Nietzsche, 2004, p. 57). Later, Lu (2005k) expressed his hope for the Chinese youth to "forge ahead and ignore the sneers and arrows", and be that sea as Nietzsche put it, for "in him your great contempt can be submerged" (p. 341). In 1921, Lu also stated that Shevyrev "does show some air of a Nietzsche-like strong man". This "air of a strong man" is "to use bombs, pistols, and all one's might and will, to engage in a lifelong battle, to resist and fall" (Lu, 2005a, p. 184).

It was not until his essay *Borrowlism* in 1934 that Lu's attitude towards Nietzsche began to change. He said: "Nietzsche boasted that he was the sun, possessing illimitable light and heat, endlessly giving without receiving from others. But Nietzsche was not the sun after all: he was simply crazy" (Lu, 2005b, p. 39). In the second year, in the preface to the second volume of fiction in the series *Compendium of New Literature*, Lu analyzed this issue further, pointing out that there were only two escape routes for Nietzsche's Superman philosophy: one was "insanity and death" and the other was "to be reconciled to emptiness or to resist emptiness, even though he in his loneliness hasn't the 'last man's' will to seek out warmth, but just to despise all

176   *The Enquiries of Lu Xun in His Early Years*

authority and be eventually reduced to a nihilist" (Lu, 2005j, p. 262). But this does not deny the possibility of Lu occasionally utilizing some of Nietzsche's ideological concepts in order to illustrate a point. For example, in 1933 in *From Deafness to Dumbness*, Lu employed Nietzsche's concept of "the last man [German: *der letzte Mensch*]" to illustrate the fact that "Children brought up on husks will never be strong, and future achievements will be yet more insignificant, like the last man as described by Nietzsche." He ranted vehemently, accusing the reactionaries in the following terms: "They want to deafen young people's ears and turn their deafness into dumbness, so that they wither away and become *der letzte Mensch*" (Lu, 2005d, p. 295).

From the above it can be seen that the early Lu adopted Nietzsche's new idealism and voluntarism as his own ideals, but his aim was for China to avoid the flaws of capitalism, reform the spirit of his compatriots, and advocate energetic self-strengthening in order to save the nation. Lu long since pointed out the fact that Nietzsche's doctrines themselves were replete with contradictions, and he adopted and adapted a few useful sections of Nietzsche's doctrines to enrich and elucidate his own points of view.

Whether it is the Theory of Evolution or Nietzsche's ideology, Lu fully embodied the precious spirit of criticizing and reforming Western thought in the light of China's actual situation and needs.

15.4 Cross-Multicultural Literary Studies

Unlike Wang Guowei, who was more focused on spiritual inquiry, Lu Xun concentrated on exploring the more immediate question of awakening the populace; therefore, he differs from Wang in his attitude to literature. Lu answered the question "what is art" in this way. Lu (2005f) stated:

> All human beings are capable of two things: to feel and to create. For the feeling part, every person other than an idiot can appreciate and feel touched by natural objects, be it the sun rising from the sea or a blade of green grass teeming with life. Equipped with appreciation and provoked emotions, one or two talents will be able to reproduce them in the forms of poems or essays. This is the creating part. Therefore, the basis of feeling is thoughts, without which there would be no art. However, the natural objects one sees are not necessarily perfect, as flowers may have withered and forests may be barren. The transformation effort during reproduction, to make it appropriate, is called beautification.
>
> (p. 50)

Lu pointed out that, on the one hand, art was the reproduction of objective things; on the other hand, only after human sensibility and creativity could the reproduction occur. Therefore, Lu claimed: "There are three elements in art, namely things by nature, thought and beautification". "The artist could compose and beautify natural objects". Lu then emphasized "things by nature" were primary, while thought was secondary. Not only did art reflect natural phenomena, but Lu also held the same opinion in the social field. Lu (2005h) stated:

> In poetry and novels, most of the protagonists are untamed. This is not a coincidence wherein the writers are merely using their imagination, but rather a precursor to the emergence of new social trends, which are reflected in literature and art.
>
> (p. 51)

This is Lu's view on the relationship between literature and society.

Based on this view, Lu wrote "On the Power of Mara Poetry" and "On Imbalanced Cultural Development" in 1907, comparing and analyzing the unique characteristics of the development of a range of ethnic literatures. He first noted that Indian, Hebrew, Iranian and Egyptian, among others, were all ancient civilizations, which were "famous at the brink of history and fashioned the dawn of culture", whose strength had waned and whose culture had atrophied to such an extent that "grand voices gradually ceased to issue from the minds of the nation" and that political decline had brought with it literary stagnation. Lu further compared these ancient countries with Russia. Russia was also a great nation and had also sunk into silence: "Russian silence; then stirring sound. Russia was like a child, and not a mute; an underground stream, not an old well." For this reason, in the first half of the nineteenth century, figures such as Gogol "inspired his countrymen with imperceptible tear-stained grief" (Lu, 2005i, pp. 65–66). By comparing a range of cultures, Lu demonstrated the significance of literature, especially poetry, to national culture and spirit. In the history of the development of Chinese literature, his kind of cross-cultural analysis of the relationship between literature and culture was an entirely new way of thinking.

Lu's main thrust in "On the Power of Mara Poetry" was to "bring attention to those, among all the poets, who were committed to resistance, whose purpose was action but who were little loved by their age". Lu named these kinds of poets Mara poets. "Moluo", generally rendered "魔罗", is the phonetic transcription of the Sanskrit word Mara, meaning devil. Southey, one of the British Lake Poets, in the foreword to his epic poem *A Vision of Judgement*, hinted at the fact that Byron was "Chief of the Satanic School", and suggested that the government ban the sale of Byron's works. Furthermore, in an essay responding to Byron, Southey publicly accused Byron of being the leader of the "Satanic School", which later included many others such as Shelley. Lu's "On the Power of Mara Poetry" was written in an effort to introduce the Mara poets' words, deeds, ideas, and the impact of their circles.

Byron was the focal point of "On the Power of Mara Poetry", which offered an exhaustive introduction to his life and works. Lu laid special emphasis on Byron's passion for freedom, his opposition to violence, and his fight for independence, liberty, and human dignity, bent upon the annihilation of all false, hypocritical, and vulgar conventions. At the same time, he

178   *The Enquiries of Lu Xun in His Early Years*

stressed Byron's well-defined likes and dislikes, his sympathy for the weak, and his capacity as "a champion of strength who gave his enemies no quarter, while he displayed sympathy toward them during the deprivations of captivity" (Lu, 2006, p. 93). He also characterized the main feature of Byron's work as being full of passion, and exhibiting a lively spirit: "I have written from the fullness of my mind, from passion, from impulse, from many motives... It becomes apparent how Byron's every word, every turn of phrase, are manifestations of his life's breath and spirit" (as cited in Yue, 2016, p. 21). Lu argued that Shelley, as a member of the "Satanic School", was also "a man of great imaginative faculties who gave unrelenting pursuit to his every ideal, never shirking or turning from his goals... an extraordinarily moral character, with ideals as lofty as the clouds; surging with irrepressible passions" (ibid., p. 21). Nevertheless, Lu highlighted Shelley's dissimilarity to Byron in that, from childhood Shelley had "loved" the artistic nature of "mountains and lakes and the sea, and the solitude of forests... harmonized the rhythm of his heartstrings with the sounds of nature, enabling him to create a body of inimitable lyric compositions" (ibid., pp. 21–22), in his pursuit of the mystery of life and death. It should be especially noted that even though he admired Byron and Shelley greatly, Lu was sharply critical in his reception of their ideas. In fact, none of the melancholic and tender sides of romanticism, such as Byron's suspicion and pessimism and Shelley's metaphysical ideology and "sympathetic yet impotent" philosophy, ever appeared at the core of Lu's vision. Moreover, Lu rarely discussed the great romantic poet Keats, who was closely associated with Shelley, because his poetry lacked a "Maran" flavor.

When Lu mentioned any other poets who focused on the topic of rebellion, he invariably stressed their individual differences. For example, when discussing Pushkin, Lu argued that "while exhibiting Byronic features, his works diverge quite markedly from that style". This "uniqueness" demonstrated itself first and foremost in "the transferal of Pushkin's affections away from the Byronic hero to the ordinary people of his ancestral land". According to Lu's analysis, the reason for this was the different character of the Russian state and its people and the different dispositions of Pushkin and Byron (Lu, 2005i, p. 90). Lu further analyzed Pushkin and Lermontov:

> Pushkin and Lermontov were to Byron as water drawn from the same stream, and yet they greatly differed. Pushkin took on the outward manifestations of Byron's Weltschmerz, while Lermontov inherited his ethic of remaining in the opposition. Thus, Pushkin eventually submitted to the Tsar's authority, choosing reconciliation, whereas Lermontov fought on to the end, without retreating or wavering in the least.
>
> (Ibid., p. 91)

Lu went on to say:

> Lermontov, too, loved his country deeply, but this differed significantly from Pushkin's brand of patriotism in that he avoided reference to

The Enquiries of Lu Xun in His Early Years   179

Russia's military power in any description of his nation's greatness. His truest love was for the villages and the steppes; an attachment to the country folk that extended to the natives of the Caucasus as well, a region that had risen against Russia for the sake of its own freedom.

(Ibid., p. 93)

In addition, he also compared their different attitudes to Napoleon and their different attitudes to nature. Apart from these, he used the same method to introduce the three Polish poets Mickiewicz, Slowacki, Krasiński and Hungary's Petőfi. This comparative analysis of grouping works with similar themes and similar spirits is one of the methods used in comparative literature's thematology.

In analyzing the "Satanic poets" led by Byron and Shelley, Lu paid special attention to their dissemination and influence. Lu (1996) noted:

Then Byron and Shelley, as we know, took up the fight. With the power of a tidal wave, they smashed into the pillars of the ancient régime. The swell radiated to Russia, giving rise to Pushkin, a poet of the nation; to Poland, creating Mickiewicz, a poet of revenge; to Hungary, awakening Petőfi, a poet of patriotism; their followers are too many to name.

(p. 108)

Lu pointed out that Pushkin was deeply influenced by Byron. When Pushkin was exiled to the south of the country,

he began to read Byron's poetry and was deeply affected by its greatness, something that accounts for transformations both in his own thought and writing style. His narrative poems also took after Byron, of which his most extraordinary works were *The Prisoner of the Caucasus*, and *Childe Harold's Pilgrimage*.

(Lu, 2005i, pp. 89–90)

Moreover, "it was through Pushkin that the Byronic mantle of Mara thought passed on to Lermontov": "By the time Lermontov had risen to the rank of major in the Elite Guard of the Imperial Hussars, he began to imitate the style of Byron's oriental tales and developed a great admiration for the character of the poet", and at the same time

Lermontov's character was also akin to that of Shelley. Shelley's *Prometheus Unbound* had a strong effect on him, and he grappled with the same set of questions about life and the struggle between good and evil that had tormented Shelley, but in verse, he never imitated him.

(Ibid., pp. 91–92)

Lu noted both their similarities and differences. Additionally, he analyzed the influence of Byron and Pushkin on Mickiewicz, as well as the unique features

180 *The Enquiries of Lu Xun in His Early Years*

displayed in Slowacki's works, which "must surely have been found among Byron's Oriental poems", and Petőfi, who "had studied the poetry of Byron and Shelley; his verse speaks boldly of freedom and his fervor and abandon have much in common with the temperament of the two poets" (Ibid., p. 100). Strictly speaking, despite covering a multitude of cultures and discussing the spread and influence of the "Satanic School" led by Byron and Shelley from England and Russia and to Poland and Hungary all in one breath, and analyzing its sources and spread Lu's research cannot be termed empirical. However, at least he used the methodology of "influence research" to reach previously unachieved results.

In sum, Lu firmly believes that "to praise the true greatness of your native land takes introspection and knowing others, and that awareness comes from careful comparison. Once awareness finds its voice, each sound strikes the soul; clear, articulate, unlike ordinary sounds" (ibid., p. 67). This statement not only bears testimony to the young Lu Xun's ideals and aims, but also shows that the main technique adopted by Lu is comparison. The domain he mostly concentrates on is literature, so he has to immerse himself in a range of comparative literatures during his research. No matter whether it is interdisciplinary cultural and literary research or cross-cultural comparative research, or research into reception and influence, his contribution is always unique, and it can be said that it was the flood that opened up China's comparative literature. All the above clearly demonstrate that China's comparative literature is not entirely innately pre-existing, nor is it imported in from abroad, but rather, it is a response to the demands of the development of Chinese literature itself.

Note

1 See: Nietzsche, F. (2006). On the land of education. In K. Ameriks & D. M. Clarke (Eds.), *Thus spoke Zarathustra* (A. Del Caro, Trans.). New York: Cambridge University Press. pp. 93–95.

References

Guo, M. R. (1959). *Collected works of Guo Moruo* (Vol. 12). Beijing: People's Literature Publishing House.
Lenin, V. I. (1975). Democracy and Narodism in China. In *Lenin collected works* (Vol. 18) (pp. 163–169). (S. Apresyan, Trans.). Moscow: Progress Publishers.
Lu, X. (1996). On the power of Mara Poetry. In A. D. Kirk (Ed.), *Chinese literary thought: Writings on literature, 1893–1945*. Stanford: Stanford University Press.
Lu, X. (2005a). After the translation of *Worker Shevyrev. Collected works of Lu Xun* (Vol. 10). Beijing: People's Literature Publishing House.
Lu, X. (2005b). Borrowlism. *Collected works of Lu Xun* (Vol. 6). Beijing: People's Literature Publishing House.
Lu, X. (2005c). Brief outline of Chinese geology. In *Collected works of Lu Xun* (Vol. 8). Beijing: People's Literature Publishing House.
Lu, X. (2005d). From deafness to dumbness. *Collected works of Lu Xun* (Vol. 5). Beijing: People's Literature Publishing House.

The Enquiries of Lu Xun in His Early Years   181

Lu, X. (2005e). Lessons from the history of science. In *Collected works of Lu Xun* (Vol. 1). Beijing: People's Literature Publishing House.

Lu, X. (2005f). Letter on the promulgation of the fine arts. In *Collected works of Lu Xun* (Vol. 8). Beijing: People's Literature Publishing House.

Lu, X. (2005g). Miscellaneous memories. In *Collected works of Lu Xun* (Vol. 1). Beijing: People's Literature Publishing House.

Lu, X. (2005h). On imbalanced cultural development. *Collected works of Lu Xun* (Vol. 1). Beijing: People's Literature Publishing House.

Lu, X. (2005i). On the power of Mara Poetry. In *Collected works of Lu Xun* (Vol. 1). Beijing: People's Literature Publishing House.

Lu, X. (2005j). Preface to *Compendium of new literature*. *Collected works of Lu Xun* (Vol. 6). Beijing: People's Literature Publishing House.

Lu, X. (2005k). Random thoughts (41). *Collected works of Lu Xun* (Vol. 1). Beijing: People's Literature Publishing House.

Lu, X. (2005l). Toward a refutation of malevolent voices. In *Collected works of Lu Xun* (Vols. 1 & 8). Beijing: People's Literature Publishing House.

Lu, X. (2006). On the power of Mara Poetry. In P. G. Zarrow (Ed.), *Creating Chinese modernity: Knowledge and everyday life, 1900–1940*. New York: Peter Lang.

Lu, X. (2011). Toward a refutation of malevolent voices. (J. E. von Kowallis, Trans.). *Boundary 2, 38*(2), 27–65.

Lu, X. (2013). On the power of Mara Poetry. In J. E. von Kowallis. Translating Lu Xun's Māra: Determining the "source" text, the "spirit" versus "letter" dilemma and other philosophical conundrums. *Frontiers of Literary Studies in China, 7*(7), 422–440.

Nietzsche, F. (2004). *Thus spoke Zarathustra (Selections)/Also sprach Zarathustra (Auswahl): A dual-language book*. (A. Stanley, Trans.). New York: Dover Publications, Inc.

Tao, T. (1939). Mixed opinions of Lu Xun. *Lu Xun Style 1939*(1), 24.

Yue, D. Y. (2016). *China and the West at the crossroads* (S. Geng, & D. Dorrington, Trans.). Beijing: Foreign Language Teaching and Research Publishing Company, Limited & Singapore: Springer Science+Business Media Singapore.

16 Zhu Guangqian and His Contribution to Comparative Literature in China

16.1 Zhu's Accumulated, Inclusive Cultural Consciousness and Literacy

Zhu Guangqian, a descendant of the great Southern Song philosopher Zhu Xi, had been immersed in Chinese accumulated cultural consciousness from a very early age. He was born in Tongcheng county, Anhui province, a place with a profound cultural legacy. His grandfather presided over Tongxiang Academy, and his father, who spent his lifetime running a private school in his hometown, was quite open-minded. His father befriended the advocates of New Learning (*xinxue*) and would hang couplets at home upon which were written words that demonstrated his open-mindedness. In childhood, Zhu had read and memorized most of the traditional elementary learning classics and he taught himself works that included *Records of the Grand Historian* and *Strategies of the Warring States*. Zhu (1987d) once said: "I have already read and recited since young, long essays such as *Biographic Sketches of Xiang Yu*. I also found Wang Yinglin's *Record of Stories from Arduous Learning* delightful in some ways" (p. 441).

At fifteen, Zhu Guangqian was admitted to a local Western-style school, Kongcheng Advanced Elementary School, which was providing education in a new fashion. After only one semester's study, he entered the renowned Tongcheng High School founded by Wu Rulun, a well-known representative of the homonymous literary faction, the Tongcheng School. Wu Rulun aimed to nurture intellectuals proficient in both Chinese and Western learning. The high school's couplet motto inscribed by Wu reads: "In decades, or one century hence forth, all types of great talents will emerge; they are all found growing right here on this campus in their embryonic years, as it were; we aim at merging and synthesizing the essences of learning of all nations, eastern or western, through cultivation and discipline."

The couplet is accompanied by a plaque reading: "To cultivate pillars of the nation." Those words manifested the importance Wu attached to the blend of Chinese and Western cultures. In short, his elementary and secondary education not only laid a solid foundation for Zhu Guangqian's classical Chinese studies, but also introduced him to "New Learning" from the West.

DOI: 10.4324/9781003356240-16

Zhu Guangqian's Contribution to Comparative Literature in China 183

In 1918, at the age of 21, Zhu Guangqian received a government scholarship to study at the University of Hong Kong (HKU) where he studied English, Education, Biology, and Psychology. His study of psychology back then had a tremendous, lifelong influence on his academic research. The exceptional achievements he later made to the psychology of tragedy and of literature and art are mainly attributed to the aforementioned education. During his stay at HKU, Zhu's favorite subject was English literature. He became familiar with Shakespeare's *Hamlet* and *King Lear*, Milton's *Paradise Lost* and *Paradise Regained*, Dickens' *David Copperfield* and *A Tale of Two Cities*, among others, and especially admired English Romanticism represented by Wordsworth and Coleridge, having a deep resonance with the advocacy of individuality and the sentimental, melancholic tones in their works. He said: "I want to do my bit to let my students cherish the value of spirit" (Zhu, 1987f, pp. 186–187). Through his study at HKU, Zhu Guangqian's knowledge structure of both Chinese and Western learning was established.

In 1925, with the benefit of another government scholarship from Anhui province, Zhu enrolled in the Faculty of Arts at the University of Edinburgh and studied English Literature, Philosophy, Psychology, Ancient European History, and History of Art. During his eight academic years in the UK, he made in-depth studies on figures such as Croce, Nietzsche, Schopenhauer, and Kant, and was profoundly influenced. "Romantic poetry was my first contact with Western literature," Zhu once said. "What is essential for Romanticism is the unfettered extension of personal emotional imagination." He then added: "I was studying literary criticism, and thus I first came across Croce, a dominant figure in bourgeois aesthetics at that time. Subsequently, I used his lens to view others including Kant, Hegel, Schopenhauer, Nietzsche and Bergson" (Zhu, 1987e, p. 15). Here, Zhu systematically revisited the origin of the influence of Western thoughts he was subjected to.

As mentioned above, Zhu Guangqian already possessed a considerably deep foundation of Chinese culture when he came into contact with Western culture, enabling him to choose his starting point and growth point in terms of what could be considered as time-space coordinates, and he strove thus to include ancient and modern, Chinese and Western cultures without bias.

16.2 "All Values are Derived from Comparison"

Having grown up in such an inclusive cultural context, Zhu Guangqian (1987d) stressed: "All values are derived from comparison" (p. 176). In his "On Taste", Zhu (1987c) argued:

> Art and literature are not necessarily accessed through one only path. The landscape in the east can only be seen by those heading eastward, while that in the west seen by those heading westward. When the former travelers hear the latter praising the scenery in the west, they feel it is being exaggerated and they simultaneously pity the latter for not having beheld the beauty seen in the east, and vice versa. This is so often the

184 *Zhu Guangqian's Contribution to Comparative Literature in China*

case, which need not be made a big deal out of. Ideal spectators are those who would turn west and have a look after they have explored the east so that they are able to experience the charm of both ways. Only they are worthy appraisers to assess the merits and demerits of the east and the west.

(pp. 346–347)

Zhu (1987f) was explicit in stating:

Generalizing about the merits and demerits of Chinese and Western poetry is like generalizing about the merits and demerits of Chinese and Western cultures; it is quite difficult to be unbiased. Chinese poetry is superior to Western poetry in some ways, while it is inferior to its Western counterpart in other aspects. Both have their advantages, which can be verified through mutual reference.

(p. 209)

Zhu (2012a) then summarized his academic experience:

Speaking of my personal experience, I first learnt classical Chinese and then turned to learn vernacular Chinese, during which I encountered considerable conflicts and struggles. As I began to be fascinated by vernacular Chinese, a repulsion for classical Chinese grew in me; yet later, after much groping, I came to realize the indelible value of classical Chinese. At first I learned it from the Tongcheng School masters and then imitated literati of classical Chinese in criticizing works of the Six Dynasties for their ornateness; afterwards, when I had acquainted myself a little more with literatures during that period, I realized they had an advantage over those of the Tang and Song dynasties in certain ways. In terms of poetry, I started from Tang poetry, finding Song poetry tasteless, yet later, with more reading of the latter, I discovered its unique flavor. Similar is my experience of learning foreign literature; often going from preferring A without a full understanding of B to understanding B and reassessing A.

(p. 176)

From the above, we can at least learn the following three things.

Firstly, the foundation of literary research lies in "knowing" (*zhi*). As Zhu argues, "not knowing the least" is tantamount to "spiritual incapacity", and those with this problem miss most of life; "knowing the false" leads to "deplorable taste", or "spiritual poisoning", which could lead to thorough spiritual corruption; "knowing but not to the full" leads to "narrow taste", or "being spiritually shortsighted", and those with this problem are often criticized as always "looking at the sky from the bottom of a well and falsely accusing the sky of being too insignificant". Zhu maintains that comparison should always be, above all, based on an all-sided understanding of the object

Zhu Guangqian's Contribution to Comparative Literature in China   185

in question. Various theories are just like photos taken from different angles, and, in some cases, only an insignificant part of the object has been captured. Thus, if obsessed with one certain theory, one will form a partial view, and for a clear understanding of something in its entirety, a comparison of all the photos taken from different angles is required.

Secondly, regard shall be paid to the peculiarities as well as the ins and outs of what is being compared. Zhu (1987f) notes:

> All great poets have their predecessors and successors; such is the so-called "source and course". Mere reading of works by a poet without knowing the person's background or purpose can by no means result in a thorough understanding of the poet's contributions. Poetry of every nation has a life history as a prolonged, unbroken whole. Putting together accomplishments of all ages, we will have a complete, lively organism, within which there are veins to trace.
>
> (p. 205)

According to Zhu, every successful piece of work has its peculiarities and sometimes even works of the same genre differ considerably. It is necessary to "expand our horizons and deepen our understanding through comparison". Thus, comparing requires, not judgement of different works by the same measure, but in-depth comprehension and broad referencing so as to identify their "distinct features" and "common literary mind".

Thirdly, comparison can not only generate new knowledge, but also enable "mutual reference", that is, an understanding of B enables reassessment of a previously known A. Taking himself as an example, Zhu (1987f) writes:

> It was when I had read a few Western poems that I began to take pleasure in Chinese poetry and appreciate its grace. My research on Western poetry gave me an insight into the artistic quality and techniques in poetry, and I somewhat learnt how poets view life and the world and how they wield the language. With those in mind, I looked again at Chinese poetry and derived much more in the poems I had recited repeatedly. Consulting previous critiques or treatises on poetry, I secretly found resonance with some of the opinions of my forerunners and, on occasion, found out that mine was without precedent. As a dabbler I was able to yield such results, and a deep exploration should produce more significant results. Therefore, I suppose anyone studying Chinese poetry may likewise read Western poetry in its original language (poetry defies translation). A wider reading of the latter may promote a more proper understanding of the former. Western poetry can be where its Chinese counterpoint should be mirrored.
>
> (pp. 209–210)

In fact, this is what is under much discussion in comparative literature, namely, mutual elucidation.

186 *Zhu Guangqian's Contribution to Comparative Literature in China*

16.3 *On Poetry*: The Pioneering Work on Sino-Western Comparative Poetics

In 1933, Zhu Guangqian finished his first draft of *On Poetry* in Strasbourg, France, and his dissertation *The Psychology of Tragedy* with which he earned his degree of Doctor of Letters. In July of the same year, he returned to China, and joined the faculty of the Department of Western Languages at Peking University as professor. Zhu (1987c) recalls:

> At that time, Hu Shi was head of the Department of Chinese Literature. He held a rather unpopular view among his contemporaries on literature education in China, believing that professors of foreign literature shall be invited to deliver some of the courses at the Department of Chinese Literature. Therefore, after reading my original draft of *On Poetry*, he invited me to teach at his department for a year. After the War of Resistance against Japanese Aggression, I came all the way to Wuhan University, where Mr. Chen Tongbo, who was in agreement with Hu Shi, invited me to lecture on *On Poetry* in their Department of Chinese Literature for another year. Every time I gave a lecture, the original script would undergo drastic revision.
>
> (p. 4)

Under such circumstances, his monograph, also titled *On Poetry*, was not published until 1942. Between 1934 and 1935, Zhu's important publications on Chinese–Western comparative poetics included "Comparison between Chinese Poetry and Western Poetry in the Context of Feeling", "On Taste", "Why Epic Poetry Fails to Flourish in China" and "Defending Chinese Art from the Perspective of the 'Theory of Distance'".

In the preface to the war edition of *On Poetry* written in 1942, Zhu Guangqian (1987c) again stresses:

> All values are derived from comparison. A lack of comparison is a lack of basis for judging. As Western poetry and relevant theories are being spread into China, our materials for comparison are in greater abundance than before. We should take advantage of this opportunity to probe what on earth are our strengths and weaknesses in previous poetry creation and theories, and whether Western achievements can be used for reference.
>
> (p. 4)

By reference to Western poetics, *On Poetry* provides an in-depth causal analysis of similarities and differences in social, historical and ethico-moral terms. With Chinese literature as its focus, the monograph offers an all-round discussion on a vast scale, covering the origin of poetry, poetry and comical allegories, poetic appeal and imagery, the relationship of thoughts and feelings with language, poetry and prose, poetry and music, and poetry and painting, among others.

Zhu Guangqian's Contribution to Comparative Literature in China   187

In general, Zhu's studies on Chinese–Western comparative poetics have the following traits.

Firstly, how Chinese and Western literature coincide or differ is always illustrated in detail with a multitude of examples, and rarely by a single piece of evidence. When comparing Chinese and Western romantic poetry, for instance, Zhu (1987c) points out:

> Most Western poetry of human relations is centered on romantic love, whereas despite the large portion of such productions in Chinese poetry, other human relations are not eclipsed by this kind of sentiment. Friendship and the bond between sovereign and subjects, insignificant in Western poetry, are almost comparable with romantic love in Chinese poetry. Works by those great poets like Qu Yuan, Du Fu and Lu You, if without their patriotism, loyalty to the throne or concern for their fellow-men, would be deprived of their quintessence for the most part.
>
> (p. 74)

He further argues that ancient China attached much less importance to romantic love than today, and when it comes to poetry, friendship was a subject much more valued. Zhu (1987c) writes:

> Works of presentation and response account for the greater part in work collections of many poets. Friendships between eminent Chinese poets such as Su Wu and Li Ling, the seven scholars of Jian'an, Li Bai and Du Fu, Han Yu and Meng Jiao, Su Shi and Huang Tingjian, or Nalan Chengde and Gu Zhenguan have been extolled far and wide from ancient times to the present. In contrast, despite well-known friendships between Western poets, for example, Goethe and Schiller, Wordsworth and Coleridge, Keats and Shelley, and Verlaine and Rimbaud, their collections rarely include works on the delight from the company of friends.
>
> (p. 75)

Zhu (1987c) goes on to say:

> Most Western love poetry is written before marriage, and they are hence always intended to praise beauty and show affection; conversely, Chinese love poetry is mostly productions after marriage, so the best among them tend to be those lamenting separation or death. The former is most skilled in showing affection, and Shakespeare's sonnets and short poems by Shelley, Browning, among others, reach the best of it. The latter, on the other hand, is best at lamenting, and its prime examples include The Cocklebur [from *Guo Feng*], Cypress Boat [from *Classic of Poetry*], The Distant Cowherd Star [from *Nineteen Ancient Poems*], A Song of Yan by Cao Pi, Autumn Thoughts of a Lovesick Wife by Emperor Yuan of Liang and Long Yearning, Feelings of Resentment and Spring Thoughts by Li Bai.
>
> (p. 76)

188   *Zhu Guangqian's Contribution to Comparative Literature in China*

From an artistic perspective, "Western poetry triumphs in frankness, and Chinese poetry in euphemism; the former in profundity, and the latter in subtlety; the former in extravagance, and the latter in elegant simplicity" (Zhu, 1987f, p. 485). Such knowledge of both the other and the self is strengthened through a host of examples of phenomena in poetry, examined by way of all-sided comparison.

Secondly, Zhu is not satisfied with mere enumeration of phenomena, but rather he delves deeper into the social, historical, and ethico-moral reasons for differences observed. For instance, he analyzes why love poetry of China and the West differ, revealing three points:

> First of all, Western society, though appearing to be united in the form of a state, is partial to individualism in essence. Thus, romantic love, the main preoccupation of each individual's life, has been given commitment to the full so that it overshadows all other interpersonal relations. Chinese society, on the other hand, appears to be family-based, but it essentially stresses nation-wide virtue. Accordingly, the literati tended to spend most of their lives either in officialdom or exile, and "wife relocated to a county apart" was commonplace for them. Women were not their daily companions, but colleagues and pen friends were.

Furthermore, influenced by the code of chivalry in the Late Middle Ages, the Western world featured a relative high status of women, who had access to decent education, and thus were congenial to men in scholarship and interest. The delight Chinese literati derived from friends was always available in the West from women. Under Confucian thoughts, the position of women was comparatively low in China. Conjugal love was often based on ethical considerations, while the pleasure from a congenial companion was hardly possible between couples. Moreover, China's social ideal leaned towards scholarly honor or official rank, and to throw oneself at a woman's feet was regarded a matter of shame in Confucianism.

Lastly, Eastern and Western attitudes towards love differed greatly. Westerners valued romantic love, as is indicated in sayings like "love is best of all". Chinese people, however, had greater regard for marriage than love, and real love tended to happen at lovers' rendezvous. Only those frustrated and depressed, and with a pessimistic and even world-weary attitude, for example, talented and romantic emperors, including Yang Guang and Li Yu, were willing to publicly abandon themselves to sensual pleasures, and they invariably became objects of public denunciation for generations (Zhu, 1987c, p. 75).

Thirdly, in line with Zhu's effort to avoid one-sidedness and absoluteness in comparing Chinese and Western poetry, to neatly summarize the features of a certain culture or type of poetry is hardly attainable. For example, Zhu concludes the inclination of Western poetry to be for strength and Chinese poetry for delicacy, as is evidenced by the large portion of natural description of seas, storms, precipices, valleys, and daylight views in Western poetry and lakes, willows, breezes, drizzles and night views in Chinese poetry (ibid., p.

Zhu Guangqian's Contribution to Comparative Literature in China 189

77). Such distinctions are evidential, nevertheless, they are not immune from the accusation of overgeneralization. Zhu was also aware of the limitations of generalized comparison, explaining that Western poetry is not void of delicacy, nor Chinese poetry of strength, but the two qualities are not typical of the respective domains (ibid., p. 77). More importantly, comparison by generalization is bound to involve subjectivity and preconceived ideas from the person who has drawn the comparison such that subsequent re-comparison requires these factors to be included among the objects of comparative analysis. To give an example, Zhu (1987c) concludes:

> Western poetry is broader and more in-depth than Chinese poetry because of the philosophical and religious nurture of greater breadth and depth that it receives. If it were not for Plato and Spinoza, and the idealism and pantheism displayed by Goethe, Wordsworth, and Shelley would not be possible; similarly, in the absence of religion, there would be no Greek tragedy, or Dante's *Divine Comedy*, or Milton's *Paradise Lost*. Therefore, it is for sure a pleasant surprise that, from stark, barren soil, Chinese poetry exhibits its marvelous splendor, which yet, is not entirely satisfactory compared to Western poetry. I'm very much delighted with Chinese poetry, and believe Western poetry fails to equal it in terms of grace, subtlety, and elegance. However, as to magnificence, I could not defend it.
>
> (p. 79)

Inevitably, such a conclusion embodies personal opinions and preferences of the agent of comparison, especially in the appraisal of Chinese literature with Western literature as the standpoint. This might not be applauded by many, but can make an object of research *per se* and even an excellent frame of reference in later attempts at comparing poetry in the East and the West.

16.4 Zhu's Elucidations

Upon the publication of *On Poetry*, renowned scholar Zhang Shilu remarks:

> In the discussion of different issues in poetics in each chapter of Zhu's work, he refers to Western literary and artistic theories for cross-reference and comparison with those inherent in China and examines examples from Chinese poetry for verification. This is an adequate indication of a necessary approach to studying Chinese literature. Meanwhile, Zhu does not follow Western theories blindly, but gathers a multitude of theories, makes critical selections, and picks the most proper one as the yardstick. Moreover, on occasion, he makes corrections to defects in Western theories based on the observation of realities in China and in the light of indigenous Chinese theories. This could be said to be digestion of imported scholarship.
>
> (Zhang, 1947)

Recalling Zhu's course of Psychology of Art and Literature at Tsinghua University, Ji Xianlin (1987) comments:

> This course was exceptional and was the one I found most satisfactory. It was incomparably superior to all those convened by professors from the UK, the US, France, and Germany... When he introduced literary and artistic theories prevailing in Western countries, he would at times cite examples from ancient Chinese poetry, which we did not find a little far-fetched and could easily understand. He was well able to make sense of eccentric theories, engrossing me all the time.
>
> (pp. 28–29)

Likewise, speaking of what Zhu Guangqian achieved in academic research, Luo Dagang (1986) gives special praise for his use of examples from Chinese literature (for the most part poetry) and art (mostly painting) to elucidate basic concepts in Western aesthetics, which Luo believes is an approach worth advocating and developing. It is thus evident that, at the time, the practice of interpreting Chinese literary phenomena by way of using Western literary theories and elucidating those theories through instances from China was widely accepted. Such attempts, for one thing, contributed to brand new interpretations of literary phenomena native to China, and for another, render those "eccentric" Western theories more acceptable and accessible.

Zhu Guangqian (1987c) observes:

> There has always been *shihua* but no *shixue* in China[1]. *The Literary Mind and the Carving of Dragons* by Liu Hsieh, though neatly arranged, is not confined to poetry. *Shihua* is mostly composed of random notes taken down on the spur of the moment. Being concise, pertinent and approachable at the same time is its virtue, but it is also accused of being disorderly piecemeals and sometimes being biased towards subjectivity and other times towards blind faith in tradition; being insufficiently based on scientific spirit and method.
>
> (p. 3)

Literary criticism, as Zhu sees it, has been a weak link in the development of Chinese literature. In his "Uncharted Territory in Chinese Literature", completed shortly after his arrival in Britain for study, Zhu underscores that the most significant turn Chinese literature should take, after being re-examined in the light of Western literature, is literary criticism, and that in this regard, it is more desirable to "borrow stones from other hills", namely to learn from others' experience, which could constitute a more concrete and intelligible comparator. He further points out that to inscribe the top margin with comments like "unworldly loftiness and indulgent leisure" or "setting off from detachment and ending up with an abrupt halt" is inclined towards overgeneralization and disorderliness such that it is hardly of use to literary researchers.[2] The establishment of a theoretical framework of modern Chinese literature and art is an important goal Zhu Guangqian has always been pursuing in his academic research. Such a theoretical system could no way be built out of nothing, and Western theories are a natural point of reference. In Zhu's time, theories prevalent in Western literary circles included Croce's intuitionism, Lipps's concept of empathy, and Edward Bullough's theory of distance. These theories not only prevailed in the West at the time, but also fit well with some traditional Chinese notions.

For instance, Zhu Guangqian took Croce's "intuition of form", not only because it enjoyed wide currency in Europe at the time, but also due to its compatibility with Chinese ideas, including the realm where "the subject and the object are dissolved" (*wu wo liang wang*, also translated as "forgetting both self and things") and the belief that "if viewed with a calm spirit, all would be content; the pleasure of the four seasons is like that of man". Croce (2019) states, in the opening chapter of *Aesthetic as Science of Expression and General Linguistic*, that "Human knowledge has two forms: it is either intuitive knowledge or deductive knowledge" (p. 8). Zhu Guangqian (1987c) argues:

> Aesthetic experience as the intuition of form proposed by Croce is relatively well-grounded, because it involves the two elements of aesthetic experience: self and things. In terms of the self, aesthetic experience is characterized by intuition, and in terms of things, by image.
>
> (p. 409)

He further explains that aesthetic experience is intuitive experience, and its object is the "form" as aforementioned, and that aesthetic experience is therefore the intuition of form (Zhu, 1987a, p. 208). Such intuition is but image contemplation, and it has nothing to do with logic, judgment, or value. He argues, by quoting Laozi, that "Learning consists of adding to one's stock day by day; the practice of Tao consists of subtracting day by day" (Laozi, 1999, p. 103). He then explains:

> Learning is about knowledge from experience, while *Tao* is about the possibility of intuitive form in itself. The more one knows about something, the more difficult it is to focus on its form, to intuit its form, and thus more difficult to stimulate a real, pure sense of beauty. The aesthetic approach here involves decreasing learning to increase *Tao*.
>
> (Zhu, 1987a, p. 210)

For instance, when beholding at a tree, if one always thinks about its worth in monetary terms, or on its botanical classification, one will hardly feel its beauty intuitively. Therefore, "intuition" in Croce is what is called "spiritual concentration" in the Chinese tradition. Zhu argues:

> Aesthetic experience is a state of mental or spiritual concentration when the subject not only forgets to appreciate the world external to the object,

192 *Zhu Guangqian's Contribution to Comparative Literature in China*

but also forgets the subject's own existence. In pure intuition, self-aware-ness is void, because the state of real spiritual concentration is only pos-sible when the subject is forgetful of the self-thing distinction, this distinction being the origin of self-awareness... In brief, aesthetic experi-ence is characterized by the total oblivion of the self-thing distinction.

(Ibid., p. 213)

Zhu further explains:

Such forgetfulness results in the identity of self and things. Due to aes-thetic exultation where the subject cannot distinguish its self from things, the life of the subject and that of things begin to communicate in a con-tinuum, and therefore the subject unconsciously infuses its traits of char-acter into things and, conversely, "absorbs" the poise of things. When appreciating an old pine tree, the viewer, in the deepest of its concentra-tion, tends to carry the evoked images of uprightness and chastity over to the pine and in the meantime draws on the forceful elegance of the pine and literally humanizes the pine and materializes the viewer. In short, in aesthetic experience, the distinction between self and things completely dissolves: self merges into nature and nature finds its way into self; therefore self and nature out there reaches oneness, evolving interac-tively and resonating.

(Ibid., p. 214)

"Self and things" has been a commonly-used pair in Chinese poetry and poetics. As early as the Song dynasty, Huang Che, in his "Preface to *Gongxi's Remarks on Poetry*", commented on Du Fu's poems: "Every line Du wrote and sang was without exception out of concern about the country and the people with the boundary between self and things blurred." This remark aligns "the boundary between self and things" with "concern about the peo-ple and the country", the former representing the communication between man and nature, and the latter the relationship between man and society. Many works of remarks on poetry in later times, including *Night Chats Facing My Bed* (by Fan Xiwen), *Generalization of Art* (by Liu Xizai), and *Words on Poetry* (by Shen Deqian), address the "self–thing" duality as a most important notion. The concept of "self and things" embodied in traditional Chinese poetry is used by Zhu Guangqian; against this concept he elucidates Croce's "intuitionism", and vice versa. His attempt leads to the following achievements. First, Croce's ideas, previously new to China, were brought in, while the Chinese understanding of the "self and things" theory was deep-ened and renewed. Secondly, the commonality and complementarity between the two, to some extent, demonstrates the common "poetic mind" and "liter-ary mind" in Chinese and Western literatures, and proves that they share common principles. Thirdly, the bidirectional elucidation also serves to rem-edy the shortcomings of the both theories with new theories subsequently emerging.

Zhu Guangqian's Contribution to Comparative Literature in China   193

To further elucidate the "self–thing" relationship, Zhu goes on to introduce Bullough's theory of distance and Lipps's concept of empathy. The theory of distance is the one Zhu discusses and utilizes most. For instance, he provides detailed analysis in his monographs, including *The Psychology of Tragedy*, *Letters on Beauty*, *On Poetry*, and in his articles on aesthetics and literary issues such as "Distance between Tragedy and Life" and "Defending Chinese Art from the Perspective of 'Distance Theory'". In the second chapter of *The Psychology of Art and Literature*, Zhu Guangqian points out that distance alters the relationship between self and things from a practical to an appreciative one. He writes:

> In terms of self, distance means "detachment"; in terms of things, distance means "isolation". Poets are invariably praised for their natural, unrestrained disposition, for their unworldly-mindedness, and for their transcendence, all of which converge in one essential point: they were able to view things at certain "distances". Conversely, to criticize someone for being enslaved or fettered by worldly comforts (possessions, fame, or personal interests) is an indication of the excessive relevance they attach to the interests derived from things, with no "distance" left between self and things.
>
> (Ibid., p. 218)

Clearly, what the theory of distance stresses is consistent with the understanding that aesthetic experience is the intuition of form. Both aim to skip over the pragmatic realm so that the emergence of aesthetic experience becomes possible. However, Croce (2019) believes that human beings are naturally capable of intuition, and thus "homo nascitur poeta" [a human is born a poet] (p. 15). He somewhat strips aesthetic experience from life in its entirety; exaggerating its purity and independence. It seems that whenever a form or image is generated from intuition, the person only presents his or her existence in the aesthetic sense, and not in the least as a "scientific" or "pragmatic" existence. Yet, in fact, the three senses of existence are one and the same person. "Intuition of form" or aesthetic experience only occurs when an aesthetic attitude is adopted towards real life—to keep and view the object at a psychological distance. Zhu Guangqian supplements intuitionism with the theory of distance. For one thing, he explains the prerequisites for the occurrence of aesthetic intuition, so that Croce's intuitionism as an abstraction is brought back to earth, without "conditions favorable or detrimental to its initiation and maintenance" being neglected (Zhu, 2012b, p. 290). For another, his exposition of the distance theory also expands the theory's own meaning. Zhu states:

> He [Bullough] does not seem to realize the full extent of his theory's significance in breaking down the narrow confines of formalistic aesthetics and in extending the psychology of art to cover a much larger field than the abstract pure aesthetic experience... the idea of "distance", as

194   *Zhu Guangqian's Contribution to Comparative Literature in China*

developed in the present Chapter, though mainly echoing his view, has been extended in such a way as he might not have foreseen.

(Ibid., pp. 290–291)

With such an aesthetic distance in place, that is, the condition for aesthetics satisfied, how on earth is specific aesthetic perception produced? To elucidate this question, Zhu Guangqian introduces Lipps's concept of "empathy". Lipps's elucidation on "empathetic function" is not well-developed, which is regarded as the unidirectional projection of subjective emotion onto an external object, as if the object experiences the same emotion. Zhu (1987b), on the other hand, argues:

> Not only is the empathetic function of aesthetic experience exerted from the self to the object, at the same time, it is exerted in such a manner, the other way around. Not only is the subject's disposition projected onto the object, the object's stance is absorbed by the subject. The so-called aesthetic experience is, in fact, nothing more than a repeated, bidirectional flow of appeal between self and things happening when the subject is fully attentive.
>
> (p. 22)

He goes to illustrate his point of view:

> For example, when I enjoy the sight of an ancient pine… the image of the pine conjures up the association with high and upright character… and I unconsciously transpose this quality onto the pine, as if it originally had such a presence. Meanwhile, I, in turn, am unconsciously influenced by this quality of the pine and get uplifted, imitating its venerable and vigorous stance. In this case, an ancient pine becomes a man, and vice versa. Genuine aesthetic experience is all alike, featuring a unity between self and things, where the empathetic function is most readily activated.
>
> (Zhu, 1987b, pp. 22–23)

Zhu believes that it is such bidirectional communication that fosters the actual creation of the empathetic function.

Evidently, the pivotal reason why Zhu is able to suggest the two-way exchange between self and things, and mutual emotional interaction between the two based on Lipps's theory of unidirectional empathy, lies in the fact that he receives and elucidates Western literary theories with the traditional Chinese concept of "self-thing" unity ("man–nature" unity) already serving as a foundation. Along with his reception and elucidation, Zhu also queries and revises the Western literary theories that he introduces. Zhu is outspoken about this. He remarks in the eighth chapter of *The Psychology of Art and Literature*: "When analyzing aesthetic experience, most of the time we adopt the way of thinking derived from Kant to Croce"; that is, to "delimit aesthetic experience as an independent area for research" and to "believe that

Zhu Guangqian's Contribution to Comparative Literature in China 195

'intuition of form', 'isolation of imagery', and 'disinterested contemplation' are almost beyond criticism." However, he points out that there are two fundamental flaws here. In artistic activities, intuition alternates with contemplation, and the progression trajectory can be represented by dashed lines. Formalistic aesthetics picks out the intuitive section from this dashed line, and names it aesthetic experience, taking it as isolated and insulated. Yet this is methodologically wrong, because artistic activities, which are indeed inseparable as an entire process of development, cannot be generalized by intuition (Zhu, 1987a, pp. 314–315). Therefore, formalistic aesthetics cannot avoid the accusation of hasty generalization and being illogical. Furthermore, Zhu argues:

> For sure, we can tell apart "scientific", "ethical", and "aesthetic" elements and their distinctions among the entire psychological activities, but they can by no means be segmented and isolated. In fact, a person in the "aesthetic" sense is also one in the "scientific" and "ethical" senses.
>
> (Ibid., pp. 315–316)

This sober understanding is precisely the supplement and revision of Western formalistic aesthetics through the bidirectional elucidation of Chinese and Western poetics.

As Zhang Shilu states, Zhu Guangqian takes Western literary and artistic theories and aligns them with relevant theories native in China for cross-reference, making comparison and using examples from Chinese poetry for examination and verification. He manages to blend a multitude of theories, making critical selections, and, at the same time, correcting some of the shortcomings in Western theories. Chinese culture and the realities in the country have always been Zhu's foothold. Professor Mario Sabattini (1970), a renowned scholar in Sinological studies, praises *The Psychology of Art and Literature* for transplanting the "flower" of Western aesthetic thoughts to the "branches" of traditional Taoist literary and artistic ideology. At the point where Croce seems to diverge from cultural thoughts found in Taoism, Zhu Guangqian would invariably disregard Croce's theory without hesitation or make corrections that he deems necessary. If the "traditional Taoist literary and artistic ideology" Sabattini mentioned is a general reference to traditional Chinese literary and artistic thoughts, then it is reasonable to believe that he is right: Zhu has been trying to advance Chinese literary and artistic theories as such. Sabattini points out that Zhu misunderstands Croce's theory in quite a few places; and it is reasonable again to believe it natural that cross-cultural reading gives rise to misunderstanding, because under filtration, through the cultural perspectives of the author and the reader, both the focuses and perceptions are unlikely to make exact matches. What matters is whether the divergency makes sense and has its value. Sabattini (1970) also criticizes that the corrections Zhu makes are always such as to demolish the foundation of Croce's theory. If what is desired is not a "complete transplantation" of a certain theory, whole and intact, but rather its further spread and

196 *Zhu Guangqian's Contribution to Comparative Literature in China*

development elsewhere, then alterations of the original theory should not be regarded as destruction, but renewal instead. The dialogue between Zhu and Croce is not such that one party merges or unifies the other, but it is a generative dialogue that produces emergent properties through interaction. From this perspective what Sabattini criticizes is perhaps the creative contributions Zhu has made via his elucidation research on Chinese and Western poetics. With regard to those contributions, Zhu further carried forward both traditional Chinese poetics and Western formalistic poetics represented by Croce in the twentieth century.

Notes

1 "Shihua" [诗话] is poetry criticism or remarks on poetry and "shixue" [诗学] means poetics.
2 Zhu, G. Q. (1987). *Collected works of Zhu Guangqian* (Vol. 8). Hefei: Anhui Education Press. pp. 139–141. Qian Zhongshu revealed the common problems of the "theoretical system" from various angles in his *Discourses on the Literary Art*, and at the same time, fully affirmed the academic value of "fragmented ideas". He pointed out that "remarks on poetry" are a "fragmented" form of literary criticism. It is just a series of fragments without any direct or logical connection. Although the structure is relatively loose, and the content is quite heterogeneous, the author's mysterious ideas, aesthetic perceptions, aesthetic taste and tastes of life can be presented in a more authentic way; therefore, it is closer to human's life experience, and the works being analyzed, with high "literariness" and "readability".

References

Croce, B. (2019). *Aesthetic as science of expression and general linguistic*. Glasgow: Good Press.

Ji, X. L. (1987). He realized the value of life: Tribute to Zhu Guangqian. In Q. M. Hu et al. (Eds.), *Commemorating Zhu Guangqian*. Hefei: Anhui Education Press.

Laozi. (1999). *Tao Te Ching* (A. Waley, Trans.). Beijing: Foreign Language and Research Press.

Luo, D. G. (1986, May 26). An intellectual worker worthy of respect: Praising Zhu Guangqian's learning attitude. *People's Daily*, p. 7.

Sabattini, M. (1970). "Crocianism" in Chu Kuang-ch'ien's *Wen-i hsin-li-hsueh*. *East and West*, *20*(1/2), 179–197.

Zhang, S. L. (1947). Commentary on Zhu Guangqian's *On poetry*. *Guowen Monthly*, *1947*(58), 15–23.

Zhu, G. Q. (1987a). *Collected works of Zhu Guangqian*. (Vol. 1). Hefei: Anhui Education Press.

Zhu, G. Q. (1987b). *Collected works of Zhu Guangqian*. (Vol. 2). Hefei: Anhui Education Press.

Zhu, G. Q. (1987c). *Collected works of Zhu Guangqian*. (Vol. 3). Hefei: Anhui Education Press.

Zhu, G. Q. (1987d). *Collected works of Zhu Guangqian*. (Vol. 4). Hefei: Anhui Education Press.

Zhu, G. Q. (1987e). *Collected works of Zhu Guangqian*. (Vol. 5). Hefei: Anhui Education Press.

Zhu, G. Q. (1987f). *Collected works of Zhu Guangqian.* (Vol. 9). Hefei: Anhui Education Press.

Zhu, G. Q. (2012a). *Me and literature and others: On literature.* Beijing: Zhonghua Book Company.

Zhu, G. Q. (2012b). *The psychology of art and literature.* (Chinese-English Version). Beijing: China Publishing House.

Index

Pages in **bold** refer tables and pages followed by n refer notes.

Acta Comparationis Litterarum Universarum (ACLU) 103
aesthetic wisdom 27
Aldridge, A. O. 108
al-Qadhafi, Mu'ammar 5
American culture 6–7
American dream 37; *vs.* European dream 41–44; friendliness 39; personal freedom and success 39; political theology 40; private property 38; spiritual principles of 38–39
American global multiculturalism 57
American hegemony 8–9
American society 18, 38
The Americans: The Colonial Experience 39
Ames, R. T. 17–18, 71, 88, 99
An Anthropological Interpretation of Chinese Culture 117
Anticipating China: Thinking Through the Narrations of Chinese and Western Culture (1995) 71
anti-utilitarianism 155
Asian civilizations 2
Axial Age 1–3

Babbitt, Irving 25–26, 29n4
Bakhtin, M. M. 55
Balakian, A. 108
Baldensperger, Fernand 104
Bassnett, S. 121–124
The Battle of Seattle 12
Bauman, Z. 20, 24, 77, 86
Bell, Daniel 138, 159
Bellow, Saul 65
Berry, Thomas 29
Betz, Louis-P 104

bidirectional elucidation 116, 192, 195
Bobbitt, Philip 9
The Book of Changes 93, 95
The Book of Shang: Hong Fan 95
The Book of Shang: The Canon of Yao 90
Boorstin, D. J. 39
Bové, Joseph 13
Boyuan, Li 129
Briggs, J. 93
Brunetière, Ferdinand 103
Buddhism 1, 18, 80–81, 101, 130
Byron G. G. 53–54, 105, 149

Carré, J. M. 105
Chandler, Frank W. 106
Charter of Human Responsibilities (2001) 13
Cheney, Dick 9
Chen, L. Q. 101
Chen, M. Y. 101
Chen, S. H. 32, 54
Chen, X. P. 101
Chen, Y. Q. 81
China: an aesthetics of diversity 75; comparative literature 83; Confucianism 91; cross-cultural dialogue 75; cultural isolationism and cultural relativism 80; ethical concepts 81; foreign fiction 129; French symbolistic poetry 81; growth in economic and technological power 78; need for sincere cultural consciousness 88–90; Opium Wars 74; postcolonial era 80; rise of 5; transition 101; Western missionaries came to preach in 74

Index 199

China as the Other: mutual interpretation approach 72; process of comprehension 71; Western and Chinese thinking 71
Chinese: belief of harmony 92; reasonability 31; thought pattern 94; world literature 31
Chinese Academy of Social Sciences (CASS) 46
Chinese civilization 87
Chinese Comparative Literature Association (CCLA) 32, 126
Chinese culture 28, 30–31, 99; cultural consciousness 88–90
Chinese dream: China's liberation in 1949 46; Confucius' dream of Great Unity 45–46; future of humankind 49; knowledge 47–48; Laozi's dream of non-doing 45; modernization 44–47
Chinese humanism 26
Chinese literature 31–34; *see also* comparative literature; comparative literature in China (1900–1910)
Chinese poetry 112, 116, 137, 155, 184–190, 192, 195
Chinese *renwenism* 22–23, 25, 28
Christy, Arthur 106
civilizations, clash of: development of 7–8; Huntington's theory 1–7; New Empire theory 8–9
Classic of the Way and the Virtue 95
Cobb, J. C. 30, 100–101, 102n2
cognition 59–61
cognized subject 68–69
Cold War 6–7
Comparative Linguistics and Comparative Mythology 154
comparative literature 64; century-long history 110; in China 112–115; China's academic culture transformation 110; Chinese and Western 126; *Comparative Literature: Matter and Method* 108; death of 121–122; France and Europe 111; history of international literary relations 105; learning from foreign 114; nature and scope of 122; orientation of 108; rise of 119; in United States 106, 115; Western and Eastern literatures 109; and world literature 51–53
Comparative Literature and Culture of Peking University 75

Comparative Literature as a Discipline of Decolonialization 88
Comparative Literature in China 31
comparative literature in China (1900–1910); fiction translation 130–134; Lu's past and present of China and West *see* Lu, X.; Wang Guowei's literature 135–141
Confucian civilizations 3
Confucianism 44, 91, 156
Confucian tradition 27
Confucius' dream of Great Unity 45–46
Confucius' philosophy 71
Confucius's Aesthetic Educationism 157
Confucius's proposition 92
consciousnesses 32
constructive postmodernism 52
Cooper, Robert 9
The Crisis of Comparative Literature 107
Croce, B. 123
cultural consciousness 88
cultural diversity and symbiosis 57
cultural hegemony(ism) 14, 99
cultural homogenization 31
Cultural Revolution 25, 37, 66

Damrosch, D. 33
Dao (the "Way") 61
Daoism 156
The Davos World Economic Forum 6
The Decline of the West: Perspectives of World-History 3, 86
Derrida, J. 11, 33
Descartes' system 93
Dewey, John 18
Discourses on Governance of the States: Discourses of Zheng 60
Don Quixote 56
A Dream of Red Mansions 73n1, 138–140, 157, 159–161
The Dream of Red Mansions 59
Du Fu 155
Du, X. Z. 82

Early China/Ancient Greece: Thinking Through Comparisons 88
Eco, Umberto 75
Empire: form of 7–8; old and new 8
Empire 7–8
Engels, F. 53
entropy 65–66
Euro-American fictions 134
Eurocentrism 12, 105
European culture 71, 87

200　*Index*

Europe and China 48–49
European dream: *vs.* American dream
41–44; attainment of freedom 40;
high-quality life 40; multiculturalism
and global ecological consciousness
40; second Enlightenment 41;
sustainable civilization 40
The European Dream 28, 37, 48

Fairbank, John K. 98
Fei, X. T. 78, 88–89
Feng, Y. L. 157
fiction translation 130–134
Fleischmann, W. B. 108
Foreign Literature Review 33
Forest of Fiction 129
Foucault, M. 31
French fiction 131
French School of Comparative
Literature 104, 124
Fu, Yan 133

Gayley, Charles M. 106
*The Geopolitical Aesthetic: Cinema and
Space in the World System* (1992) 72
globalization 7, 9–10, 12, 41, 43, 55–56,
71–72, 76, 78, 81, 86, 89, 97–98, 100,
113, 117, 119, 121–122, 124n1
Gnisci, A. 88
Goddess Nv Wa 73n1
Goethe 31, 53, 105, 133, 138–139,
158–160, 187, 189
Guangjian, Wu 129
Guillén, C. 108
Guisheng, Zhou 129, 131
Gulag Archipelago 25, 37
Guyard, Marius-François 105

Habermas, J. 11
Hall, D. L. 17, 71, 88, 99
Han Yu 155, 163n1
Hardt, M. 7
harmony without homogeneity 75, 78,
88, 90–92
Heaven 26, 59, 92
Hegel 14, 59, 72
hegemony 12; American 8–9; cultural
94, 99, 113, 119; and terrorism 85;
Western 79
History of Chinese Literature 130
History of Chinese Philosophy 154
A History of Western Philosophy 14
Hongming, Gu 133
Huangong, Zheng 91
Hui, Zhang 33, 56

human-centrism 24, 26
humanism 22–23, 52
humanitarianism 22
humanity 22, 35, 49, 79, 83, 86, 99,
113, 169
human society and order 25
The Human Use of Human Beings 65
Hundred Days' Reform (1898) 129
Huntington, S. P. 1–7, 20n4

imperial homogeneity: global civil
society 12–14; globalization and
development 9–11; unilateralism and
European Renaissance 11–12
imperialism 8–10, 123, 146, 166, 174
Institute of Comparative Literature and
Comparative Culture 51, 75, 87
interactive cognition 68–69; cognitive
style transformation 14–15; E. F.
Schumacher: *Small Is Beautiful*
18–20; François Jullien: Why We
Westerners Cannot Avoid China in
Our Study of Philosophy 16–17, 87;
literature and natural sciences 64–67;
natural sciences and humanities
61–64; patterns of cognition 59–61;
phenomenological paradigm 15;
Roger T. Ames and David L. Hall:
confucius thinking 17–18
inter-cultural communication 2
inter-cultural literary research 113
interdisciplinary literary research 116
International Comparative Literature
Association 73, 107

Japanese Comparative Literature
Association (JCLA) 126
Jaspers, K. 1
Jiang, Yang 56
Jianren, Wu 129
Jianzhong, Ma 132
Jing'an Collection 158
Jinghan, Chen 129
Jingwen, Zhong 115
Jin, Zhang 33
Ji, Xianlin 114, 116, 118
Journey to the West 59
Jullien, F. 16–17, 51, 71, 100
Jung, C. G. 19
Junwu, Ma 129

Kagan, R. 9
Kang, Y. W. 127
Kant 12, 136–137, 154, 157, 159, 162,
183, 194

Index 201

Kantian epistemology 136, 154
Karlgren, Bernhard 98
Kemu, Jin 56
Kristol, W. 9
Kumarajiva 56
Kuwaki, Genyoku 134

La Littérature Comparée 105, 114
Laozi 2, 28n2, 45–46, 70, 92, 94–96, 191
Leibniz 101
Lenin, V. I. 141
Levinas 82
Liang, Q. C. 114, 127–131, 133
The Liberation of Literature 32, 54
Lin, Shu 111
literariness 107, 122, 124, 196n2
literary anthropology 117
logical cognition: interactive cognition
    approach 68–69; interpretation of
    literature 68; narrative
    compositions 68
Logocentrism 76
Loliée, F. 105, 114
Lusheng, Tian 129
Lu, X. 31–32, 53–54, 72, 141; analysis of
    social history 144; Byron's poetry
    148; elements in Western culture 142;
    On Imbalanced Cultural
    Development 143; on indigenous
    Africans and aboriginal Australians
    142; literature 145; materialism 142;
    past and present of China and West
    141; On the Power of Mara Poetry
    148; relationship between literature
    and society 147–148; respecting
    individuality 146; theory of evolution
    144–145
Lu You 155, 187

Mailer, Norman 65
Manshu, Su 129
Marx, K. 31–32, 53, 62–63
Mearsheimer, John 9
Médecins Sans Frontières 12
Meltzl, Hugo 103
Mickiewicz, Adam 54
Miner, Earl 73
Ming Dynasty 81
Mi, Wu 26
Modernity and the Holocaust 20, 24,
    77, 86
Morin, E. 9–11, 24, 51, 77, 86
Motora, Yujiro 135
Moxi, Huang 129
multiculturalism 6–7, 70–72

mutual interpretation: and China as the
    "Other" *see* China as the "Other";
    impalpable and incommensurable 70;
    macro-narrative 69; self and the
    other 70
mutual understanding 70

narrated history 15
National News 127, 130
natural sciences: and humanities 61–64;
    and literature 64–67
Negri, A. 7
Neo-Confucianism 81
neoconservatism 9
neo-humanism 23–25; fundamentals of
    25–28
neo-imperialism 8–9
The New York Times 31
Nietzsche, F. 140, 145–146, 163
non-equilibrium of literature 66–67
non-Western cultures 72

*On the Power of the Satanic School of
    Poetry* 31
outsider view of the "Other," 70

Pageaux, D. H. 52, 75, 87
The Peach Blossom Fan 139
Peat, F. D. 93
Petőfi, Sándor 54
Philosophy and Education Theory 157
political fiction 128
Pope Urban II 4
Posnett, H. M. 103
post-Cold War 1
post-modernism 30–35, 73, 119
Prigogine, Ilya 66
The Principle of Fiction 128
principle of interaction 15, 60, 70, 77
principle of the other 15, 60, 70, 77
principle of universal applicability 77
Project for the New American Century
    (PNAC) 9
Pushkin 54, 105
Pynchon, Thomas 65

qing 25, 27, 28n3, 31
Qing government 111
Qinghua, Chen 101
Qingyi Bao 127
Qu Yuan 157, 187

Reflections on Comparative Literature
    in the Twenty-first Century 122–123
Remak, H. 64, 107

202 *Index*

Renjian Cihua 157
renwen 22–23
Revel, J. F. 18
Ricard, M. 18
Ricci, Matteo 74, 84n1
Richard, Nisbett 44
Rifkin, J. 28, 37–38, 41–44, 49
Rinrigaku (Ethics) 135
Rorty, R. 12, 87
Rosemount, Henry 44
Rumsfeld, Donald 9
Russell, B. 14, 93

Saussy, H. 121–122
Schiller, Friedrich 137, 158
Schofield, W. H. 106
Schopenhauer, A. 136–137, 140, 157, 159–160, 162–163
Schumacher, E. F. 19
Schwartz, Benjamin I. 98
scientism 25
Scott, Walter 105, 134
The Secret of the Golden Flower 19
secularization 11
self-affirmation/self-gratification 77
self and the other 56–57
self-consciousness 141, 167–170
self-enclosed Eurocentric model 72
self-examination 34, 141, 144, 167–170
self-suppression 26
Shackford, Chauncey 106
Shelley, P. B. 53–54, 149
Shi, Hu 39
Shi, Su 17, 60
Shu, Lin 129, 133
Shuyuan, Qiu 127
Sidgwick, Henry 135
sinology: and *guoxue* 98, 100–101; phases of development 98–100
Social Darwinism 144
social reform 126, 129, 137, 158
Songcen, Jin 130
Song Dynasty 17, 60, 136, 154, 192
Sontag, Susan 66
Soviet Union 4, 6
Spengler, O. 3, 20n2, 86
Spivak, G. C. 121–123
sustainable civilization 26, 40

Tang Dynasty 78
Taoism 61
Taoist philosophy 70
Tao Te Ching 61, 70
Tetsugaku-gairon (Introduction to Philosophy) 134

Texte, Joseph 103
Thatcher, Margaret 47
The True Meaning of the Lord of Heaven 74
Thinking from the Han: Self, Truth and Transcendence in Chinese and Western Culture (1998) 71
Thinking Through Confucius 71, 88, 99
Tianzhen, Xie 31
Toynbee, A. J. 3, 20n3
traditional Chinese culture 25, 27, 30, 45; harmony without homogeneity 90–92; patterns that encourage diversity 93–96; relationship between man and society 96–97; world created out of chaos 92–93
traditional Chinese medicine 25, 30, 52
traditional Western culture 123
The Tragedy of Great Power Politics 9
Tu, Weiming 79

United States 4–7, 9, 12, 18, 24, 99, 106–107, 113, 115, 126–128
universalism 30
University of North Carolina 107
Updike, John 65
U.S. armed forces 9

Vandermeersch, L. 99
Van Tieghem, Paul 104–105, 114
Villemain, Abel-François 103
Voltaire 101

Walter, Xavier 99
Wang, G. W. 100, 112, 115; aesthetic intuition 157; Chinese and Western literature 154; Chinese learning and Western learning 135; Chinese literary criticism 137; Chinese literature *vs.* Western literature 158; classical Chinese studies and Western learning 153; Comparative Linguistics and Comparative Mythology 136; confluence of China and West 157; contribution to Chinese philosophy and literature 136; demerit of Chinese literature 158; *A Dream of Red Mansions* 161; exalting pure philosophy and art 137; finiteness of human beings 140–141; infinity of the universe 140–141; knowledge of Western philosophy 136; liberation 160; literature for living 156; literature for ornament 156; moral and political philosophies

155; national boundaries of learning 135; old *vs.* new and China *vs.* West 153–154; opera and fiction 137; Refutation of Doubts about Philosophy 154; *Tetsugaku-gairon (Introduction to Philosophy)* 134; theoretical exploration 136, 154; traditional Chinese culture 140, 163; True 156–157; Western cultures philosophy and art 155; Western learning 154

Weber, Max 72
Wellek, René 107
Western academia 95
Western and Eastern cultures 27
Western centralism 72
Western civilization 3, 11, 24, 77, 86, 143; Sinic Civilization 5, **5**
Western colonialism 52, 88
Western comparative literature 72–73, 122
Western culture 19, 30, 46, 71, 86, 93, 111, 122–123, 126, 128, 130, 133, 141–142, 144, 149, 155–156, 163, 165, 167–168, 170, 182–183
Western dualistic thinking 100
Westerners 3–5, 16, 19, 32
Western humanism 23–26
Western imperialism 10
Westernization 3, 89, 175
Western liberalism 99
Western universal civilization 5
Wiener, N. 65
Wolfowitz, Paul 9
Woodberry, George E. 106

World Assembly of Citizens, 2001 13
world literature 53–54; and comparative literature 51–53, 55–56
The World of Education in 1903 154
The World of Thought in Ancient China 98–99
World Social Forum 6, 12–13
World War II 42, 76, 106, 110
Wukong, Sun 59

Xianlin, Ji 56
Xiaoping, Deng 44, 47
Xia Ren 162
Xia, Z. Y. 127–128, 130
Xinshu: The Art of the Dao 90
Xi, Zhu 26, 93
Xuanzang 56
Xu, Dishan 114

Yan, F. 127
Yang, Z. H. 32, 116, 126
Yiliang, Zhou 101
Yin-koh, Tschen 100, 114–115
Yongxing, Wang 101
Yuehong, Chen 33–34, 55

Zedong, Mao 46–47
Zhang, Pei 32–33, 54
Zhao, T. Y. 46–48
Zhen, Dai 96
Zhenduo, Zheng 133
Zhongqi, Wang 129
Zhongshu, Qian 118
Zhuangzi 91, 156
Zufen, Shen 129
Zuoren, Zhou 115, 134

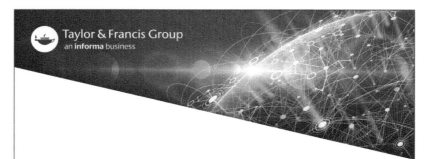